Praise for *In the Vall*

An Amazon Bes

"*In the Valleys of the Noble Beyond* is ⸱⸱⸱⸱⸱⸱⸱⸱ ⸱⸱⸱⸱⸱⸱⸱⸱ ⸱⸱⸱ ⸱⸱⸱out how we see what we want to see and don't see what we're not prepared to see." —*Washington Post*

"Searching for an elusive ape, Zada has a knack for meeting unforgettable humans." —*Globe and Mail*

"Full of dramatic, tense chase scenes—the book is, quite literally, an adventure story." —*The Millions*

"Despite the towering creature at its heart, the genius of *In the Valleys of the Noble Beyond* is most often its human pathos . . . Odd, winning gravitas." —*Open Letters Monthly*

"For lovers of nature writing who also definitely want to know about the Sasquatch (so, everyone)." —*Literary Hub*

"Zada's entry is a beautifully rendered account of a mist-shrouded world suspended between myth and modernity: its people, culture, ecology, and for receptive readers, its most mysterious denizen." —*Amazon Book Review*

"The strength of Zada's story is the writer's own humility. He is alert to the possibility (or likelihood) that as a Torontonian tramping through what most of us would call wild country—though it is, in fact, home to many people—he is capable of missing the point: that the search for the Sasquatch is a settler's fever dream . . . The attempt not to tell a story but to listen to one is the greater theme of the book." —*Literary Review of Canada*

"An entertaining, provocative exercise in cryptozoology." —*Kirkus Reviews*

"Fascinating . . . Zada's fun, well-written travelogue will interest environmentalists and armchair adventurers alike." —*Publishers Weekly*

"Zada strikes an engaging balance between curiosity and skepticism, letting the locals' convincing stories speak for themselves while probing the science behind misperceptions and cultural beliefs. While fringe-watchers will relish Zada's Sasquatch research, nature buffs will also enjoy his lush descriptions of the Canadian Pacific Northwest wilderness." —*Booklist*

"John Zada is one of those rare writers who conjures spellbinding prose through an acute sense of nature's significance and the mythologies we all inhabit. A profound debut." —Robert Twigger, author of *White Mountain: A Cultural Adventure through the Himalayas* and *Red Nile: A Biography of the World's Greatest River*

"John Zada's prose is an utter delight, and his observances are shrewd and often extraordinary. But most of all, Zada has the ability to suck readers in deep, so that they're right there with him on the trail of the Sasquatch. I recommend *In the Valleys of the Noble Beyond* more highly than any other travel book I have read in years. With time it will become a classic, and Zada will be recognized as the foremost chronicler of what is surely one of the most beguiling preserves in all adventure." —Tahir Shah, author of *In Arabian Nights* and *The Caliph's House*

"Finally a truly talented writer approaches a subject matter that has been otherwise relegated to a cultural punchline thanks to, primarily, reality television. John Zada's quest for this holy grail and his compulsion for emotional narrative is nothing less than a modern-day mythical journey; and he shares it with us in a perfect blend of poetic prose and creative story-telling. Zada completely captures the essence of what you experience: the landscape first, followed by the people and their rich culture, and finally the human mind as it tries to make sense of what might be the world's most bewildering phenomenon. Only after that journey is completed, as John did, does one finally meet the creature itself." —Survivorman Les Stroud

"A fascinating and unique account of the Bigfoot phenomenon that is equal parts memoir, psychology, travelogue, cultural commentary and manifesto on nature. Totally gripping and unputdownable. Destined to be a classic of adventure and a standout among the more conventional works on the Sasquatch." —Jason Webster, author of *A Death in Valencia*

In the
VALLEYS
of the
NOBLE
BEYOND

In Search of the Sasquatch

JOHN ZADA

Grove Press
New York

for the people of the coast.

Printed in the United States of America

First Grove Atlantic hardcover edition: July 2019
First Grove Atlantic paperback edition: May 2020

Quotations from *Caravan of Dreams* (© 1968, 2015 Idries Shah) and *Learning How to Learn* (© 1978, 2017 Idries Shah) printed with permission of The Idries Shah Foundation
Quotation from *Mystical Poems of Rumi* (© 1968 by A. J. Arberry) printed with permission of the University of Chicago Press

This book was designed by Norman E. Tuttle at Alpha Design & Composition. This book was set in 12.5-pt. Bembo by Alpha Design & Composition of Pittsfield, NH.

Library of Congress Cataloging-in-Publication data is available for this title.

ISBN 978-0-8021-4898-8
eISBN 978-0-8021-4716-5

Grove Press
an imprint of Grove Atlantic
154 West 14th Street
New York, NY 10011

Distributed by Publishers Group West

groveatlantic.com

20 21 22 23   10 9 8 7 6 5 4 3 2 1

AUTHOR'S NOTE

The journeys chronicled here took place before the most recent changes in government in Canada and British Columbia, and among First Nations mentioned here; the narrative is told in the present tense and reflects some political and economic details specific to that period. In addition, a few names have been changed to respect the privacy of individuals living in the smallest of communities I visited.

CONTENTS

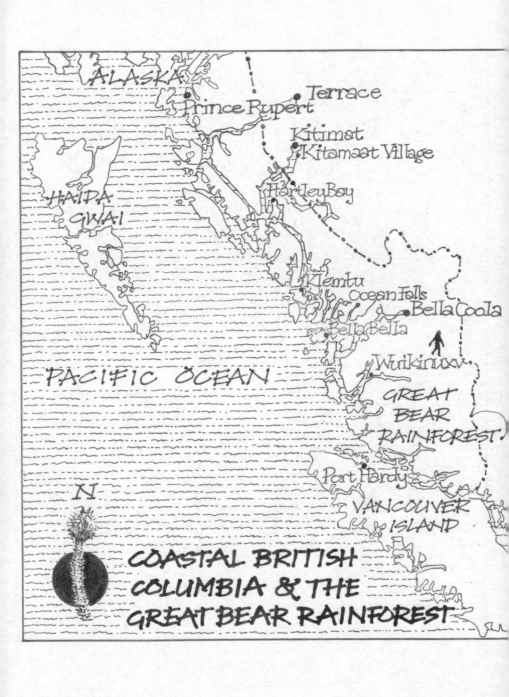

ALASKA

Terrace

Prince Rupert

Kitimat
Kitamaat Village

Hartley Bay

HAIDA
GWAI

Klemtu

Ocean Falls
Bella Coola

Bella Bella

PACIFIC OCEAN

Wuikinuxv

GREAT
BEAR
RAINFOREST

Port Hardy

N

VANCOUVER
ISLAND

COASTAL BRITISH
COLUMBIA & THE
GREAT BEAR RAINFOREST

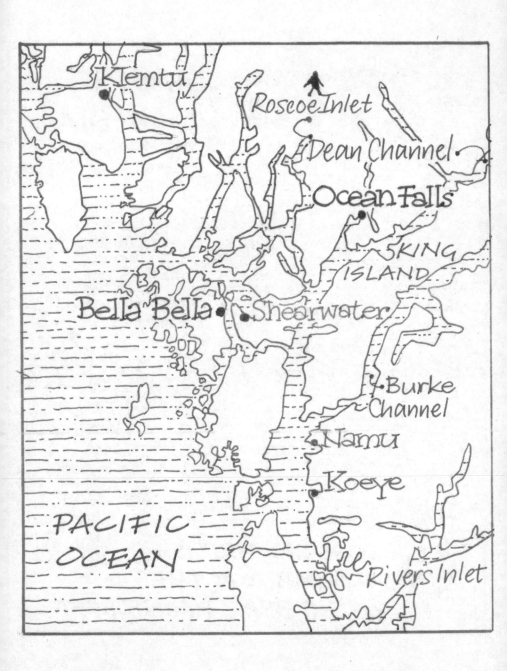

Klemtu

Roscoe Inlet

Dean Channel

Ocean Falls

KING ISLAND

Bella Bella • Shearwater

Burke Channel

Namu

Koeye

PACIFIC OCEAN

Rivers Inlet

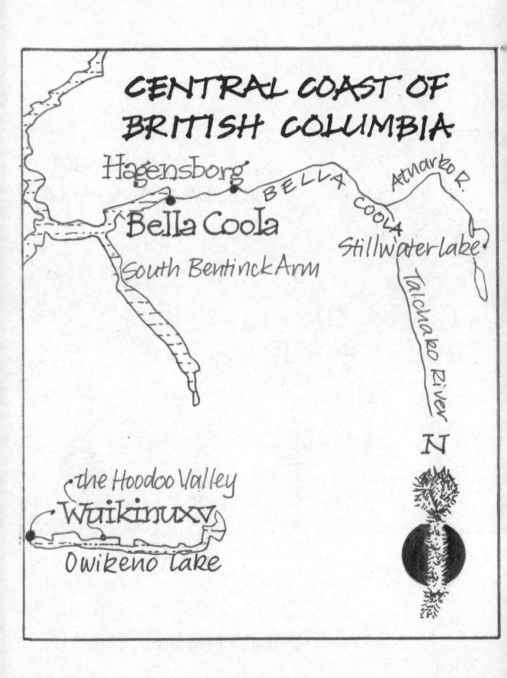

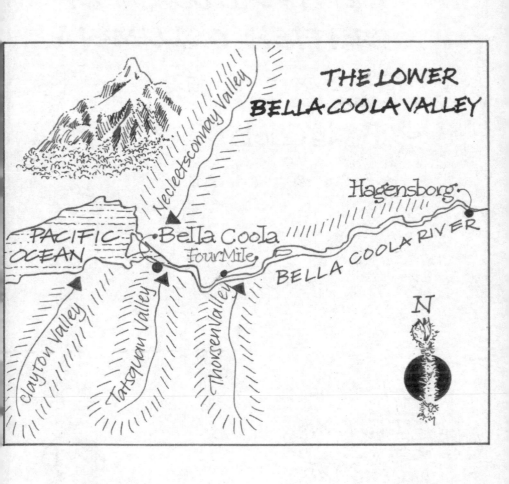

They said, "He is not to be found, we too have searched."
He answered, "He who is not to be found is my desire."
　　　　　　　—Jalal ad-Din Rumi, *Masnavi-i Ma'navi*

All Faith is false, all Faith is true:
Truth is the shattered mirror strown
in myriad bits; while each believes
his little bit the whole to own.
　　　　　　　—Sir Richard Francis Burton,
　　　　　　　The Kasidah of Haji Abdu El-Yezdi

PART I

THE BECKONING

In any field, find the strangest thing and then explore it.
—John Archibald Wheeler, physicist

A froth of dark, roiling clouds churns above the swaying canopy. The rain begins, but as a gentle caress.

I am trudging through ground moss and rotting blowdown to the symphonic pitter-patter of reconstituted sea. Shouldering a flimsy daypack and holding a single-barreled shotgun, Clark Hans, my hiking partner, leads me along a high, forested bluff overlooking an expansive valley. We reach a lookout on the edge of the bluff with a commanding view across the floodplain, where limestone mountains dressed in a patchwork of cedar, spruce, and hemlock vanish under strangleholds of mist. To our right, the river meets the ocean, a sullen, blotted-out void.

Clark stares into the distance.

"Here is right where it stood," he says. "Where it looked down at me."

I say nothing, bearing witness to a reverie I can barely understand.

A cool gust of wind washes over us. The rain increases.

"Let's go," Clark says, coming out of his trance. "We'll follow the creek back."

"The creek?" I say. "But you said there's bears there. Why don't we go back down the rock face?"

"Too slippery now from the rain."

Clark heads back into the forest and marches in the opposite direction from which we came. I follow behind him, barely able to keep up. We come to the edge of a steep ravine, the slopes of which are filled with colonies of devil's club, a spiky shrub as tall as a man. We skirt around the sharp-spined, broad-leaved plant, grasping at smaller trees and shrubs to avoid slipping down the hill in the ever-intensifying downpour.

We reach the bottom of the ravine, a narrow gully between the moss-encrusted walls of two mountains. We're completely drenched. All around us, a nightmarish tangle of salal and salmonberry bushes rises above our heads, partly concealing enormous conifers reaching for the narrow opening of sky above the gorge. We can hear the nearby creek running, but it is nowhere to be seen.

Clark, exhaling plumes of foggy breath, scours the surroundings. Suddenly his eyes dart left. There is a rustling in the bushes up the gulch. It's followed by the sound of something heavy moving.

Da-thump. Da-thump. Da-thump.

Fear clenches my chest. Clark remains frozen, his head cocked in the direction of the sound.

Da-thump.

There is something near us, waiting, watching, listening. I pick up what I think is a gamy animal smell mingling with the aroma of drenched evergreen. Clark takes hold of his gun with both hands. In almost zero visibility, the weapon offers little, if any, protection. Clark turns to me with an expression of muted alarm, trying to gauge my reaction.

Then: *Da-thump! Da-thump! Da-thump!*

"*Go!*" Clark yells, dashing through the berry bushes to a faint game trail. As I run behind him into the thicket sharp branches tear at my face and rain gear. All I can see is Clark's backside a few feet in front of me.

A heaving, growling bark explodes around us.

WOOF-WOOF-WOOAHHF!

WOOF-WOOF-WOOAHHFFF!

I break into a sprint with my arms held up to my head to protect myself from whatever beast is nearly upon us. The barking resumes—louder now—and the terror spikes. Then I realize it's Clark making the noises. He stops and cups his hands to his mouth.

"Hey, bear! Hey, grizzly-grizzly-grizzly!" he hollers at the top of his voice, a ploy to ward off any bears nearby.

Clark drops his arms and ducks into a waist-high tunnel-like trail in the brush. We're forced to crawl on our hands and knees, past sprawling blooms of wet, rotting skunk cabbage, making loud noises, and occasionally having to untangle ourselves from the branches that snag our packs. I realize that at any moment we might be ambushed and mauled by a startled grizzly. I'm awash in regret for what feels like a foolish undertaking—revisiting the perch of a legendary creature that also happens to be in the heart of bear country.

We come into a relatively dry enclosure of gargantuan Sitka spruces. Beneath a few of the trees, the forest floor is packed down. Clark wanders over to one of the impressions and moves his open palm over it.

"Day bed," he says. "A mother and cub were just here."

Clark gets up and heads into the younger brushy alder forest at the edge of the spruces, barking and yelping like a man possessed. I follow into yet another gauntlet of thorns. The novelty of exploring one of the last intact wilderness regions on the planet gives way to silent cursing.

And then reprieve. We emerge, bleary-eyed, from the darkness onto a bright, open estuary dotted with driftwood, mature berry bushes, and half-eaten salmon carcasses. Several bear trails interweave through the tall sedge grass. The invisible creek we were following appears, emptying into a wide, fast-moving river running gray with glacial silt into a fjord-like Pacific channel to our west. Clark stops, rests the butt of his gun on the ground, and turns to me with the smiling satisfaction of a man grateful to have come through.

"Nickle-Sqwanny," he says.

Before us is the confluence of the Necleetsconnay River and the Bella Coola River, which drains an epic, fifty-mile-long valley of the same name. We are in the Great Bear Rainforest, a wilderness region the size of Ireland located along Canada's rugged British Columbia coast. The partially protected area, touted as the largest expanse of unspoiled temperate rain forest left in the world, extends some 250 miles between Vancouver Island and the Alaska Panhandle.

Days earlier, I had arrived in the town of Bella Coola—a Nuxalk Nation community situated just a short distance from where we're standing. A series of serendipitous encounters led me to Clark, who, people told me, had once seen a Sasquatch—a member of the alleged race of half-man, half-ape giants believed by some to inhabit the wilds of North America. The reputed hair-covered bipeds, known more colloquially as Bigfoots, don't officially exist. No physical specimen, living or dead, has ever been produced. Because of that, mainstream science scoffs at the idea of such creatures, which are also considered by most people to be no more real than fairies or gnomes.

But like other residents of the Great Bear Rainforest, Clark Hans, a soft-spoken, fifty-one-year-old father of four, and erstwhile hunting guide turned artist, is convinced that the animals exist—and that he saw one. He agreed to take me to the location of his sighting; a spot he had been too afraid to revisit since the incident thirty years prior.

On that day in the spring of 1983, Clark had been on a duck-hunting trip in the Bella Coola estuary with two of his cousins. Upon arrival there, the group decided to split up. Clark would remain at the mouth of the Bella Coola River, and the others would head up the Necleetsconnay River. They agreed to meet later back at their boat.

Clark remembers that day as being eerily quiet. Nothing moved.

"All day I never seen a bird, I never seen a duck, I never heard nothing," he said, recounting the story before taking me up the bluff. "It was just silence all day. And I couldn't make no sense of it."

The experience was made stranger by a memory from the week before, when Clark had ventured up the creek alone to check his animal traps. While there he had felt an unusual presence. Some-one, or something, he felt, was watching him. He then discovered a cluster of young alders whose tops had been snapped back at the nine-foot level. It was something he'd never seen before, nor could he explain it.

The day he was hunting with his cousins, Clark continued to scour the estuary but found no birds. As he decided what to do next, his eye caught a distant movement on a moss-covered bluff on the mountain facing him. He saw what looked like a person moving into and out of the trees. Clark thought it might be one of his cousins, but he couldn't tell for sure. Whoever it was kept weaving amid the foliage. After disappearing again, this time for much longer, the figure reemerged along the bluff closer to Clark. He estimates it was no more than two hundred feet away when it stepped into the open.

But what he saw caused him to shake his head and blink in disbelief. Directly ahead was not a person but a large, muscular humanoid, covered in jet-black hair, with wide shoulders and long arms, standing on two legs. Though it looked human, it had a menacing, bestial appearance.

"I never seen any person that big before in my life," Clark said. "It was massive. It just stopped on the mountain and stared at me. And I stood there frozen."

Clark thinks the encounter lasted one whole minute. But at the time, he said, it felt infinitely longer. Though he couldn't make out the eyes in the general blackness of its face, the creature seemed to impale him with its gaze. A deep chill ran through Clark's body. His legs became wobbly. And for a moment he felt as though he might pass out. Then the animal released Clark from its visual grip and casually shuffled off.

"It walked into the bush in just a few strides," he said. "It didn't run. It just calmly walked away like it couldn't care less. They tell you not to be scared, but I was afraid."

Clark had known about these creatures his whole life. Nuxalk traditional tales, passed down through the generations, speak of a pair of supernatural beings known as *Boqs* and *Sninik*, humanoids that are analogous to Sasquatches. Some in the community considered the animals to be a bad omen. Others claimed the creature's very gaze could trigger a coma—or even death. As Clark stood stunned in the aftermath of his sighting, his mind flooded with scenario after terrifying scenario. Was the monster still watching him? Was it planning an ambush? Had it already cursed him? He'd heard that some people who had looked into the creatures' eyes had gone mad. Maybe his spiraling fear was evidence that he too was now losing his mind.

The mortifying possibilities swirled into a vortex of dread. Clark had to flee. He tore off all his clothes and in an adrenaline-fueled feat of endurance crossed an ice-choked Bella Coola River delta, while holding his shotgun and clothes aloft to keep them dry.

Back in town, Clark's uncle and grandfather found him slumped at the doorway, frazzled, wide-eyed, and teetering on the brink of hypothermic collapse. When they asked Clark what had happened, he tried to relate his story. But his speech was garbled and nonsensical. What little they did understand of his chattering gibberish was enough to alert them to what had happened.

The men did all they could to warm Clark up and calm him down. Later they burned sage and sang traditional chants to purify him of any negative emanations absorbed from the creature.

"I was naked during the ceremony," Clark said. "They took my clothes and smoked those too—so the creature wouldn't bother me. So it wouldn't haunt me. But it still did."

Clark's fear and anguish deepened, and he was hospitalized for anxiety. After being discharged, days later, he underwent a complete transformation. Clark quit both smoking and drinking. He started going to church, and he took up drawing and painting. For a year he refused to go anywhere near the forest. Until he led me on the hike that afternoon, Clark had not once returned to the spot where he'd seen the creature three decades earlier. Neither had he climbed the nearby bluff where the animal, looking down on him, had so deeply altered the course of his life.

"I'd heard lots of Sasquatch stories before," Clark said. "I used to tell people: 'I'll believe it when I see it.' I never disbelieved it. I just said: 'I'll believe it when I see it.' And when I did see it, I said: 'Why me?'"

Ten days before meeting Clark, I had traveled from Toronto to British Columbia to work on a magazine story about the Great Bear Rainforest. After gaining a small amount of environmental protection in 2006, this lofty stretch of rugged coastline (best known for the white Kermode bear, or "spirit bear") had been insinuating itself into the mind of the outside world. I had come to write about the area as an up-and-coming travel destination for those interested in seeing grizzly bears, going on hikes in primeval forests, and learning about the first peoples, who have inhabited this coast for at least fourteen thousand years.

But as is often the case with plans, little went as intended.

In the town of Bella Bella, on Campbell Island, the seat of the Heiltsuk First Nation, I found myself more interested in the people—and local goings-on—than in taking part in any touristy adventures on offer at the nonindigenous-owned local fishing lodge. While engaging with residents, I heard about a frightening incident. Months earlier, a monstrous humanoid had been seen on the edge of the community's youth camp, located nearby at the mouth of the beautiful Koeye River on the mainland coast. It wasn't the first such incident at the camp, I was told.

Deeply intrigued, I talked to two of the key eyewitnesses, a brother and sister in their teens, and implored them to tell me their stories. The mere mention of the incident caused them to stiffen and etched onto their faces something of the visceral fear they had experienced. They were hesitant to speak at first, but then they agreed. What stood before them that night, they insisted, was not a bear standing on its hind legs, as a few skeptics in the community had alleged—but a Sasquatch. The Koeye valley, they added, was one area Sasquatches inhabited.

At first I thought I'd come across an isolated incident—a spooky bump-in-the-night episode gone sideways. But from that moment forward, without my having made so much as a suggestion or query, Sasquatch stories jumped out at me—both in Bella Bella and in neighboring towns. My arrival on the coast, it seemed, was coinciding with a cyclical rash of creature sightings in every nearby community. And contrary to what I expected, people itched to talk about it.

In the Kitasoo/Xai'xais First Nation community of Klemtu, thirty miles north of Bella Bella, residents claimed that someone, or something, was banging on and shaking their homes in the middle of the night. Bloodcurdling, high-pitched screams emanating from the forest above the town were reported on a weekly basis. Two construction workers from southern British Columbia, newly arrived and ignorant of the experiences of the local residents, told me that they often heard a hollering and stomping on the mountainside above their trailer. Both claimed to be lifelong woodsmen and said it sounded like no animal they knew.

Meanwhile, in the Bella Coola valley, people traveling along the two-lane highway reported large humanlike forms crossing the road in their headlights at night. The gargantuan, lumbering figures were said to be of such enormous stature that they stepped across the highway in just three strides before melting into the blackness. Large, humanlike tracks, some measuring up to eighteen inches in length and pressed deep into the earth, appeared along the bushy byways between unfenced homes in two indigenous neighborhoods. These were only a few of the stories.

By the time I met Clark, I was awash in these tales. I had done little of the outdoor adventuring planned for my travel story and was instead obsessively following a trail of yarns, strangely synchronized as if they'd been deliberately laid out for me.

As a child I had been obsessed by stories about Bigfoot. I grew up in the 1970s and early '80s, a time when Sasquatch had become a pop-culture icon after a string of movies and television shows exploited the public's apparent fascination with the creature. I became literate by reading some of the first books published on the subject. For years the creatures, which I had come to believe in wholeheartedly, even appeared to me in my dreams at night. They were otherworldly, existing far beyond the pale, yet fit perfectly into the fabric of my mental universe.

I mostly grew out of this obsession, but part of it remained with me. Now, through no will or decision of my own, my old interest had resurfaced—like an amnesiac's memory returning. But now, the faded old yarns printed in dusty library books were turning into real-life experiences shared trustingly with me—a writer and journalist—by the people who lived and breathed them. I felt compelled to investigate and make sense of this mystery, which, to me, had languished in inexplicability for far too long. Maybe I could discover something that others had not found. When Clark told me his story and offered to take me to the very spot he'd been fearfully avoiding for three decades, I couldn't say no.

While I stand on the banks of the Bella Coola, the rain lets up before beating down again, this time with the feel and ferocity of sleet. Clark wades waist-deep into the river to fetch our aluminum rowboat, which has been picked up by the rising tide and dragged downstream. When he returns, we climb in and push off, hitching a ride on the swift current. Clark rows as I bail out rainwater from the bottom using an empty laundry detergent container with its top sawed off. A young bald eagle cuts a path directly over us, its wing flaps reverberating in the air. The bird lands atop a rotting tree stump sticking out of the inundated estuary. I turn my gaze to take in the valley and the mountains that line it. I have not left yet, but the desire to return to the Great Bear begins to take hold of me.

The river current slows as fresh water and salt water collide. Clark leans over the side of the boat, reaches down into the water, and pulls out a large eagle feather. He holds it close, admiring it, before handing it to me with a satisfied grin.

As we drift into the head of the inlet with sights set on the distant shore, a firm resolve takes hold of me.

I start making plans for my return.

2

THE STRANGEST THING

*It's like you walking down a back alley and bumping into a
Frankenstein monster. Everybody knows there's no such thing, but
you've just seen him.*

—Bigfoot eyewitness in John Green's
Sasquatch: The Apes Among Us

Several months after my adventure with Clark, I'm back in the
bosom of the West, speeding in a rental car along the tree-lined shores
of Vancouver Island. I'm heading for the town of Port Hardy—an
air and sea hub linking to the remote wilderness communities and
logging camps strung along British Columbia's rugged coast. Tucked
into my passport, on the seat beside me, is a plane ticket to Bella
Bella, where I will kick off a maritime journey taking me through
towns and villages with roots going as far back as the celebrated
civilizations of antiquity.

The Great Bear Rainforest occupies the upper two-thirds of
British Columbia's long, sprawling coast. It is a region tangled with
inlets, passes, and islands that add up to some thirty thousand miles
of shoreline—a length greater than the circumference of the earth.
Nodes of human habitation are few and far between. I'm taking the
summer and early fall to visit as much of the area as I can without
the benefit of my own boat. The general plan is to begin my trip in

island-bound Bella Bella on the "outside coast" and hopscotch my way between communities to Bella Coola on the mainland, where I ended my previous trip. Floatplanes, ferryboats, and whatever other flotation devices I can hire or commandeer will serve as transport in a place whose fundamental characteristic is its mind-boggling profusion of trees and water.

As I drive along the edges of forest on Vancouver Island, I get a taste of the coastal wilderness I'll fully experience in the Great Bear. But pull back these tree-lined facades, and you'll be faced with the shocking reality of the island today: a preponderance of clear-cuts. Vancouver Island's productive old-growth wilderness has been logged to the brink of extinction. Ugly bare patches cover huge swaths of the island. The Great Bear Rainforest, though having suffered some deforestation, has remained comparatively inviolate. The uniformity of its intact areas, seen from the air, is as astonishing a sight as the rapacious clear-cutting on Vancouver Island.

In the early 1990s, plans by lumber companies in British Columbia to ramp up their operations on the central and north coast triggered a response from environmentalists tantamount to a small crusade. A group of battle-hardened activists, emboldened by fresh victories against logging companies on Vancouver Island, drew up new battle lines. To galvanize global support for their fight, they coined an emotive epithet for the little-known stretch of coastline they were trying to protect: the *Great Bear Rainforest*. For years this mostly blank area on maps had been known as the "Mid and North Coast Timber Supply Area"—phrasing that reflected the view by outsiders that the area was just an economic commodity. The new name, inspired by the region's high population of grizzlies, evoked a kind of mythos. And it gave activists an edge.

Years of battles ensued, culminating in a deal in 2006. Environmentalists, industry, government, and First Nations signed an agreement that, in actuality, protected one-fifth of the ecologically fragile Great Bear forest. A subsequent agreement a decade later that made headlines around the world shored up that accord. The 2016 Great Bear Rainforest agreement provided various levels of protection across 85 percent of the region. That deal, which still allows for tourism, old-growth logging, and other industrial activities, was celebrated in the media as a grand compromise: a framework for sustainable development and a model for the resolution of other land-use conflicts.* However, the two agreements did nothing to address an issue whose stakes, residents assert, dwarf those tied to logging.

Since around the time of the first Great Bear agreement, plans have been set in motion by Canadian fossil-fuel companies to build a number of pipelines and seaport terminals on the north coast. There, liquefied natural gas (LNG), extracted by fracking, and diluted bitumen—a thick, watered-down crude mined in the infamous tar sands of Alberta—would be loaded onto supertankers for the long journey across the Pacific to energy-hungry markets in East Asia. For coastal residents, pipelines and tankers are a peril, the ultimate threat. The fear is that any of those ships, transiting the rough, narrow channels of the Great Bear region and the notoriously tumultuous waters beyond it, could get into an accident, resulting in a spill from which a widely affected area might never fully recover.

It is into this wild and immaculate landscape, marred by the gathering storm clouds of human discord, that my journey in search of the Sasquatch is taking me. As I drive along the edge of the forest, past patch after patch of enormous clear-cut, it becomes obvious just how destructive unmitigated capitalism can be. For many, the Great Bear area represents a frontier territory, entirely up for grabs,

---

* Only 38 percent of the Great Bear Rainforest enjoys full, core protection under the law. The remainder is under stringent management guidelines.

IN THE VALLEYS OF THE NOBLE BEYOND 17

whose sole, underlying, purpose is to provide salable resources and incomprehensible wealth for a select few.

Running up against the avarice of Big Oil is the iron will of residents. Their determination is reflected in a Heiltsuk First Nation art installation on display at the University of British Columbia's Museum of Anthropology in Vancouver: a cedar mask depicting the supernatural sea creature Yagis. The round and slightly hook-nosed face, draped in a mane of horsehair, stares in wide-eyed, inconsolable rage. In its jaws, about to be crushed, is a plastic model of a supertanker. The ship sits tilted and moribund, like a salmon trapped in the fangs of a bear. The installation comes across as a harbinger and prophecy, as it rests amid the wealth of indigenous artifacts looted in the same impulse of greed about which it forewarns.

I grew up in a suburb of Toronto, Canada's largest city. Though leafy and spacious, my neighborhood was a largely dull and uninspiring place. Like many big city suburbs, mine was a monument to mediocrity, a lazy arranging of things whose hallmarks are almost always an affront to creativity: from the fanatical separation of commercial and residential life to car-centric dictates on movement to the sprawling rows of insular cookie-cutter castles.

There was one redeeming quality, however, that mitigated the ennui felt across our residential tundra: a wooded ravine through which a creek ran. It has become a vogue for suburban developers building on former woodlands to leave small patches of token forest as decoration to help lure potential home buyers. Our wood was considerably more vast, one that the plastic surgeons of sprawl, either in their wisdom or out of neglect, had not entirely neutered. The ravine was part of a series of interconnected greenbelts that extended from the city and meandered north through the nascent suburbs and into the outlying fringes where forests mingled with farmland. Its mystery was enhanced by rumors, related by other kids, that it linked to some larger, deeper wilderness.

This thicket, comprising maples, spruces, ashes, and elms, turned out to be a salvation. It offered us adventures and experiences—unmitigated by parental control—that broadened our minds: a feeling of danger and risk, and the sense of achievement that comes with the successful transgression of limits. Some of those dangers were far-fetched, like the murderous recluses who were rumored to live there, hidden among the trees. Others were considerably more real, the dangers implicit in nature, evidenced in a large eastern white pine that stood in a clearing. It had been struck by lightning, its hollowed-out trunk roasted char black. The tree, which somehow clung to life, stood as a warning to interlopers. Its message: *humans don't rule here.* Our parents understood this better than we did. But what they didn't know was that their own exaggerated account of rabid creatures, homicidal hermits, and malign shadows upped the ante of excitement for us. It made the place doubly seductive.

So we ventured there, going on micro-adventures, alone or in small groups. We roved, sifted, and explored. Built fires. Climbed trees. Built forts. Observed wildlife. Lounged in the tall weeds. Got into fistfights. Dabbled in the forbidden.

We stretched ourselves, relishing a rare sense of privacy and control.

Each incursion into that surviving woodland was a journey to a kind of underworld from which we emerged reborn, brimming with new knowledge. What these forest experiences taught me early on was that learning and adventure were inextricable, and that a dose of discomfort and risk was an essential part of that formula. It was an approach to learning that stands in contrast to the practices of our safety-obsessed, overstructured education system, with its regimented activities and endless sitting at desks.

Something else happened in this period that became apparent only later: the forest made me one of its own, in the same way it does to those growing up or living in real wilderness regions. Its essence was injected into my blood, its pattern imprinted on my brain. It didn't matter that it was a pruned pseudo-forest existing in a choke hold of suburban sprawl. The ravine was a self-contained extension of all wilderness areas—a spark from the fire of grander wilds. Because of that, my early bush experience seeded a growing desire in the years ahead to find a vaster woodland, the quintessential forest—one that retained some vestige of its original bounty and power. Nature as it once was, unknown to any memory.

That inner impulse didn't fully crystallize until later. It was to be a long and circuitous road that led to that forest, one made more mysterious and poignant by tales of savage giants.

Wild, bedraggled humanoids have been reported in hinterland regions around the world for centuries. In remote and mountainous corners of the Caucasus, central Asia, China, and Siberia, traditions abound describing unruly bipeds living on the tattered edges of civilization. The Abominable Snowman, or Yeti, of the Himalayas is the best known of these manifold Asian humanoids.*

North America too has its far-flung, otherworldly realms, and from them come stories of similar creatures, supersize and even more bestial than many of their Asian counterparts. Travelers and

---

* The Yeti, one of whose original local names was *Meh-Teh* (Sherpa for "that thing there"), is believed to inhabit the lush mountain valleys of Nepal, Bhutan, Tibet, and the Sikkim region of India.

explorers, pushing west along the frontier in the 1800s, reported encounters with rogue beings they described as "wild men." As settlers began populating the ever more rugged regions of the far west, incidents involving "skookums," "evil genies," "hairy men," "bush Indians," "apes," and "forest devils" proliferated by word of mouth and in the early North American press. Indigenous residents, when confronted with these accounts, generally laughed or shrugged their shoulders. Nothing new, they informed the settlers. Not only were these wild people known to them and their ancestors, there was even a time before the arrival of the white man when they had had dealings with them.

Had the reports petered out, all might have been attributed to a mix of colorful storytelling and sensational journalism. But the reports kept coming in. By the early twentieth century, a basic profile of these creatures had taken shape among those who believed in their existence: they were apelike, often of gigantic stature, and covered in hair, and on occasion left behind large, deep footprints. Even US president Theodore Roosevelt mentioned the creatures in his 1892 book *The Wilderness Hunter*. He described a story he'd heard about a woodsman who, reputedly, had been killed by one of the animals. Stories like these introduced more and more people to the creatures.

One big tale appeared in the press in 1929. That year, John Burns, a teacher living on the Chehalis Indian Reserve near Harrison Hot Springs, British Columbia, wrote an article for *Maclean's* magazine about a race of forest giants called "Sasquatch" that had been terrorizing people in the area. "Sasquatch" was a mispronunciation of the word *Sasq'ets*, meaning "wild man" in a local dialect of Halkomelem, a Coast Salish language. Burns had been tipped off about the creatures by a British-born teacher and anthropologist also living in the vicinity. No sooner had he started looking into the sightings than he became hooked. Burns began to document reports obsessively, becoming the world's first known Sasquatch researcher.

"I was startled to see what I took at first to be a huge bear crouched upon a boulder twenty or thirty feet away," said one eye-witness Burns quoted in the *Maclean's* article. "I raised my rifle to shoot it, but, as I did, the creature stood up and let out a piercing yell. It was a man—a giant no less than six and one-half feet in height, and covered with hair. He was in a rage and jumped from the boulder to the ground. I fled, but not before I felt his breath upon my cheek."

For the next few decades, Burns would churn out dozens more articles about the creatures, which he wholeheartedly believed in and whose protection he later advocated for—but which he never once saw. His dispatches alerted readers far and wide to the alleged animals and gave them a name that would stick.

But not until almost thirty years later, in 1958, would the subject blow wide open. Inspired by the sensationalized reports of the Abominable Snowman in Nepal a few years earlier, the growing media machine of postwar America jumped on a series of similar sto-ries coming out of a small town in northern California. A bulldozer operator named Jerry Crew came forward with plaster-of-Paris casts of gigantic footprints found on a logging-road construction site near the town of Bluff Creek. Someone—or something—had been leaving enormous humanlike tracks with monstrous strides in the dirt around the work site. The same culprit had also tossed around large machinery and equipment left overnight at the location. When the incidents caused several of his colleagues to walk away from the job, a fed-up and frightened Jerry Crew took his sixteen-inch casts to the media. The local newspaper editor used in his headline the catchy name the road builders gave the perpetrator of the tracks: Bigfoot. "An insouciant turn of phrase by construction workers had given birth to a phenomenon," writes Brian Regal, the author of a book about Sasquatch researchers.[1] The story was the gunshot that signaled the start of a race to find what would become a new holy grail of exploration.

Since then reports of the creature—and the efforts to capture and study it—have grown exponentially, culminating in what is now a de facto field of study. Successive generations of Sasquatch enthusiasts, from amateur sleuths to hunters, scientists, journalists, and explorers, have all tried their hand at solving this modern-day riddle of the Sphinx. In addition to organizing countless expeditions, this legion has cast thousands of tracks, generated a deluge of blurred images and video, recorded numerous cries in the night, collected hair and scat samples, run DNA tests, appeared in hundreds of podcasts and radio and TV programs, written numerous books, held conferences, and compiled data banks listing many thousands of reports from all across the United States and Canada.

But the creature's alleged ninja-like prowess has kept it one step ahead of the hunter-investigator paparazzi. So far no Sasquatch, living or dead, or any of its mammoth body parts has been produced. Bigfoot enthusiasts say that because the creatures are nocturnal, numerically rare, and highly evasive, it is difficult to see one, let alone capture one. No Sasquatch remains are found, they add, because bodies of animals who die natural deaths in the forest are seldom ever found. Animals usually go into hiding when sick and vulnerable. Their remains, including bones, are picked apart by scavengers, and what's left quickly decomposes. When asked why there isn't better photographic evidence than the handful of blurry, inconclusive pictures taken to date, Sasquatch enthusiasts say that it's hard to take quality pictures in high-contrast or dimly lit cluttered forests where Bigfoots, often seen at a distance, are usually exposed in the open for just a few seconds. Observers, they add, are so shaken by an encounter that most of them forget to use their cameras or phones.

Scientists, citing the lack of hard evidence, deny the existence of the animals and even deride the enthusiasts' efforts. Wild-man aficionados concede that hard proof of the Sasquatch has indeed been hard to come by—but that other clues suggest the creature is real. They say that a high number of geographically clustered sightings, anatomically sound footprints, and a convincing piece of film footage taken of one of the creatures in California in 1967 indicate that there is something real to this phenomenon.* Bigfoot's strikingly consistent physical and behavioral traits, they add, lend credence to its existence.

Covered in either black, brown, red, gray, or white hair, the adult Sasquatch stands anywhere from around six and a half to ten feet tall. In a few rare cases, the animals are reported to be taller. Some are lanky. Others are bulky and intimidatingly muscular, with broad shoulders, little or no neck, and a slightly pointed head. Their long arms drop to their knees, and they are often seen walking in a some- what stooped and exaggerated fashion. Some Sasquatches give off a wretched, indefinable smell, likened to that of a wet dog that has rolled in its own excrement and rooted in garbage. They are pri- marily nocturnal and exceptionally shy, and do their utmost to avoid humans. Though they seldom physically attack people, they are given

---

* The 16-mm Patterson-Gimlin film, shot by Roger Patterson and Bob Gimlin at Bluff Creek in the mountains of northern California, purports to show, in a roughly one-minute segment, a female Sasquatch (with breasts) quickly walking away into the trees. To this day, analysis of the film and the debate over its authenticity continue ad nauseam. However the footage has yet to be debunked. At the risk of adding one more voice to that cacophony, it's worth mentioning that the figure's rippling musculature, unusual body proportions, changing facial expressions, and bizarre gait have led Hollywood special-effects people and scientists specializing in bipedal locomotion to state that the film could not have been faked. See Meldrum, Jeff, *Sasquatch: Legend Meets Science*. New York: Forge Books, 2007, Chapters 7 and 8.

at times to terrifying displays of aggressive territorial behavior. Loud vocalizations, throwing rocks and branches, stomping, whacking tree trunks with sticks, and slapping and shaking buildings are frequently reported behaviors. Bigfoots are believed to be hunter-gatherer-scavengers par excellence. They are said to eat everything under the sun, from plant matter to salmon, shellfish, rabbits, mice, deer, and elk, as well as items looted from farms and trash cans. Some Bigfoots, especially smaller, younger ones, have been seen in large trees. They are believed to build nests and shelters in the forest, speak a kind of gibberish, and live and travel in small groups or families.

These most basic details are about all the self-proclaimed experts agree on. The Sasquatch community is known for its incessant infighting and divergent views on what Bigfoot actually is and where it falls in the grand scheme of nature. Vectors of discord crisscross the entire field of what I call "Sasqualogy." The fault lines in these debates are many and the bickering is often cantankerous, if not outright vicious.

Investigators tend to fall within three main groups, believing Sasquatches are either: (a) animals, (b) spirits, or (c) extraterrestrials. Some in the first group believe Bigfoots are a surviving species of great ape, a conclusion drawn from their general appearance and apelike behaviors. These investigators have drawn a hypothetical connection between Sasquatch and an enormous prehistoric species of Asian gorilla (inferred by tooth and jaw remains) known to science as *Gigantopithecus blacki*. "Not so!" says an opposing clique, which insists the animals are far more humanlike, given their higher intelligence, behavior, and self-awareness. Their adroitness in remaining almost entirely concealed, according to this clique, is indisputable proof of that claim.

Those who take the spiritual line (b), sometimes called para-normalists, invest the animals with supernatural qualities such as prescience, telepathy, trans-dimensional movement, and the ability to shape-shift into other objects (or animals) or inflict injury or death by psychic means. For them, the creatures can be benevolent or malevolent depending on the eyewitness's spiritual condition and intent. Though evasive, Bigfoots will communicate with humans that they deem worthy enough. Some members of the newest generation of Bigfooters have recorded and posted online pictures and footage showing the results of reported gift exchanges with Sasquatches. Orbs woven from twigs, marbles, and squirrels with their heads bitten off are among some of the goodwill offerings.

Of course, stories of UFOs and space aliens also tend to elbow their way into discussions about Bigfoot. The extraterrestrial proponents (c) claim Sasquatches were dropped off on our planet aeons ago for purposes ranging from Earth-colonization to the study of human behavior.

Every difference of opinion between researchers eventually finds expression in online fisticuffs. One group believes a Sasquatch should be shot and killed to prove its existence. Another faction, outraged, says Bigfoots are an endangered species and must be protected at all costs. Somewhat famous and well-paid reality-TV Sasqualogists endure murmurs of envious criticism from their cash-strapped counterparts who work in obscurity. Debates have even raged over the plural form of *Bigfoot*. Is it Big*foots*—or Big*feet*? Or is it simply Big*foot*? Sensitive Sasqualogists insist the term *Forest People* is more politically correct than the moniker *Bush Indian*. Every significant shred of data and every hypothesis put forward by a researcher draws its inevitable detractors from some other camp. Even interesting and creative conjectures, like those positing that Bigfoots emit paralysis-inducing infrasound in their vocalizations (as tigers do to stun their prey when they roar before attacking) or that they generate bioluminescent light from their eyes to see in the dark (explaining eyewitness accounts of eyes shining at night) are eventually derided.

This frenzy of antagonism, reminiscent of the bickering common in academia, can at times mimic a battle-royal scene out of professional wrestling, with dozens of athletes pummeling one another, each in an attempt to emerge the lone victor. Meanwhile, the hardened skeptic, a combatant in his own right, stands at ringside, pointing to the spectacle as proof that what Bigfooters say exists simply cannot.

I don't recall the exact sequence of events, or the watershed moment, when I was captured by the Bigfoot mystery as a kid. But certain memories stand out. The main one is reading a cache of Sasquatch books from the local public library during my primary and early high school years, hardcover tomes sporting pseudoscientific titles superimposed over illustrations of footprints or shadowy woods with silhouetted humanoids peering out of them:

On the Track of the Sasquatch
The Sasquatch File
Sasquatch: The Apes Among Us
The Search for Bigfoot: Monster, Myth or Man?
Wildmen: Yeti, Sasquatch and the Neanderthal Enigma
Do Abominable Snowmen of America Really Exist?

The Bigfoot and Yeti books were slotted into a crowded section in the back corner of the library and shared space with other cryptozoological gospels. They were bracketed by titles on the Bermuda Triangle at one end and a larger collection of books on UFOs at the other. I grew up during a time when Sasquatch fever ran rampant. It was the 1970s, a cultural epoch in which receptivity to paranormal subjects and "the unexplained" was particularly high. Bigfoots and Yetis, despite their rarity and their elusive nature, appeared everywhere—in books, television, movies, and even consumer products.* You couldn't avoid them if you tried.

One popular 1970s TV series, *The Six Million Dollar Man*, featured the most memorable fictional cameo involving the Sasquatch. In a two-part episode, the show's protagonist, a bell-bottomed cyborg secret agent named Steve Austin, fought a scraggly-looking, cave-dwelling Sasquatch (played by the seven-foot-four-inch-tall wrestler André the Giant). That bearded, white-eyed, feral beast, who turned out to be a robot created by space aliens, and whose image, I'm certain, bore into the consciousness of millions of young people like me, derived its spellbinding horror from the fact that it looked and acted more like a human than an ape. It was cognizant, a "wild man" in the truest sense of the term.

Steve Austin's Bigfoot may have set the stage for my obsession, but it was the real-life accounts I read about in the emerging Sasquatch literature that hooked me. The most memorable tales were set in the mountainous and exotic Pacific Northwest. The region's wildly picturesque expanse made it a kind of fantasy world where anything seemed possible.

The Sasquatch books I read were not innocuous bedtime stories for entertainment's sake. They were frightening catalogs of alleged real-life monsters encountered by traumatized people. The accounts were interwoven with compelling arguments for the existence of the animals. The books pushed an agenda. The authors sought converts for their worldview, and my young, malleable

---

* I owned a pair of Bigfoot sneakers, made by the Buster Brown shoe company, which featured a humanoid barefoot sole (for making footprints in the mud) and came with a whistle that mimicked Sasquatch vocalizations.

mind, thirsty for the possibility of some expanded reality, took the bait. The books convinced me to believe in the creatures, even though I had no objective, experiential knowledge of whether they existed or not.

We know from studies involving conditioning that high emotional arousal makes us susceptible to the ideas and opinions of others. Fear, anger, sadness, and excitement function as trance states that focus and lock our attention. When we're overtaken by these emotions, we're unable to discern subtleties or think rationally. Emotion puts the gatekeeper of our thoughts, our devil's advocate, to sleep, opening the door for messages to imprint onto our minds. When the same messages repeat over and over, the risk of thought engineering is especially high.*

My belief in these creatures seemed reasonable at the time. How else could one explain the sheer number of sightings? And the huge, deep tracks? Could thousands of people claiming to see the same thing actually be wrong? Was this all a great hoax spanning centuries and distant corners of the continent? Surely not. There had to be something to it.

But as time passed, no definitive answer emerged. As with all things cyclical, Bigfoot's popularity ebbed. For a long stretch of time, coinciding with my transition into adulthood, Sasquatch fell from the public eye. I remained intrigued by the subject but didn't give it much more thought. But a trip to British Columbia in 1998 brought it all back.

---

* Dictators and demagogues often whip crowds into an emotional frenzy using a number of cues and techniques to lock their attention while bombarding them with messages and agendas.

In 1998, I visited the town of Nelson in the Kootenay region of British Columbia's southern interior. It was my first trip to the province. Nelson, a historical silver-mining town nestled in the heart of the Selkirk Mountains, is a sort of promised land. Life in the isolated community is tranquil and unhurried. The mountains guarding it have a rugged, ageless disposition, bristling with lush forests and peppered with crystal deposits and hot springs.

This also happens to be serious Sasquatch country, though a lot of people don't know it. Unlike some places with more obvious Bigfoot tie-ins, Nelson doesn't have a widespread reputation for being a wild-man hub. But its Bigfoot bona fides are merely less conspicuous. This I learned later—I was simply there to visit a friend who had recently made Nelson his new home. It was the middle of winter. The town was covered in a blanket of freshly fallen snow, the kind that floats down in clumps the size of silver dollars, muffling all sound and rendering everything inert. It was a lazy kind of week; we had no real plans other than lounging around, drinking beer, and frequenting the town's sushi restaurant and vegetarian cafés.

Then one day we decided to go for a hike.

The trail we chose began at the top of my friend's street on the edge of town and curved its way around the slopes of Silver King Mountain. We stepped out in the crisp, pine-scented air and made our way up the snowy road to the trailhead. Above us, the forested mountain grew ever more deeply white until, alabaster and heaving with snow, the high slopes vanished behind voracious clouds. The farther we went, the whiter the world became. Every branch of every tree along the trail was loaded to capacity with snow, a thousand miniature avalanches in waiting.

Over an hour in, we stopped to rest. It was midafternoon. A premonition of dusk hung in the air. The woods were uncomfortably still. We had seen no other people on the trail that day.

"How much farther should we go?" I asked.

Before my friend could answer, something caught our attention. Above and behind us, in the distance, we could hear movement. It was a diffuse rustle at first but grew louder and more methodical. Something, or someone—it had to be someone!—was walking, almost marching, through the snow toward us, and was covering ground fast.

Crunch-crunch . . .

    Crunch-crunch . . .

        Crunch-crunch . . .

Soon the sound was almost directly upon us. It had an excruciatingly heavy presence. Deep panting accompanied every thundering step, which resonated surreally, as if in surround sound. It was so close—whatever it was—it seemed as if we could reach out and touch it. Yet we couldn't see a thing. Not a single moving tree, or a cloud of snow thrown off branches. Just a heavy plodding, like a locomotive chugging past us. The jolt of intense, heart-stopping fear didn't kick in until after the sound had started to recede around the mountainside. My friend and I turned to each other, wide-eyed.

We spent the next few moments in terror-fueled speculation, trying to determine what had walked past us. We had just ruled out woolly mammoths when the presence began plodding back toward us—this time from the other direction—as if it had forgotten something.

Crunch-crunch . . .

    Crunch-crunch . . .

With it came that same deep, seething panting.

It sounded agitated, almost as if it were deliberately announcing itself with stomps and anxious pacing. The floodgates of dread blew wide open. It was too much to handle.

In perfect synchrony, the two of us broke into a panicked sprint. Like ultra-athletes, we ran nonstop all the way back to Nelson.

I may have fled the forest with lightning speed, but I was nowhere near fast enough to outrun my latent beliefs, which were waiting for me at the head of the trail. By the time I stepped back onto the concrete, I was convinced I'd rubbed shoulders with a Sasquatch. My friend, although also sure we'd skirmished with something rare and untoward, eventually got tired of talking about it and lost interest.

But I couldn't let it go. I started to make inquiries around Nelson. After a bit of sleuthing I found myself at an artisanal coffee shop sitting across from the local Sasqualogist, a man in his early fifties named Robert Milner. He was the first Bigfoot researcher I'd ever met, and, contrary to expectations, he had no weird quirks. He was a normal guy who spoke openly and matter-of-factly about Bigfoots as if he were talking about his vegetable garden. He'd never seen a Sasquatch, he said, but had concluded from years of in-depth research that the animals lived in a dense cluster within a fifteen-mile radius of the nearby Kokanee Glacier.* Sasquatches, he added, had been seen a few times on the edges of town, but he insisted—for no particular reason—that what my friend and I had heard was most likely an elk passing above the trail.

I casually brushed off his dismissal as envy and, eager to confirm my bias, asked him how many people in town had seen the animal.

"More than are willing to admit," he replied, with an air of mystery. Forest rangers, loggers, a former policeman, and the owners

---

* The Kokanee Glacier is an iconic feature of the Selkirk range. It's also the namesake of a local beer that has pressed the Sasquatch into service as its corporate mascot. Robert said that if you spent several days camped alone anywhere in that wide radius around the glacier and played the harmonica or broadcast recordings of children playing in a schoolyard, those sounds would draw Sasquatches near and virtually guarantee an encounter. It was an idea he had recently come up with, but had not yet tested.

of a local hot springs resort were among the eyewitnesses who had confided in him.

"One hunter I know," he said, "had a distant Sasquatch in his rifle sights but chose to lower his gun rather than shoot."

"Why?" I asked.

"For the same reason that all hunters in the same situation do: he couldn't pull the trigger."

"Because he was paralyzed by fear?"

"No, because it was too human-looking. At one point the thing casually turned its head and stared straight at the guy through the crosshairs of his scope for a full minute."

My mind took in that eerie moment. Then a disturbing thought came to me. "How far away was the Sasquatch?" I asked.

A look of affirmation came over Rob's face. "Several hundred yards," he said, pausing before delivering his denouement. "The Sasquatch *knew* he was there."

In the years after Nelson, several people I met, or knew, came out of the woodwork with personal tales of their own. The first was a Toronto acquaintance with Pakistani roots who told me that a group of *Shino Mohenu*, or "men of snow," raided his mother's village in the Kashmiri Himalayas when she was a child. The creatures made off with armfuls of chickens and goats during a particularly bad winter. That was followed by a story from a friend in Vancouver who claimed to have seen a reddish-brown Sasquatch running between trees as she and a friend were hiking in the nearby Coast Mountains. A third, shell-shocked account came from a female work colleague in Toronto who had seen a huge, hairy biped cross a wooded rural road near the Niagara Escarpment, three hours north of the city. The strange thing was that the last two eyewitnesses had had almost no foreknowledge of the Bigfoot phenomenon—yet their descriptions of the animals, down to the most minor details, matched those of classic reports. Though I'd moved on from that incident in Nelson, each story had the effect of rekindling my interest in the subject. By the end of my first trip to the Great Bear Rainforest, where I had met Clark Hans while on assignment, my lifelong curiosity about the mystery had reached fever pitch.

Why are many otherwise normal people from different walks of life seeing giant, hair-covered humanoids? And why do scores of others who haven't seen them believe in them anyway, with an unshakable conviction? It seems to be more than just some passing vogue. The Bermuda Triangle, the Loch Ness Monster, crop circles, spontaneous human combustion, lizard men, and the Chupacabra all had their popularity spikes before falling off the radar like one-hit wonders. Not so with the Sasquatch. It has survived the test of time as successfully as it has avoided capture. Scores of blogs and websites track the latest research developments and eyewitness accounts. Citizen sleuths, armed with the best in affordable technology, have taken up the search in their own backyards—or in secret wilderness "habituation zones," where they claim to play cat-and-mouse games with the creatures. Documentaries on the subject continue to pour forth and capitalize on an insatiable thirst for wonder. One reality show called *Finding Bigfoot*, which follows the semi-staged exploits of four Sasquatch hunters in the field, has developed a cult following. The series inspired several offshoots, and for a while garnered some of the highest ratings for the broadcaster, Animal Planet.

There has to be a way to make better sense of the phenomenon: one that doesn't rely on ready-made positions rooted in unquestioning belief or disbelief; one that moves past the pop-culture veneer and rhetoric of opposing camps and into the more nuanced territory where psychology, culture, history, literature, and indigenous experience overlap. If primeval nature and collective memory are places where the Sasquatch continues to thrive, where better than the Great Bear Rainforest, and its deep-rooted communities, to go in search of it?

3

SASQUALOGY

In the half century since big, upright creatures, leaving hundreds of tracks, were seen in the high snowfield on the north side of Mount Everest by a band of British mountaineers, the ye-teh, or yeti, has met with a storm of disapproval from upset scientists around the world. But as with the sasquatch of the vast rain forests of the Pacific Northwest, the case against the existence of the yeti—entirely speculative, and necessarily based on assumptions of foolishness or mendacity in many observers of good reputation—is even less "scientific" than the evidence that it exists.

—Peter Matthiessen, *The Snow Leopard*

In 1963, John Bindernagel, a third-year wildlife biology undergrad at the University of Guelph in southern Ontario, visited his local barbershop. Before taking a seat in the chair, he rummaged through a stack of magazines on a nearby table and pulled out a copy of *Argosy*—an American men's magazine that featured "true" adventure stories.

As the barber went to work, Bindernagel flipped through the magazine. Halfway in, something grabbed him: it was a story about a race of undiscovered ape-men that people were claiming to see in the British Columbia wilderness. The author was Ivan T. Sanderson, an eccentric Scottish American biologist, who was making a name for himself investigating mysterious creatures and paranormal subjects. The story, brimming with eyewitness accounts and colorful illustrations of the shaggy creatures, fired Bindernagel's imagination. New species were being discovered all the time—but an anomalous, unclassified primate in North America promised to be the discovery of the century.

Bindernagel was so taken with the mystery that he decided to bring it up in his wildlife management class a few days later. Raising his hand, he asked his professor what the strange ape-men, seen by people across the Pacific Northwest, could possibly be. He had barely spoken his last words when the lecture hall erupted in peals of laughter. Bindernagel looked on as his fellow students keeled over in convulsions of cackling. The answer, the professor said, stepping in to adjudicate, was simple: Bigfoot was a hoax. With a reproachful glance, he added that the subject wasn't fit for serious discussion in class, and that it shouldn't be brought up again.

Rejected by his peers, the angry and embarrassed undergrad resolved to pursue the topic quietly on the side for as long as it took to yield answers. The subject would eventually consume him, becoming his life's obsession.

In 1998, more than three decades later, Bindernagel, a career wildlife biologist, published a book entitled *North America's Great Ape: The Sasquatch*. In it, he argued that the reported physical and behavioral attributes of Bigfoot are so similar to those of known primates that the creatures are almost certainly an undiscovered species of great ape. It was a deliberate act of demystification reflected in the book's subtitle: *A Wildlife Biologist Looks at the Continent's Most Misunderstood Large Mammal*.

I reached out to Bindernagel, now living in British Columbia, before leaving on my trip. He was thrilled by my interest and invited me to stop in at Courtenay, the laid-back community on the east coast of Vancouver Island, to spend the day with him.

Not only would I gain insight into the Sasquatch from the perspective of a scientist working on the subject—there are only a handful of such scientists in the world—but it would also provide access to the mind of a man who, for most of his life, has known the relentless pursuit of a creature that the wider world, including his own colleagues, insists does not exist.

When I pull up to Bindernagel's home—a small, aging bungalow in a leafy subdivision on the edge of town—both he and his wife are waiting on the front lawn. Bindernagel, who brandishes a toddler's smile and keeps his hands glued inside his pockets, looks very much the academic, with his wiry gray beard, beige slacks, and denim shirt. Joan, his wife, a petite and innocent-looking blonde, stands by his side, also smiling shyly.

The image and demeanor of the wildlife biologist couldn't be any further from the monster-hunter stereotype: the outspoken and abrasive alpha male decked out in commando-style bushwhacking gear and battlefield accoutrements. I'd always known that Bindernagel embodied a different archetype. Even so, I was surprised by how polite and deferential he was on the phone. His endearing use of the fading interjections of mid-twentieth-century English, like *my goodness, gee whiz,* and *shucks,* only sets him further apart from the pushy gaggle of bounty hunters. But when we shake hands, I catch a flash of stubborn determination and restless agitation rising from beneath the old-fashioned niceties. This is someone questing for a grail.

"I just came back from checking the camera traps," he says, as we stroll toward his home, referring to the battery-operated digital trail cameras that Sasquatch enthusiasts strap to the trunks of trees in the hope of photographing the creatures by chance. "That's my latest project. I've been getting loads of great images of black bears, deer, and even cougars."

"No Sasquatches?" I playfully ask.

"They're a bit more camera shy, as you can imagine," he says chuckling. "But, gee, you know, we're just weeks away from the salmon coming in. That's when the Sasquatch come down from the mountains for that first bit of rich protein after a dry summer."

We step inside and Bindernagel leads me into his living room, which resembles a flea market. Stacks of books, mounds of paper, and cardboard boxes teeming with knickknacks are heaped on top of retro 1970s furniture. Joan apologizes for the mess, saying they're in the process of moving.

When I look down, I see assembled neatly on the floor several white plaster-of-Paris casts of gigantic, humanoid footprints— Sasquatch tracks. Most of them are a foot and a half in length, and considerably wide at the sides. Some look very human. Others are more mushroom-like, with splayed toes. They are all unsettling.

Bindernagel takes a step back and gauges my reaction. I pick up a cast, the most intact and symmetrical of the bunch. It's lean and muscular, with unusually long toes and a slight hourglass shape to it.

"Joan and I came across that one in 1988 during a hike in Strathcona Park, not far from here," he says. "They're the only tracks I've ever found myself. That one's sixteen inches."

I eye the details of the heavy plaster cast as if it were some rare artifact.

"Tracks are the best evidence we have," he adds, gently taking the cast from my hands and placing it carefully on the ground before I'm finished with it. "People sometimes laugh at us for making these casts. But when it comes to studying other mammals, we biologists depend more on tracks than on sightings."

"How do you reconcile these tracks with the fact that people have been known to hoax footprints?" I ask.

"I'll show you," he says, with confident enthusiasm, picking up another cast, with much shorter toes. "This is one of a series of tracks in which the Sasquatch had a very flexible foot. It would scrunch, or curl, its toes while it walked. You couldn't fake a track like this."

I examine the cast. The toes are spread out asymmetrically.

"We have others, similar to this, that show the animal climbing up a steep hill, with its toes moving from track to track—and with little or no heel registering in the soil. In some cases, you'd need to carry hundreds of pounds just to make a deep enough impression in the ground. That's too big of a job for a hoaxer."

I'd heard similar arguments. The late Grover S. Krantz, a paleo-anthropologist at Washington State University who had researched Sasquatch from the early 1960s until his death in 2002, alleged that some purported Sasquatch tracks revealed a perfect alignment of joints and bones—the same range of anatomical features that reflect the necessary biomechanical redesign of the foot to carry a mass that large. He also showed some tracks that contain dermal ridges: skin patterns on the sole of the foot similar to fingerprints.* Dr. Jeff Meldrum, a professor of anatomy and anthropology at Idaho State University and the inheritor of Krantz's scholarly Sasquatch mantle (including his collection of Bigfoot casts), continues to plug those arguments.

"If this is all so incontrovertible," I say to Bindernagel, "then why aren't other scientists looking into this?"

---

* Krantz showed his dermal-ridged tracks to fingerprint experts around the world—including those in law enforcement, who were much intrigued by them. One renowned fingerprint guru, John Berry, who was also the editor of the fingerprint community's journal, *Fingerprint Whorld*, told Krantz that Scotland Yard had concluded the prints were "probably real." See Regal, Brian, *Searching for Sasquatch: Crackpots, Eggheads, and Cryptozoology* (New York: Palgrave Macmillan, 2011), p. 138.

"That's the $64,000 question," he says. "The answer: ignorance of the evidence. And it's also the implication of the evidence—that we're dealing with an existing mammal. Scientists can't handle that."

In full stride Bindernagel picks up another massive plaster cast of the splayed-toe, mushroom-like variety.

"Scientists will look at this track, but then a theoretical problem crops up. How can we have an upright ape in the world? And, of all places, here in North America? To them it's just a preposterous claim."

"But maybe it is preposterous," I suggest. "What if the Sasquatches don't exist? Where are they? Isn't that the $64,000 question?"

Bindernagel's eyebrows furl. "The question no longer is: Does the Sasquatch exist? That one's been solved. It exists. The question now is: Why is it scientifically taboo?"

My line of questioning has pushed a button. The biologist's calm, jovial manner transforms into an agitation that becomes personal.

"Do you know that there's been almost no recognition of my books? The only reason I can live with this is that once the animal is proven, people will ask, 'Why didn't we see this coming?' And I'll say to them, 'We did! I wrote about it years before in those books that all of you have ignored!'"

Joan, who is listening with her back to us at the other end of the room, turns to give her husband a commiserating look. Bindernagel shoots her a pained expression before returning his gaze to me. His eyes are now glazed; his chin quivers ever so slightly.

"Look at me. I'm not a young man anymore. I'm seventy-two years old, and the clock is ticking."

John Bindernagel's unceasing half-century quest to get the Sasquatch included in the lexicon of North American mammals has
been nothing short of an odyssey for personal vindication.

In the years after his humiliation at the university, Bindernagel
scoured every library looking for any information about giant ape-
men. At first he found no more than a few tongue-in-cheek reports
in old newspaper clippings. Pithier material in books about the
Abominable Snowman or Yeti of Nepal also fell into his dragnet.
But Bigfoot's cousin in the Himalayas was both too geographically
distant and too nebulous in terms of evidence to be of any use to
Bindernagel.

When a British Columbian journalist from Harrison Hot Springs
named John Green, a pioneering Bigfoot researcher, started publishing serious books on the subject in the late 1960s, Bindernagel found
what he was looking for. Green's encyclopedic tomes—repositories
of impeccably researched eyewitness accounts from across the Pacific
Northwest—made him realize that the Sasquatch phenomenon was
far more prevalent and widespread than he had even imagined. All
of this came at a crossroads for the young wildlife biologist. With his
graduate work behind him, Bindernagel was now trying to find his
specialty in a field in which original research topics were quickly
grabbed by the flood of academics coming out of school. One of
Bindernagel's role models, the American field biologist George
Schaller, had become famous for his research on the African lion and
mountain gorilla. Bindernagel, who was still without expertise on
any animal, knew he had to act fast if he wanted to make his mark.

"Here's George, the first serious biologist to write about large
mammals, and I'm thinking: Is there going to be anything left for the
rest of us?" Bindernagel recalls. "I was working on the African buf-
falo at the time, but someone else had made that his niche. I needed

something new. And then one day it hit me like a bolt of lightning: I could make the Sasquatch my animal of specialization!"

Bindernagel carried his epiphany with him to Tanzania, where he took a job as a wildlife consultant for the United Nations. There, a group of scientists at the Serengeti Research Institute helped cement his desire to study the reputed animals.

"I raised the subject there. And there was no laughter and no joking. They said, 'John, if I were you, and I wanted to pursue this back in Canada, I would do such and such.' These were British, Dutch, and American scientists. They were first class and were unbelievably supportive."

In 1975, Bindernagel and Joan moved back to Canada, where they set themselves up on the east coast of Vancouver Island. It was an area of frequent Sasquatch reports, and the biologist wanted to be as close as possible to his bounty. But the financial realities of life, including raising a family, meant that the nonpaying research had to play second fiddle to conventional biology gigs. To make ends meet, Bindernagel spent the coming decade piecing together wildlife survey and consultancy jobs, some of them abroad. He spent his off time pounding the pavement in British Columbia to build his dossier of ape-men reports.

"I'd look for eyewitnesses at a dock, at Port Hardy or someplace, and there would be jokes," he says. "I'd ask: 'Has anyone here seen a Sasquatch?' And people would respond: 'Just my brother-in-law! Ah-ho-ho-ho!' In those moments I felt it wasn't working. But once in a while there would be a really good report. And it went on like that for years."

By the mid-1980s, Bindernagel had assembled a large dossier of firsthand reports from across the province. He'd cut his teeth like the best of the investigators, and was becoming a local authority in the burgeoning field of Sasqualogy. But he was also losing hope that a Bigfoot would ever be brought back from the woods in chains. A physical specimen had still not been produced, and society as a whole seemed no closer to accepting a creature of tabloid farce. For Bindernagel, who was spending his own money with virtually no payback, the Sasquatch began to look more and more like a chimera. As much as he tried to keep his activities hidden from his associates in the scientific community, rumors about his part-time sleuthing had reached the ears of more and more colleagues. People in academia were beginning to talk. Suddenly, Bindernagel's reputation, credibility, and livelihood all seemed to be on the line. So the biologist did what any self-respecting scientist with a wife and two kids would do in that situation: he shelved the creature. After a solid ten-year run, Bindernagel's hobby, passion, and would-be career were dead in the water. For the first time in his adult life, he found himself forlorn and rudderless. Everything seemed without purpose.

Then in October 1988, something entirely unexpected happened. Bindernagel and his wife were helping guide a group of seventh-grade girls on an overnight camping trip in nearby Strathcona Provincial Park. During the hike in, one of the girls trailing at the back of the caravan stopped in her tracks with her eyes fixed on the ground beside the trail.

"What's *that*?" she shouted, pointing toward a patch of mud. Bindernagel approached to see what was the matter.

"When I got there," he recalls, "I looked down and—my goodness!—I was beside myself: there was a Sasquatch track!"

And not just one. There were several large humanoid footprints pressed deep into the mud on the side of the trail. Unable to do anything at the moment, Bindernagel and his wife returned to the area later to cast the tracks in plaster of Paris.

It was an eerily fortuitous moment that rekindled Bindernagel's interest with a fury. Many researchers had spent their entire lives without themselves ever seeing a Sasquatch or coming across tracks. But here the beast had all but danced across his path, as if it were taunting him. Not only were the prints in very good condition, but Joan, who had at best been lukewarm toward her husband's obsession, was also there to see them for herself. It was the vindication that Bindernagel so desperately sought.

He decided on the spot to revive his research; only this time, there would be no half measures. He would come fully out of the closet with his interest, becoming a sort of "Bigfoot biologist."

Ten years later, Bindernagel published his first book on the subject: *North America's Great Ape: The Sasquatch*. In it, he argued that Bigfoots were an unclassified species of ape that shared physical features and nearly identical behaviors with other primates in the animal kingdom, such as mountain gorillas, chimpanzees, and orangutans. Reports of Sasquatches vocalizing, throwing objects, emitting rancid odors, bluff charging, building nests, and scavenging and foraging are all part of the primate repertoire. For Bindernagel they were, in aggregate, too much to be coincidence.

"I am now satisfied with the available evidence for the existence of the Sasquatch in North America," he writes in the book's opening. "My view is that not only do we have sufficient evidence to treat the Sasquatch as a bona fide member of North America's spectrum of large mammals, but that we already know a great deal about its biology and ecology."[2]

Bindernagel broke ranks with his colleagues not only by declaring the animal extant but also by circumventing the normal avenues of peer review. It was an act of dissent that effectively made him a heretic. But because he wasn't a big-name scientist, few people paid him any attention. The book, which was issued by a small British

Columbian press, and which faced the usual uphill battles to garner publicity, didn't reach a wide enough audience. It fell on mostly deaf ears.* Without a carcass or physical specimen, few of his colleagues would take the animal seriously enough to stake their reputations on it, even with Bindernagel's erudite arguments.

Not even a second book, published in 2010 and lambasting the scientific establishment for its closed-mindedness, would stir debate in a community that Bindernagel described as being "asleep at the wheel." In *The Discovery of the Sasquatch*, a philosophical manifesto seven years in the making, Bindernagel threw everything he had at the scientific establishment. He argued that in spite of the lack of formal recognition by science, the Sasquatch had, nonetheless, already been "discovered." It was a de facto discovery, he insisted, made first by indigenous people and later by colonists and everyone else who followed. It just wasn't officially sanctioned. He went on to list all the mental impediments and misconceptions that prevented science from seeing what he and others had so easily recognized.

"The proposition put forward here," Bindernagel writes, "is that the acquisition of a sasquatch specimen will merely be additional corroboration of a discovery which can already be claimed on the basis of published testimonial evidence, evidence which has been corroborated by the archived physical evidence of tracks."[3]

But like his first book, *The Discovery of the Sasquatch* landed with a thud.

Now in the grip of disillusionment, and of his growing sense of mortality, Bindernagel is spending most of his time trying to make available every shred of his findings for when he is no longer alive, by way of the Internet. He says the upsurge in popular interest in the

---

* Bindernagel mailed copies of the book to the heads of all state and provincial wildlife units in North America, only to receive just one lackluster letter of thanks.

subject, with self-published books, reality-TV shows, and websites, largely by nonscientists, threatens to eclipse his lifework. His fear of being forgotten, postmortem, weighs on him.

"I was recently with a younger researcher from Alberta who didn't even know who John Green was!" he says. "Imagine that— *John Green!* This is the guy who literally started Sasquatch studies. I mean, gee whiz, if a guy like Green's already being forgotten, what's gonna happen to the rest of us?"

Tomorrow I leave for the Great Bear Rainforest, and in the time left with my host, I want to poke and prod at his arguments a bit more. I suggest to Bindernagel that we abandon his leafy Courtenay subdivision in favor of a place more connected to his work—a place with a bit of an edge and some Sasquatch history. We hop into his car and head to a local haunt known as Medicine Bowls, a stretch of rapids and waterfalls on the Browns River, located ten miles from town.

Medicine Bowls, Bindernagel tells me, is on the edge of a subalpine region called the Forbidden Plateau. The name for the area was coined after an incident in the late 1800s in which three dozen women and children of the K'ómoks First Nation mysteriously vanished from a makeshift camp while the men were on a war raid. No trace of them was ever found. Some in the tribe claimed that they were abducted by a race of alpine giants believed to inhabit the region.

We leave the open fields and thin patches of wood at the edge of town and drive into an ever-thicker coniferous forest. Bindernagel's demeanor changes. He is suddenly excited, gesturing with flitting, birdlike movements at areas where sightings of the creatures occurred in the past.

"A bunch of reports came in from here," he says, with a big grin, "and now I'm getting cameras set up in the area. It's a promising spot, but nothing like where you're going tomorrow on the central coast."

We turn onto a bumpy dirt road beneath a canopy of large cedars and continue to a clearing at its far end. We park the car and bushwhack down a hill until we reach the moss-covered banks of the Browns River, which is a mostly dry gash of rock careening through majestic timber. There has been no rain on the British Columbia coast for weeks, but snowmelt from the high peaks of the Vancouver Island Ranges keeps the river at a trickle.

As we scramble down the high banks, Bindernagel warns me that the gully drops precipitously in parts up ahead, creating treacherous whirlpools when the river is higher.

"I got a report some years back of a Sasquatch standing up there beside those trees, looking down at a group of people," he says, pointing at a tree-lined cliff.

"It wouldn't be that hard," I reply, "for a man in a fur suit to get up there and scare people down below."

Whatever the reality of Bigfoot, hoaxing is an undeniable part of the Sasquatch phenomenon. Shortly before my trip, a forty-four-year-old man, wearing a military-style ghillie camouflage suit, was run over by two cars and killed while crossing a highway in Montana. The man, it turned out, was impersonating a Sasquatch in a botched practical joke meant to frighten people.

"Hoaxing is taken as an explanation for all reports because it's considered more plausible than a hidden animal," Bindernagel fires back.

"But it does seem much more plausible an explanation."

"Not when you know the facts," he says. "These hoaxes would have to have been happening for centuries among the indigenous people before the Europeans arrived. And today they'd have to occur in the most unlikely places and times. During downpours, in the middle of the night, in places where there are hardly any people. Places you can only get to by floatplanes. Explanations of hoaxing are sometimes more far-fetched than explanations of a Sasquatch!"

By questioning Bindernagel, I feel myself becoming the personification of the skeptical establishment and doubtful general public. And that emboldens him. He is no longer addressing me but speaking to the rest of the world.

"When people see a Sasquatch walking," he says, imitating a Bigfoot stride, "they realize they are not looking at a human in a fur suit. They see huge size and displays of extraordinary strength. They see great speed across the landscape. They're also seeing fluidity and muscles rippling. People say, 'This couldn't just be a human in a fur suit.'"

"Yes, but how can any animal be so elusive as to completely avoid physical capture?" I say, shifting to what I take to be firmer ground. "Surely that must mystify you."

Bindernagel shakes his head.

"No?" I say.

"The animal's just hard to see. If you read about Jane Goodall in the early days with chimpanzees, or Birute Galdikas with orangutans, you'd understand that these primatologists didn't just start observing chimps and orangs in the wild. They heard noises. And when the researchers approached them, the animals ran off. They didn't get good views of these animals until after months of following them and getting them partly habituated. It's the same with the Sasquatch."

"But some researchers have been trying to habituate Sasquatches for years. And there's still no firm proof."

Bindernagel shrugs. "I can't speak for everyone's methods. These are very smart animals."

The biologist's conviction is unshakable. He has answers for everything and speaks as if reading from a memorized script. I decide to launch a bunker buster to pierce through his scholarly facade.

"Aren't you afraid you've wasted your life?"

Bindernagel's face drops. It's a punch below the belt, and I regret asking the question. His calm and composure begin to break down.

"Deep down my work is about helping people who are mentally distressed by what they've seen. It's about being able to say to them, 'I understand your distress.' In the meantime, yes, it's difficult. And my wife, Joan, has suffered even more than I have."

I refrain from responding, wanting neither to set him off nor to concede. But when his last answer fails to elicit any acknowledgment from me, the floodgates open.

"Gee whiz, John! Thousands of people are seeing this animal— and nobody wants to talk about it! All I'm saying is, there's a conservative way to explain it: this simply is an upright great ape. Great apes exist on the planet!"

Later, as we drive along the gravel road that leads out of the forest, a red pickup truck emerges in the distance. Bindernagel, who has been quiet, pulls his vehicle to the right to make room for the other to pass. The truck creaks to a stop beside us. The driver, who is rolling down his window, is a young man in his late twenties. Sitting beside him is a blond woman of about the same age.

Bindernagel, coincidentally, knows him—a family friend named Carl. And for several minutes a conversation ensues.

"I'm still doing my Sasquatch research," Bindernagel says at one point, changing the subject with a smile. "I've got trail cameras set up all around here. I'm getting some great wildlife shots."

Carl and his girlfriend stiffen at the mention of the creature and glance at each other. "It's funny you mention that," Carl says. "Just the other day, a guy I know told me he saw a Sasquatch on Sonora Island last winter."

Bindernagel's jaw drops. His eyes nearly jump out of their sockets. "Oh, my goodness!" he growls, turning to me in amazement, his face contorted with gladness. "Well, go ahead, Carl! Do tell, do tell."

"My friend was doing construction work alone outside at the wilderness resort there. At one point he glanced to his side and saw a huge hairy thing on two legs walking between him and a cement truck. My friend said it was as tall as the roof of the truck. The creature then looked at him and gave him a dirty look before making a beeline into the bush."

I watch Bindernagel with fascination as he reacts to this serendipitous, though secondhand, report. He's nearly beside himself with euphoria and breaks into a flurry of questions that are met by an equal number of shrugged shoulders and shaking heads.

"Dunno," Carl says, over and over again. "All he said was that he never believed in Bigfoot before, but now he was convinced."

Before driving off, Carl bids adieu to Bindernagel with a friendly smile, saying, "Well, I hope you find it."

When I look at Bindernagel moments later, I see his mood has soured. His face shows a mixture of expired elation, irony, and annoyance—all melded into one unsettling look that I can't decipher.

"What's the matter?" I ask.

"*Well, I hope you find it,*" Bindernagel says mockingly, enunciating each word as if he'd been slighted. "See what I mean? People have no idea."

"I don't follow."

"The Sasquatch—it's already been found!" he says, with a resentful, drawn-out sigh. "One day the vindication will come."

Bindernagel fixes his gaze on the road, shakes his head, and changes the subject, pointing out another promising location for a camera trap.

PART II

4

Bella Bella
(Waglisla)

*They believe in a race of giants, which inhabit a certain mountain off
to the west of us. This mountain is covered with perpetual snow. They
inhabit the snow peaks. They hunt and do all their work at night. They
are men stealers. They come to the people's lodges at night when the
people are asleep and take them and put them under their skins and
to their place of abode without even waking. Their track is a foot and
a half long. They steal salmon from Indian nets and eat them raw as
the bears do. If the people are awake, they always know when they
are coming very near by their strong smell that is most intolerable. It is
not uncommon for them to come in the night and give three whistles
and then the stones will begin to hit their houses.*

—Diary of Elkanah Walker, a missionary among the
Spokane people of the Pacific Northwest, 1840

The flight from Port Hardy, near the northern tip of Vancouver
Island, to Bella Bella is short, taking just over forty minutes. But
the distance covered feels immeasurable. Within moments we soar
over the blue abyss of the Pacific, crossing some invisible boundary
separating humanity's neat grids from the sprawling folds and rising humps of a free-flowing hinterland. We skip over Labouchere
Channel, banking north across the thickly carpeted mainland
coast and the islands that huddle around it like pottery shards.

Our small twin-engine turboprop flies low, revealing the landscape in the clearest detail. Long stretches of yellow sandy beach, clusters of rocks foaming with breakers, and stands of old growth—all breathtakingly intact—roll past in succession. Occasionally, fjords—cliff-lined coastal inlets of the sea—appear, snaking eastward, before vanishing into distant scrums of mountains.

This wilderness in my sights is a powerful spectacle, amplified, I suspect, by my own predispositions and experiences. I've spent much time living and working in the Middle East, with its austere, bone-dry deserts, which I've not only become accustomed to but also accepted—as a child of Arab parents—as part of my genetic makeup. The Great Bear Rainforest is the antithesis of that barren topography. Placing images of the two regions side by side, you would be hard-pressed to find a more stark contrast. Because it is so wonderfully different from everything I'm used to, the Edenic lushness below resonates deeply with me.

We dip bumpily into fingers of low-lying cloud, emerging high above gnarled, tangled treetops in miniature. Soon a road appears, then a cluster of homes. A water reservoir and a marina finally hurtle by as the plane sinks into an outlying, tinder-dry bog jungle, meeting its shadow on a solitary strip of pavement.

When I returned to Toronto after my first trip to the area and tried to describe the Great Bear Rainforest—an environment so dynamic, so complex, and so possessed of intelligence that to be in it is to be subsumed into a living, breathing thing—I got mostly blank stares and perfunctory nods from my listeners. For most people, there was no comparable point of reference.

Maps, though useful for navigation, are crude approximations of reality, visual guides to only one aspect of spatial and temporal experience. To read a description of the Great Bear Rainforest as a wilderness extending 250 miles along British Columbia's central and north coast, or to see it delineated on a map, may give some vague impression of its dimensions. But it won't convey the area's topography, its density of foliage, and its internal immensity. Even a flight over the region fails to reveal its hierarchal complexity. The Great Bear's matrix of lakes, rivers, valleys, islands, mountains, and seemingly endless tracts of tangled forest is a universe unto itself. If longevity, sustenance, and the ability to swim in numbingly cold water weren't an issue, a human could enter that wilderness and conceivably ramble through it forever. A winding trajectory would result in space turning in on itself, creating a kind of infinity for the wanderer.

The Great Bear Rainforest is the largest tract of intact coastal temperate rain forest in the world—one so rich and prolific that it supports more organic matter per square meter than any other place on the planet. Receiving as much as two hundred inches of rainfall a year, its most productive areas generate up to four times the biomass (the total quantity or weight of organisms in a given area) of the Amazon, the Congo basin, or the rain forests of Borneo or New Guinea. Wading through the fluorescent green of coniferous old growth, among trees both living and dead and thickly carpeted with mosses and lichens, must rank among the most stirring and profound of human experiences.

Some of the tallest and oldest trees in the world have grown here. Western redcedar, Douglas fir, Sitka spruce, western hemlock, shore pine, and amabilis fir are the mainstays of a great blanket of green that, in times gone by, covered most of North America's western coastline. Though many of their number have been lost to logging, these trees are capable of growing to a few hundred feet in height and can live well over a thousand years.

Those big trees are sages of the forest and veritable agents of planetary life support. They produce oxygen, sequester carbon, stop soil erosion, trap and distill rainwater, provide shelter and habitat for animals, create microclimates, foster decay that fertilizes the soil, and ultimately self-replicate—their inanimate poses belying all of this. Beneath these titans, stratified worlds and their creatures overlap and intermingle. Concealed by undergrowth and the detritus of the forest floor is the rain forest's soil. It is a repository of nutrients and a seething cosmopolis of interactions. Ants, bacteria, fungi, and a host of microscopic entities churn and mince the carbon-rich soil that is the ecosystem's pillar of health, facilitating the decomposition of organic matter and bringing rich minerals to the surface. In his book *The Clouded Leopard*, Canadian anthropologist, ethnobotanist, and author Wade Davis describes a square meter of productive rain-forest terrain as supporting approximately "2,000 earth-worms, 40,000 insects, 120,000 mites, 120 million nematodes and millions upon millions of protozoa and bacteria, all alive, moving through the earth, feeding, digesting, reproducing, and dying."[4]

Between the timeless, slow-motion gyrations of the soil and the iron steadfastness of the giants that root in it is the tangle of wild undergrowth consisting of hundreds of plant species, including edible and medicinal herbs. A host of invertebrates and amphibians dwell and travel within it, from lungless salamanders to tailed frogs to slugs growing up to eight inches long, providing food for rodents and birds. Mammals like deer, porcupines, beavers, rabbits, elk, wild sheep, and mountain goats are preyed upon by the large hunters: grizzly bears, black bears, coastal wolves, and cougars.

This seemingly endless litany of terrestrial ecology is matched in the nearby ocean. For here land and water are extensions of each other. Old-growth conifers find their underwater counterparts in vast, undulating kelp forests that give sanctuary to what Davis calls "the greatest coastal marine diversity on Earth." Countless species of fish, marine invertebrates, and aquatic mammals—dolphins, whales, seals—rove, drift, and reside, sometimes within a stone's throw of shore. The shellfish-encrusted rocks of the intertidal zone—the most fertile in the world—are exposed in a vibrant display of textures and colors: blackish-blue mussels, clusters of off-white barnacles, green anemones, and colonies of starfish painted orange, blue, and green.

Several keystone species—creatures with intense relevance to everything in the ecosystem—reside in the ocean. The five major species of Pacific salmon—pink, coho, sockeye, Chinook, and chum—range for years before returning to spawn and die in the rivers and creeks of their birth. No less miraculous than the salmon's cyclical return is the annual spawning of the Pacific herring, whose arrival on the shores of the Great Bear during the spring snowmelt is a landmark event. The fish return by the thousands of tons, each female laying up to twenty thousand eggs, which attach to underwater plants. Males discharge milt, or sperm, over the eggs in such quantities that the entire surrounding sea turns white for weeks.

As all things exist in relation to all other things, no creature or any process in which it partakes subsists in isolation here. The interrelation of all aspects of life in the Great Bear is its greatest spectacle. The sea bestows rain upon the land: rain which both sinks nutrients into the soil and in turn washes them out to sea to feed aquatic life. The big trees modulate the flow of that rain, preventing soil erosion and torrents along delicate creeks from blowing out salmon spawn. By helping the salmon survive, the big trees help themselves and other animals. Bears, eagles, and wolves feed on the salmon and deposit their carcasses, which act as fertilizer in the soil, encouraging the growth of berry shrubs.

Like complex, weaving motifs in arabesque art, each aspect of rain-forest life, each playing its own tune, combines with all the others to create a grand symphony of ecology.

I need no more than a minute to claim my bag and leave the confines of the Bella Bella airport—one of the smallest I've traveled through. The terminal comprises a small building with a check-in desk and a coffee counter situated on a strip of asphalt running through the bog forest coniferous jungles of Campbell Island.

My fellow passengers, a mix of locals and visitors, mill outside with the residents who have arrived to pick them up. We're at the foot of the road that runs into town through a rough-and-tumble forest flanked by glittering ocean on one side and a pair of mysterious-looking hills on the other.

I hop into the back of a taxi van with a few others. The young driver asks my destination.

"Alvina Duncan's bed-and-breakfast," I tell him.

"Alvina!" he exclaims, chuckling cryptically to himself.

We drive up and down thickly forested hills with views of the sea. Huge ravens crisscross the sky above us. We enter town, passing aged wooden bungalows and two-story homes that sit spaciously beside one another on plots of unfenced land. There are signs in many of the windows: No to Enbridge Pipeline. Heiltsuk Nation Bans Oil Tankers in Our Waters.

We turn onto another street and pull into the driveway of a brown-and-white two-story corner house—the B and B. When I arrive at the front door, I find a note saying Alvina, the proprietor, is out of town. There are instructions to phone someone to let me into the house. I do so, and minutes later a young Heiltsuk woman, in her mid-twenties, with short black hair and wearing a white summer dress and flip-flops, arrives.

"I'm really, really sorry," she says, as she scampers from her car, holding plastic shopping bags and fumbling for a key. "Alvina's down in Nanaimo. She'll be back in a few days."

We enter the house and climb a staircase to the second floor, where I find a nicely furnished apartment with three bedrooms. A large window in the living room overlooks part of the town and the ocean just beyond. I drop my bags in the largest of the three rooms, which are all unoccupied.

"Here's your key," the woman says as I come out. "The shower's broken, so you'll have to use the one downstairs, where Alvina sleeps. No plumbers in Bella these days."

The woman unpacks her shopping onto the kitchen counter, and then stops abruptly and turns to me.

"I'm so sorry. My name's Sierra," she says, laughing and extending her hand. "I'm Alvina's grandniece. I watch the place and cook for guests when she's away. I'd have been here when you arrived, but things have been so crazy the last few days with the fire."

"Fire?" I ask.

"You didn't hear? One of our big buildings by the wharf burned down the other day. The supermarket, the post office, the liquor store—all gone."

"Was anyone hurt?"

"No, it happened in the middle of the night. Everyone was asleep. Three girls set fire to the place. They said it was an accident. The cops are investigating."

I remember the building from my past visit. The afflicted structure also housed a café run by a local nonprofit, which I had visited.

"There was a coffee shop in that building," I say.

"Yeah, the Koeye Café," she says, frowning. "Gone as well. Including their offices and library. The whole town's upside down. Everyone's on edge. They've turned our church into a makeshift store."

I tell her about my last trip to the area, including my interest in collecting Sasquatch stories.

"There's been a lot of activity in the last few months," she says, chopping celery on a cutting board. "People hearing screams and smelling that bad stink."

I ask if she thinks the creatures exist.

She shrugs. "I don't know. The problem here is that sometimes stories get passed along from person to person and get bigger and bigger with each telling. You never really know what to believe. That's kinda how it is with small towns. And Bella Bella's no different."

Bella Bella, though small, is the largest community on British Columbia's central coast. It's a way station appearing like a mirage in the ethereal blue-green dreamscapes of the Inside Passage route to Alaska—a coastal thoroughfare for cruise ships, ferries, freighters, yachts, and fishing boats. The town sits near the outer edge of a knot of channels and passes, next to the open ocean.

Bella Bella is split between two precincts, reflecting the area's fractured landscape. The main town, straddling the northeastern corner of Campbell Island, is Bella Bella proper, the seat of the Heiltsuk First Nation. A smaller community of nonindigenous residents clusters around the village of Shearwater, a fishing lodge and marina built on the site of a World War II naval base on neighboring Denny Island. All together, some fifteen hundred people call the area home.

Geographical isolation, human catastrophes, and a history of government exploitation and abuse have left social and economic scars on the community. In the winter of 1862–63, a deadly smallpox epidemic broke out in the city of Victoria and spread—killing tens of thousands of indigenous people across British Columbia. It nearly destroyed the Heiltsuk, whose surviving members from across the territory resettled near today's Bella Bella.* Over a decade later, the Canadian government, bent on controlling and assimilating the country's indigenous populations, drove residents of First Nations onto reserves and began to set up residential schools to Christianize and "civilize" them. For more than a century, children nationwide—150,000 in all—were forcibly separated from their parents and placed in these church-run education centers, which strictly forbade them to speak their languages and practice their cultures under threat of punishment. Abuse—physical, psychological, and sexual—was rife in the schools. Thousands of students died in abhorrent, spartan conditions. Meanwhile, the logging and commercial fishing industries expanded their operations on the coast in the twentieth century, extracting huge numbers of trees and fish without much thought for the long-term environmental consequences, giving little more than employment to nearby communities.

In spite of everything, Bella Bella doesn't resemble other indigenous communities in Canada, many of which have fared worse under the same circumstances. The Heiltsuk are blessed with an abundance of resources, an accessible location, and picture-postcard surroundings that draw in tourists. The nation's territory is not ceded through any treaty, and its political life is vibrant and organized. The Heiltsuk are a proud and social people. Ethnic and family bonds are tight. Cultural events, including those tied to ceremonial food

---

* The Heiltsuk population at one point dwindled to 250.

harvesting (collecting herring spawn and seaweed, canning fish, and digging clams), only fortify that cohesion.

Unfathomably deep roots are the basis of Bella Bella's extraordinary resilience. The Heiltsuk have occupied their territory for at least fourteen thousand years.* For millennia, prior to European contact, they and their neighbors forged one of the most sophisticated nonagricultural societies on the planet. Like the ancient Greeks or the Polynesians, the Heiltsuk have always been a maritime people, known for the enormous oceangoing canoes that whisked them between coastal settlements at the mouths of creeks and rivers, and beyond into the open sea. Before disease dwindled the nation's numbers, as many as twenty thousand people are believed to have inhabited up to fifty villages and seasonal camps spread across thousands of square miles of territory.

During the previous visit for my magazine assignment, I had spent my few days in Heiltsuk territory almost exclusively at the fishing lodge on the Denny Island side. I had managed a short day trip to Bella Bella, where I'd come across that first Sasquatch report, which set my travels on the coast that summer on a new trajectory.

I first spy Alvina in her backyard on the morning of her return from Vancouver Island: a large-framed woman with short gray hair, wearing an orange sleeveless shirt and laying assault to her lawn with a droning weed cutter. She is tough and brawny, often stopping to pick up and move garden furniture and other heavy items with astonishing ease. At one point she looks up at me on the balcony as if suddenly intuiting my presence. I raise my hand to wave just as

---

* In 2017, an ancient archaeological discovery made on Triquet Island, just southwest of Bella Bella, placed it as one of the oldest sites of human habitation in North America.

she turns, uninterested, to continue her attack on the foliage. Soon the weed cutter goes silent, and the woman begins climbing the stairs to the balcony, where I'm seated eating breakfast.

"Boy, what a workout," she says. "With all the grandkids coming through this house, you'd think a seventy-year-old woman would catch a break." Once at the top, she stops and gives me a serious once-over.

"You must be Alvina Duncan," I say, breaking the ice.

She cracks a slight grin. "And you must be the Sasquatch Man."

We proceed to chat over coffee, while bumblebees and hummingbirds flit over the many potted plants and flowers around us.

There's an inexplicably grand, dignified quality to Alvina. Her charisma and confidence are of the type found in movie heroes: strong, silent, understated—yet direct. I'd heard that Alvina, a retired tribal councillor and Heiltsuk matriarch, commands much respect in the community for her purposeful, no-nonsense approach to dealing with others. Beneath her firm demeanor, however, is a warmth that frequently rises to the surface.

Our conversation, unavoidably, turns to hair-covered giants.

"Have you ever seen one?" I ask.

"No," she says. "But I've seen tracks. And Don, my late husband of thirty years—he and I once heard one whistling when we lived on Hunter Island."

"So, you're convinced they exist."

"There are too many reports. You know that. Otherwise, you wouldn't be here."

"I'm trying to weigh the arguments as objectively as possible. To get as close to the truth as I can."

"If you want the truth, just ask us," she says. "We'll tell you everything."

"What about physical proof?"

Alvina snickers. "This is our backyard. We know it better than anyone else. That should be proof enough."

"But your word alone won't convince others," I say.

"That's all right, we're not trying to convince anybody."

Despite our congenial sparring, Alvina and I have taken to each other, and I realize I'll need her help facilitating introductions with other people in town. An outsider suddenly appearing in a small, tight-knit community and asking questions is bound to cause discomfort and arouse suspicion.

I mention this to Alvina, and she responds with an understanding nod. "I'll put in a good word, whenever I can.

"I'm no expert on the Sasquatch," Alvina continues. "But there's one thing I do know for sure. And you should write this down in your notebook: there's always been an understanding between us and them."

"Between your people and the Sasquatches?"

"Yup," she says. "That's what the elders say. It's unspoken. We leave them alone, and they leave us alone. They don't bother us, and we don't bother them. That's about it, and that's the way it works."

A few days later, I go to interview my first eyewitness: a Heiltsuk civil servant named Mary Brown. In the spring of 2008, Mary and two other adults led a group of nine girls from Bella Bella on a weekend camping trip to a wilderness cabin in Roscoe Inlet, a conservancy area north of town. A waterway flanked by mountainous fjords, Roscoe is legendary for its stunning beauty. Because old village sites are found there, it's also culturally and historically important for the Heiltsuk. Mary claims she and her group had a frightening encounter with a Sasquatch during their trip to the area.

I've heard about Mary's story from someone else in the community. When I phone her, she happily agrees to share her experience and invites me to her second-floor office in what she half-jokingly calls "downtown Bella Bella," a short walk from Alvina's.

On the way there, I pass the scene of the fire that consumed the band store complex. Though still standing, the building is largely destroyed, its charred remains reeking of the wet decay of food and garbage that hadn't been consumed by the fire. The forlorn sight stands in stark contrast to my own fleeting memories of the hundred-year-old blue-and-white building with WAGLISLA (the Heiltsuk name for Bella Bella) emblazoned over the front entrance.

"It's a huge tragedy," Mary says of the fire as I arrive, greeting me with a long face. As we enter her office and sit down, she tells me she is working on the case to help the three girls accused of setting the blaze.

Mary is Bella Bella's restorative justice coordinator. She's an advocate for community members going through Canada's criminal justice system while also acting as a representative of the tribal justice arm of the band, helping rehabilitate offenders in ways more in line with Heiltsuk culture. Mary is confident and self-assured, probably in her mid-forties, and has a bubbly personality. The nine teenage girls she accompanied to the cabin in Roscoe in 2008, she says, were at-risk youth, and the camping trip was part of her work.

"I haven't told this story for a few years," she begins somewhat nervously. "I sometimes can't believe it happened—but it did. And I wasn't the only person there."

Traveling by boat, the group arrived at the bayside cabin during low tide in the late afternoon on the Friday of the weekend outing. After dropping crab traps at one end of the bay, Mary and the other adults took the girls to the cabin located at the other end. There they set up camp and showed the girls how to dig for clams on the beach. As dusk neared, Mary, the two other adults, and one of the girls got back into the boat to retrieve the crab traps. The tide was still low. The rocky, forested shore, maybe a hundred yards away at the most, rose a bit above their heads.

"As I was pulling up one of the traps I had this really eerie feeling something was watching us," Mary says. "I began to look around. The others felt the same."

As Mary pulled her trap out of the water, one of the adults, her friend Marilyn, screamed, "Look! *Look!*" and pointed toward the shore.

"I looked up and couldn't believe what I saw—there was a *Thla'thla* right at the tip of the rock!" she says.

"Sorry, a what on the rock?"

"A *Thla'thla*. That's the word in our language for a Sasquatch. It was crouched down with its arms hanging around its knees, which were up past its shoulders. It was brown in color and just huge. It looked just like that character in *Star Trek*."

"You mean Chewbacca? In *Star Wars*?"

"That's it. It was like a giant monkey with a human-shaped head. And it was watching us in what looked like amazement. It was leaning forward, just staring at us. And at first we were just in awe."

Both the boaters and the creature were frozen in shock. But then the gravity of the situation sank in. Marilyn, who had first spotted the creature, started screaming in horror, yelling hysterically at her husband to start the motor so they could escape. That surge of fright startled the animal, and it stood up. At that moment the boaters saw the creature in its full dimensions: roughly eight feet in height, with long arms, broad shoulders, and a barrel chest.

"Its arms were so long, and its hands were so big," Mary recalls. "It stood up and looked over its shoulder at us as it walked off. After three or four steps it was gone, into the forest."

The relief at seeing the animal leave turned into renewed terror when the adults realized that the girls digging clams on the beach were now in danger. Mary paints a scene of utter pandemonium, as the boaters, in an effort to alert the girls, drove their vessel at full throttle onto the beach—with the impact nearly throwing them out. They then sprinted down the shoreline yelling to the girls at the top of their lungs to get into the cabin as quickly as possible, because they'd seen a *Thla'thla*. Seeing the adults in hysterics, and well versed in old stories about Sasquatches, the teenagers were whipped into paroxysms of fright. Everyone fled inside.

Safe and in the cabin, the group went over and over the details of the encounter in amazement and disbelief. Once everyone had calmed down, a few hours later, the group agreed that the creature was likely gone and wouldn't return. As evening fell, the adults set about making dinner, while the girls climbed into the bunks in the loft area of the cabin. After dark the campers started hearing something moving through the bushes outside. They thought the smell of food had attracted a nearby bear. But whatever had come around soon crawled beneath the cabin, which was raised on stilts.

"The floorboard has cracks in it," Mary says. "And we were overcome by this incredible stench. You know how a dirty, wet dog smells, right? But this was like ten times stronger. It was so stink."

Aware of the bad smell associated with the creature, the campers concluded that the Sasquatch had returned and was now just a few feet beneath them. They became terrified. Seeking protection, the adults climbed up onto the bunks with the girls. For over an hour nobody moved, as they all listened to the animal beneath the cabin shifting around and occasionally knocking and scratching at the floor. It remained there and seemed to have no intention of going away.

"And then Marilyn lost it again," Mary says, chuckling. "She screamed, 'I can't handle this anymore! Grab the gun!' She ordered her husband to confront the *Thla'thla*. So the poor guy climbs down and takes the gun out of the case. He's literally shaking, trying to load his twenty-two. He then swings the door open—and I swear he probably had his eyes closed because he was so terrified of what would be out there—and shoots his gun into the darkness. *Bang-bang-bang-bang-bang!* He then slams the door, pushes the dining table against it, and piles any movable objects on top to barricade us in." Mary, engrossed in her own story, bursts into laughter. "As if that was going to help us," she says. "If that thing wanted to get into the cabin that night, it would have."

But it worked. The animal retreated from beneath the cabin, taking its rancid odor with it. At the crack of dawn, the terrified, sleepless campers took their things and piled into their boats and returned to Bella Bella.

When I ask Mary what most sticks out in her mind about the experience, she tells me it is the creature's face. Its expression, she says, showed no intent to harm. Instead, it revealed only an intense curiosity.

"I think the only reason we were scared is what we learned growing up," she says. "As kids we were told stories in which the *Thla'thla*—a wild woman of the woods—kidnaps children and puts them in a big basket she carries on her back. Those tales were used as cultural teachings—to teach the kids to listen to and respect their parents. And to discourage them from wandering too far off."

"Do you think the Sasquatch is a supernatural being?"

"No, they're normal flesh-and-blood creatures. The others would probably agree. I think they're just smart and cautious animals that live deep in the woods. Nothing more."

In my new capacity as the impartial Sasquatch investigator, I try to be detached as I consider Mary's story, to play the devil's advocate, as

I had done with John Bindernagel. But there are few loose strings with which to pull the story apart.

I ask if she's sure they hadn't seen or smelled a bear.

"A hundred percent," she says.

Did they look for tracks the next morning?

"No."

Why not?

"There was no time. We were running for our lives. Plus we knew what we'd seen."

I am fascinated by Mary's story. It makes sense, concordant with all I know and have heard before about the animals: the typical crouching posture, the bad smell, the sometimes mischievous behavior. Plus, four witnesses were involved in the initial sighting. It is all too compelling.

I go over the arguments for and against the creature's existence in an attempt to ground myself. In doing so, I'm reminded of how intractable the debate is. On one side you have the disciples of the rational notion that anything that can't be shown to exist physically cannot exist. On the other is the view that when something can't be seen, or can't be shown to exist, this doesn't prove it's not there. As with the scripted debates between parliamentarians, the Sisyphean back-and-forth between the two always reaches an impasse: just when one side seems to get the upper hand, the other has a comment or answer that parries it, or a maneuver to deflect it, and everyone is back to square one.

Alvina's place becomes a home away from home. Lots of people pass through on a daily basis. Grandchildren drop in, at any and all hours, for a snippet of conversation with their "Nan" while not so surreptitiously raiding her fridge. Friends, neighbors, and extended family make similarly unpredictable cameos, often just as Alvina is putting the finishing touches on some home cooking. Many come bearing gifts of seafood: jars of salmon, steamed crab, halibut, seaweed, or herring roe prepared with butter and garlic. Alvina giddily stashes the treasures deep in her fridge, only to share them with me later, selflessly, along with a glass of wine, on her hummingbird-graced balcony.

My host's generosity is not limited to the kitchen. Having an interest in my researches, she takes an active role in facilitating them, by finding stories and easing access into the community. Alvina shakes down every person who drops into her place for a Sasquatch story or for tips on whom else I might speak to. After a while, I can barely keep up with the leads. I accumulate my own dossier of reports and quickly become familiar with many of the names and places in the territory. In my mental map, and later on Google Earth, I plug tacks into every creek valley, secluded cove, clam beach, and old village site tied to the creatures. Sasquatches, if they exist, seem to be omnipresent on the coast. No island or islet is too remote. No valley is free of their potential presence.

One night, during a backyard barbecue at the house, Alvina appears behind me and grabs my arm. "I want you to meet someone," she says, leading me to a bonfire around which several people are seated on lawn chairs. She introduces me to her former son-in-law.

"Tell him your Stryker Island story, Larry," Alvina says, before smiling at me and disappearing into the dark.

The tall, heavyset man in his late fifties is reluctant to speak at first but then tells me that he and his father had encountered an albino Sasquatch on the island. It happened, he said, while the two men were clam digging.

"Suddenly, Dad came running to me, all hysterical, saying a white Sasquatch had come after him," Larry says. "He said it was trying to protect its clams." Larry goes silent, reliving the memory.

"Then what happened?" I prompt him.

"The thing chased us outta there is what," he says. "My dad was really affected by it. He got really freaked out after. So I performed a smoke ceremony to cleanse him."

"Did he recover?"

"He was, well, different after."

I notice a man beside us listening intently to the conversation, his stern, heavily contoured face reflecting the dim orange light coming from the embers of the fire. He is staring at me, and I turn my gaze to meet his.

"You say you're some kinda writer?" he interjects.

"I am."

"You're on an Indian reservation and this is the kind of thing you want to write about?" His tone is hostile.

"It's for a book project. I'm collecting stories—"

"Look around you!" he says, cutting me off. "We're hurting here! There aren't any jobs. Groceries are expensive. Do you know how much it costs to buy a bottle of ketchup? *Ten bucks!* And that was back when we had ketchup! Our goddamn band store just burned down and no government is lifting a finger to help us. The next-nearest supermarket is a hundred miles away!"

Everyone around the fire is listening now. The truth of what he's saying dawns on me, and I suddenly feel embarrassed and a bit ashamed.

"You come from the big city, and all you can do is ask about Sasquatches!" he says. "Sasquatch this, and Bigfoot that! I have news for you: there is no Sasquatch! It doesn't exist! Why don't you do everyone a favor and write about what life is like around here—and how tough things are?"

He stands up, flicks his beer bottle into the fire, and walks away.

Prior to my trip, people acquainted with the coast told me that I'd face an adjustment period. That things work differently here. That the pace and tempo of coastal life are radically at odds with those of the city. I find that to be true. Life in Bella Bella is less structured around clock time. Outside of official business, there is less emphasis on setting up and holding to firm appointments. Plans with others have an almost hypothetical quality to them, until they actually happen. When I complain to Alvina and others that some scheduled meetings don't come to pass, they all tell me to forgo plans and just go look for people, show up unannounced. More often than not, they add, I'll find them. And experience bears that out.

The rhythms of life here are also different. People are more relaxed. They walk slowly and tread lightly. Dialogue is easygoing and peppered with natural pauses. It is also not hampered by loud ambient noises—traffic, construction, music, and the ruckus of crowds—that compel people in cities to raise their voices unconsciously. More than once, embarrassingly, I have to ask people to repeat themselves because I can't hear their quiet words.

Because of their hard opposition to the Big Oil projects on the coast, the Heiltsuk have garnered a reputation, a stereotype even, among those who don't know them, for being naturally antagonistic. But I find Bella Bellans to be friendly, open-minded, and extroverted. Nearly every driver who passes me in the street waves. People strolling by on the road also say hello and ask how I'm doing.

If a conversation is struck up, and I mention that I'm staying with Alvina, who is widely respected, there is an instant happy glimmer of recognition. My interest in Sasquatch further bridges any real or perceived chasms. I quickly gain the nickname "Sasquatch Man," which I wrongly believed was Alvina's coinage and usage alone.

But just when I think I've reached acceptance in the community, I'm reminded of the limits of being an outsider. Rumors reach my ears that some people in town think I'm an informer, trying to infiltrate the community to report on any threatening activist opposition to those Big Oil megaprojects. My supposed affiliations vary depending on the person harboring the suspicion: the police, the government, the Big Oil companies. Most of the rumors have me working for Enbridge, the Canadian multinational energy-transportation company, whose Northern Gateway pipeline program the Heiltsuk and other First Nations are determined to stop at any cost. The whole "Sasquatch getup," I am told, is believed to be a clever ruse to help me gain access to the community.*

One Saturday night, I head to the Fisherman's Bar and Grill in nearby Shearwater—the main watering hole in the area. Dance-floor revelers bounce to a live band playing 1980s covers, while scruffy-looking commercial fishermen from out of town, wild-eyed and worn by time, brood idly in the corners, nursing their beers.

I grab a drink at the bar and get invited to a game of pool with some new friends I've made. Sasquatch almost invariably comes up, and throughout the night people share names of contacts and places related to Bigfoot sightings. I jot down the small leads and anecdotes in my notebook.

---

* To be fair to the Heiltsuk, in 2013 the mainstream media revealed that the domestic intelligence arms of the Canadian government had been spying on indigenous activists who opposed the big energy projects slated for the west coast.

Within days word gets back to me that I've acquired a new nickname: "The Notetaker." And I hear from some that my scribbling in the bar that night has aroused further suspicions. Perhaps I'm reporting on certain people?

In the more conspiracy-prone Middle East, I faced similar allegations—the often good-humored, half-joking quips about espionage made by local friends and colleagues that are de rigueur in that part of the world. As in the Middle East, the history here of damaging interactions with exploitative outsiders makes the reflex understandable. But it also makes me wonder what would happen if a critical mass of suspicion were to gather around me. I do my best to shake these thoughts and redirect my attention to an important and promising meeting.

If anyone knows the mazelike interstices of the Great Bear Rainforest, it's environmentalist Ian McAllister. Originally from Victoria, the award-winning photographer, filmmaker, and author of several books on the Great Bear is also the director of Pacific Wild—a coastal conservation group he cofounded with his wife, Karen, in 2008. Ian was part of a clique of environmentalists who came to prominence during the Vancouver Island anti-logging protests of the 1980s and 90s and went on to wage the campaign that eventually created the Great Bear Rainforest in 2006. He also coined the area's name.

Ian's famous, jaw-dropping photos of coastal wolves and grizzlies come at the price of weeks alone in the bush, often sitting hidden with his camera in estuary grasses or in stands of old growth—endlessly watching and waiting. Much of his work takes place in some of the areas where sightings of Sasquatches have been reported.

Ian's forty-six-foot catamaran and field operations center, *Habitat*, docked at his Denny Island home, is strewn with diving equipment and gizmos. He and an assistant are on board packing duffel bags. Sunburned from his time out on the water, the forty-nine-year-old, with his curly red hair and freckles, projects the image of a relaxed surfer. But there's also something imposing and brazen about his manner.

"We're gearing up for a multiday expedition to monitor a pod of fin whales that appeared on our remote cameras," Ian says.

At a table covered in marine charts, he finishes telling me about his involvement in the anti-logging protests at Clayoquot Sound, on the western coast of Vancouver Island, in the late 1980s and early '90s. Those demonstrations, known as the War in the Woods, received worldwide media attention and propelled Ian into his current role, fighting for the Great Bear.

"After Vancouver Island, we thought for sure that when the public saw this place, it would only take a few years to protect it. But it didn't work out that way. It took some really heavy hands to get the government to even recognize that this was a special place. They spent an incredible amount of time trying to convince the public that it didn't exist."

"In what sense?"

"In an official sense. They're on record as saying, 'There is no such place as the Great Bear Rainforest.' So we responded, 'Well, then there's no such place as the Great Barrier Reef—or the Grand Canyon.' People have names for places. And they're not necessarily gazetted or legal names. Fortunately, the idea that Canada was destroying this fabled wilderness full of spirit bears, salmon, and towering trees in order to sell products to Europe and the United

States was totally unacceptable to the public," he says. "And so we managed to force an agreement."

"It's a big achievement."

"Yeah, except we're now back to square one."

"The pipeline?" I say, referring to the Northern Gateway project.

"Pipe*lines*. Plural. Several have been proposed. They effectively want to drive hundreds of supertankers carrying liquefied natural gas and bitumen condensate right through the very heart of this rain forest. The impact would be catastrophic if one of these fully laden tankers slammed into a reef. Statistically it will happen."

"What do you plan to do?"

"What we've done before. Dig in. Fight till the end."

"You have your work cut out for you."

"Well, there are a few conservationists, like myself, roaming about. We're hardly an army. And the communities here are some of the smallest and most isolated in Canada. If you consider the sympathetic and highly motivated provincial and federal governments, the resources of China, and every major oil company in the world that's heavily invested in the Alberta tar sands, it's pretty hard to come up with a bigger level of opposition. It's a pure David-and-Goliath situation."

Ian turns to look at his assistant, and I can tell he is impatiently gauging how much time he has left to give me. "So, you're here for some other information," he says, moving the discussion forward.

I tell Ian about my interest in Sasquatch. I feel almost silly doing so, in light of the seriousness of the conversation we've just had. I expect Ian, a de facto biologist and a practical, hands-on man, to make a dour or mocking face. But he maintains his well-honed professional, almost diplomatic, composure. He seems to mull his next words before speaking.

"Are you a believer?" he asks.

"I'm trying to decide where I stand."

He nods, sympathetically. "Well, I haven't seen anything myself. And I've been everywhere on this coast. I don't entirely discount the existence of such animals. Parts of this place could easily support them. On the other hand, a bear standing on its hinds on a foggy morning reaching for crab apples can look incredibly humanlike. I've seen it myself."

I nod.

"With all the remote-camera sites in estuaries and creek mouths, and with all the academics doing fieldwork around here, you'd think there'd be some better evidence."

Everything he says is compelling—in the way that Mary Brown's story was compelling. There's weight and authority to his words. But I'm left with a pang of disappointment—as well as the stirrings of bewilderment.

In the world of Bigfoot, there are stories. And then there are *stories*. The former involve encounters of the run-of-the-mill variety. They are the brief, unexpected, and often perplexing brushes between man and beast that occur with little fanfare and end all too quickly, leaving a trail of questions in their wake. The discovery of tracks, the screams, the glimpses of fur and form, the sound of footsteps around the tent at night—these are the more common, dime-a-dozen experiences. Had my early exposure to the phenomenon been limited to a few of these sorts of accounts, Bigfoot perhaps would not have left its indelible impression on me.

The bigger and brasher tales—the classics, as they're called—are what fueled my journey to believerdom. These yarns were so outlandish, so seemingly preposterous, that they could only be relegated to that borderland where reality segues into fantasy.

No Bigfoot connoisseur worth his night-vision equipment doesn't know the story of Albert Ostman—a Sasqualogy *cause célèbre* second only to the 1967 Patterson-Gimlin film. Ostman, a Swedish Canadian logger, claimed he was kidnapped in his sleeping bag one night while prospecting in the wilderness at the head of Toba Inlet, British Columbia (just south of the Great Bear), in 1924. Ostman alleged that after being picked up in his bag and dragged through the mountains for most of the night, he was dropped in a clearing in a small valley where the light of the rising sun revealed a nuclear family of Bigfoots—a father, mother, son, and daughter—staring at him in the faint light of dawn. His otherwise curious and mostly benevolent hosts, chattering in an incomprehensible patois, kept him prisoner there for almost a week. Ostman finally made a successful dash for freedom after poisoning "the Old Man," as he called him, by feeding him a can of chewing tobacco he happened to have in his sleeping bag.

In 1957, Ostman came forward and related the incident to journalist John Green, just before the humanoid tracks discovered in Bluff Creek, in northern California, propelled Bigfoot into popular awareness. "I Was Kidnapped by a Sasquatch," the title of Green's dead-serious newspaper story on Ostman's encounter, appearing on the front page of the *Agassiz-Harrison Advance*, foreshadowed every chintzy supermarket-tabloid headline to ever appear on the subject.[5]

Soon after Ostman's tale came to light, another yarn, also reported to have occurred in 1924, resurfaced to take its rightful place in Sasqualogy's annals of the unforgettable.

On July 13, 1924, the *Oregonian*, a Portland daily, reported that a group of five miners, prospecting on the southeastern slopes of Mount Saint Helens in Washington State, had been attacked in their cabin by a group of "Mountain Devils." The story later came to be known as the "Ape Canyon incident," named after the gorge where the attack took place and where gorilla-like creatures had been seen for as long as anyone could remember.*

Early Sasquatch investigators found and interviewed the last surviving member of that drama, Fred Beck, after digging up the old *Oregonian* article in the mid-1960s. Beck told them the assault on the cabin came in response to the prospectors' firing on creatures that had been shadowing them in the woods for several days. The account of the cabin attack, which came in the dead of night and continued in unrelenting waves until daylight, is worthy of its own horror film. The mob of ape-men swarmed the outside of the cabin, banging on its door and walls, stomping on the roof, pelting it with rocks, and reaching in with their shaggy arms through gaps in the logs. The terrified miners barely kept the creatures at bay, firing their rifles at the walls and ceiling all night, until the attack finally came to an end with the rising sun. The *Oregonian* reported that the miners "were so upset by the incidents of the night, they left the cabin without making breakfast." The forest ranger who was assigned to that district, and who claimed to have met the men as they were fleeing, later told investigators, in the 1960s, that he'd never seen grown men more frightened.[6]

Stories like these fed my fascination when I was a child. What sets them apart from other Sasquatch tales is the drama, danger, and emotional tension built into them—and a narrative flamboyance that fires the imagination. Raising the emotional pitch, research shows, leads to gullibility and conditioning. But something fundamental to these tales is key to understanding every

---

* Mount Saint Helens, an active volcano in the Cascade Range in Washington, has long been considered an important node of Sasquatch activity. When the mountain erupted cataclysmically in 1980, much of its northern face was obliterated. Apocryphal stories emerged afterward that US Army helicopters venturing into the disaster zone were airlifting out Sasquatch corpses to undisclosed military facilities.

Sasquatch enthusiast's fascination. These stories depict Bigfoots as quasi-human, intelligent, self-aware, and calculating. Even more, they insinuate a shadowy and almost forbidden parallel world, which the creatures inhabit.

When I was a kid, there was no skepticism, no weighing of evidence, no sense of whether any of it jibed with reality. At no time while reading these stories did I find it strange that Ostman, in the account of his kidnapping, never said he felt fear or terror. Or that despite also having a gun in his sleeping bag, he didn't attempt to shoot his way out. Or that the creatures that attacked Beck and his colleagues didn't simply break through the cabin door, or ambush the men later during their retreat (or indeed why most Sasquatch encounters do not—as far as we know—end in violence or death). Nor would my opinion have changed had I known that in 1966, Beck, infected by the growing vogue of Eastern religious cults sweeping the Western world, had self-published a New Age manifesto entitled *I Fought the Apemen of Mt. St. Helens*, in which he claimed psychic powers, argued for the existence of UFOs, and alleged that his party made contact during their Ape Canyon trip with native spirit guides wearing buckskin.*

The Committee for Skeptical Inquiry, a science-minded organization of debunkers, has run articles in its flagship publication, *Skeptical Inquirer*, taking potshots at claims of the existence of Sasquatches. The idea the magazine espouses most frequently, to which Ian McAllister alluded, is that Bigfoots are often no more than misidentified bears.

---

* Somewhat to his credit, Beck wrote in his manifesto: "No one will ever capture one, and no one will ever kill one.... These questions cannot be answered by expeditions. It can only come by man knowing more about his true self and more about the universe in which he dwells." See http://www.bigfootencounters.com/classics/beck.htm.

"Mistaken identifications," writes Joe Nickell, the author of one such piece, "could be due to poor viewing conditions, such as the creature being seen only briefly, or from a distance, in shadow or at nighttime, through foliage, or the like—especially while the observer is, naturally, excited."[7]

The idea that Sasquatch is nothing more than a misidentified bear isn't new. But this argument gained significant traction after the publication, in 2000, of *My Quest for the Yeti*, by Italian alpinist Reinhold Messner. The celebrated mountain virtuoso and explorer—known for the first solo ascent of Mount Everest without supplemental oxygen, in 1980—has spent his life exploring the Himalayan region. His conquest of all fourteen Himalayan peaks that top eight thousand meters, the highest on earth, has made him a legend among alpinists. After scaling every major summit in the area, the mountain-obsessed Italian turned his sights to a formidable new challenge: the mystery of the Yeti.

In his book, Messner claims that he encountered a Yeti in eastern Tibet in 1986. The incident took place in the evening, while he was on a solo expedition, tracing an old Sherpa route through a series of valleys. As he was trekking up a forested ravine, trying to reach a clearing above the tree line, Messner was startled by a fleet-footed, upright silhouette, which was stealthily darting back and forth between the trees. At first he thought he'd come across a yak and its owners, but the nature of its movements soon convinced him otherwise.

"It moved upright," he writes. "It was as if my own shadow had been projected onto the thicket. For one heartbeat it stood motionless, then turned away and disappeared into the dusk."[8]

Messner then found large tracks going up the mountainside, before the same or a similar creature reappeared and now whistled angrily at him. This time Messner got a slightly better look at it: "Covered with hair, it stood upright on two short legs and had powerful arms that hung down almost to its knees. I guessed it to be over seven feet tall. Its body looked much heavier than that of a man that size, but it moved with such agility and power toward the edge of the escarpment that I was both startled and relieved. Mostly I was stunned. No human would have been able to run like that in the middle of the night."[9]

After making inquiries with villagers, Messner discovered that he had encountered what locals referred to, fearfully, as a *chemo*—a creature comparable to the Nepalese Yeti. Messner was fascinated. He decided to embark on a new mission to find and make sense of the mysterious animal.

After twelve long years of research and excursions with local guides in both Pakistan and Tibet, the alpinist concluded that the animal he had encountered in 1986 was not the Yeti but none other than the rare and elusive Tibetan blue bear (thought to be a subspecies of brown bear). The bear's mix of unusual qualities and behaviors matched those of the alleged man-beast:

1. The Tibetan bear often walks upright. When on all fours, it places its back foot into the print of its forepaw (as bears in North America occasionally do), causing the two tracks to merge into one humanoid-looking footprint.
2. It is nocturnally active.
3. Its vocalizations are high-pitched.
4. It is known to kill yaks with one blow of its paw (yak predation is another purported Yeti pastime).
5. The Tibetan bear is red when young, becoming black when it grows into adulthood. So too is the Yeti.*

---

* Messner's thesis was even backed by Ernst Schäfer, the German zoologist, hunter, and erstwhile Nazi SS officer who spent much of the 1930s in the Himalayas at Heinrich Himmler's behest, looking for evidence of a proto-Aryan race of giants. Schäfer told Messner that he

To Messner, his discovery made absolute sense. The Tibetan blue bear was no regular bear. The animal was highly idiosyncratic, and when people were influenced by ignorance, fear, and superstition, it morphed into a beast of the imagination whose reputation spanned generations and continents.

"I hasten to add that this is an extraordinary animal—fearsome and preternaturally intelligent, as far as possible from the cuddly image people in the West sometimes have of bears," he writes. "These animals are nearly impossible to track, and for all their reality they remain deeply enigmatic. They avoid all contact with humans and are partly bipedal, nocturnal omnivores."[10]

American conservationist Daniel C. Taylor, who lived and worked for much of his life in the Himalayas, spent sixty years meticulously researching the Yeti mystery, starting long before Messner and beginning as a wild-man enthusiast himself. After traveling in the region's most remote valley systems and himself coming across a set of mysterious tracks, he concluded similarly that snow prints purported to be Yeti impressions were made by Asiatic black bears and other local bear species. He demonstrated convincingly that the tracks, including an iconic set of prints photographed by explorer Eric Shipton on the Nepal-Tibet border in 1951 (photos that set off the worldwide Yeti craze), were double impressions of a bear's forepaws and hind paws. Taylor even managed to find a never-before-published photo of the Shipton tracks that shows claw marks in the snow—which are not seen in the famous photo.[11]

Since it's assumed by most people that the Yeti and the Sasquatch are generally the same creature, these bear theories have been taken

too was convinced the Yeti was no more than the Tibetan bear, two of which he had shot and brought back to Berlin as specimens. Schäfer added that he kept his Tibetan bear thesis to himself out of fear of being executed by the Nazis, since it contradicted notions at the time that Yetis were Aryan ancestors. See Chamberlain, Ted. "Reinhold Messner: Climbing Legend, Yeti Hunter," in *National Geographic Adventure*, May–June 2000.

up and applied wholesale to Bigfoot. Reinhold Messner himself personally led the charge. "Believe me," the mountain climber declared in an interview with *National Geographic Adventure* magazine on the eve of his book's publication in 2000. "Bigfoot is in reality the grizzly. Somebody will prove it like I proved the Yeti story. It's very logical, the whole thing."[12]

Even if Himalayan bear theories are correct, which I suspect they are, the Himalayas are not the Pacific Northwest. The grizzly bear is not the Tibetan bear. And amorphous impressions in the snow are not the same as detailed humanoid tracks in dirt or mud. Time and again in my discussions with eyewitnesses in the Great Bear Rainforest, I am told in no uncertain terms: *We live with bears. They are our relatives. We know how they look and act. Believe me: what I saw was no bear.*

One of the more frequently brandished and more convincing arguments for the existence of Sasquatch is its apparent presence in North American aboriginal folklore. More than a few indigenous communities, particularly in the Pacific Northwest, allege that Bigfoot-type creatures do exist and can cite names and descriptions for them in their own traditions. For proponents of the Sasquatch, this is almost tantamount to hard proof; if such a species exists, it would have been known to local inhabitants before European colonization.

When early Bigfoot researchers managed to get past walls of secrecy and reticence, they were told by indigenous people that the creatures were greatly feared and respected. Some cast them as cannibal spirits. Others described them as thief-like, preying on women and children. In most depictions, the animals were said to have special powers, including the ability to hypnotize, induce insanity, and cause physical harm. The power to shape-shift or trans-form into other creatures, many said, is what accounted for their elusiveness. These sorts of cultural beliefs were often of secondary importance to conventional Bigfoot investigators, who were—and still are—more interested in confirming the apelike qualities of the animal, as evinced in some indigenous carvings, masks, and dances.*

There are many permutations of indigenous wild-man beings along the North American west coast. The Sasquatch, of course—its name derived from a Coast Salish word, *Sasq'ets*, meaning "wild man"—is the most famous. Among the Heiltsuk, as Mary Brown told me, the creatures are known as *Thla'thla*.† In folklore, the *Thla'thla* is depicted as a large, hair-covered, forest-dwelling super-natural humanoid. Stories usually cast it as female. Its trademark quality is a penchant for abducting and eating children. It carries a large basket on its back with an inwardly spiked lid in which to stash abductees and transport them back to its lair. Parents often used the stories of the *Thla'thla* to prod or frighten their children into obedience. Mary's memory of those childhood tales added to the terror she and the others experienced that day in Roscoe Inlet.

For a long time, like many Sasquatch enthusiasts, I'd taken it for granted that any humanoid or bogeyman-type creature that is part of an indigenous group's pantheon of supernatural beings must be the same as what people today call Bigfoot, since some, like *Thla'thla* and *Sasq'ets*, seem to fit the bill.

---

* One Nisga'a First Nation carving from the Nass River valley of northern British Colum-bia, made in 1914, is widely recognized by Sasqualogists for its monkey-like appearance, with high brow, deep-set eyes, and thin lips located far below a flat nose. Aboriginal stone carvings of heads found in the Columbia River basin in the United States have a similar primate-like appearance.

† To pronounce *Thla'thla*, place your tongue where your front teeth and inner gum line meet and speak the word through your cheeks. Interestingly, the name *Thla'thla* has the same root as the Heiltsuk word for strength or power.

A few of the beings nowadays equated with the Sasquatch are the *Gagiit* of the Haida, a human who has succumbed to fatigue, cold, or hunger to become a ghostly wilderness dweller; the *Kooshdaa Khaa* of the Tlingit, who is likened to a land-dwelling otter and is believed to be the embodiment of a drowned or lost relative; and the *Wendigo* of Algonquian-speaking peoples—a troublemaking spirit of the woods that can possess people and cause them to perpetrate acts of insatiable greed, murder, and cannibalism.

There may be something to these linkages with Sasquatch. After all, much indigenous oral history and traditional knowledge has been shown to be accurate—long antedating the same scientific or academic "discoveries." But is it possible that the Sasquatch—simply one indigenous version of the wild man, whose name was Anglicized by nonindigenous people—has become so prominent and universal a story in its own right that it has come to be mixed up with and grafted onto other unique aboriginal traditions? Could the deluge of media coverage and the long-standing pop-cultural aspects of the Sasquatch story have influenced some indigenous people, and also Sasqualogists, to see more of "Bigfoot" in some supernatural beings than is actually there? Several such creatures don't overlap much with Bigfoot apart from being humanoid or semi-humanoid.

Muddying the waters is the fact that common forest creatures are, in certain native stories, imbued with human qualities. Some can transform themselves into humans. The idea of a creature that bridges the human and animal spheres is in a sense commonplace.

When I ask Alvina if she can tell me more about the *Thla'thla*, she replies, "Maybe you should go to Old Town."

I ask what that is.

"It's the name we give to our old village site on the island," she says. "It's just south of here, down the main road near McLoughlin

Bay. It's where the *Thla'thla* is seen the most. Who knows, if you spend enough time there, you might see one yourself."

The next day I phone Ian to tell him that I've left my mini camera tripod on his boat. He tells me his assistant is going to the Heiltsuk Elders Building in Bella Bella that day for a meeting and suggests I pick up the tripod from her there.

When I arrive at the single-story cedar lodge, I find a gathering in progress. Alberta representatives from the energy multinational Chevron are giving a presentation on a liquefied natural gas project in Haisla Nation territory, up the coast. The project will transport natural gas that has been extracted by fracking along a pipeline to a coastal facility, near the port town of Kitimat, that will cool the gas into a liquid for shipping in supertankers to buyers overseas. Chevron's presentation about tanker safety is meant to win over the Heiltsuk, who vehemently oppose the project.

It's an exceptionally tense scene. Six clean-shaven men, dressed in loafers, impeccably ironed button-down shirts, and slacks, some wearing spectacles, sit rigidly in front of microphones at a large table at the front of the hall. On a large screen behind them, a PowerPoint presentation churns out fancy diagrams and blueprints of various supertankers. The men brag that these new, state-of-the-art ships, some over a thousand feet long, are virtually accident-proof. Not only are the boats built to international safety standards, they say, but they also have double hulls that can withstand huge impacts. They add that the ships will be driven by local pilots familiar with the tricky coastal passages they must navigate. Over and over they tell the audience that there is nothing to fear. Even if an accident were to occur, the gas, they say, would simply evaporate from the water. Presto! No mess! This isn't oil.

The audience looks restless, gloomy-faced, and unimpressed. A palpable sense of fear and foreboding hovers over the room. After an endless succession of blueprints, diagrams, graphs, pie charts, and factoids plugging the virtues of the indestructible superships, the PowerPoint ends.

"Does anyone in the audience have questions?" the panel asks, with a hint of trepidation. A flurry of hands shoots up. A microphone is brought to the floor. One by one, audience members make their voices heard:

Greed is running this boat. All you people want is to come here and take what you want—and then just leave! We can't even watch Hockey Night in Canada anymore without being bombarded by oil company commercials saying how great they are!

An older woman takes the microphone and stands. Her lips begin to quiver as she speaks:

We live off of this land. We fish and harvest seaweed. This is all we have. It defines who we are. If there's a spill, who will look after us? Who will help us? What . . . what will we do?

She breaks into tears, and sits down sobbing. People gather to console her. The panel members stare uncomfortably. Another man reaches for the mic:

You people have no idea! Even with five or six tugs, those tankers are going to be in a lot of trouble in a storm. One spill would probably devastate hundreds of miles of coast. If that happens we'll never see anything for it. This whole community, which has fended for itself for thousands of years, will then be standing on its last legs. We'll be living off wieners and beans!

An uncomfortable murmur rises from the audience. The distraught panel members, who have been listening in stunned silence, thank the community for its hospitality and feedback before abruptly ending the meeting and scattering.

The strong sense of kinship in Bella Bella, the level of cohesion in the community, is new and astonishing to me as a city person who has spent little time in a small town. Within weeks I notice that everyone I meet is related or somehow connected to at least one other person I've previously met. Bella Bella's human landscape turns into a vast web of interconnectivity. This latticework of relations extends to other nearby communities, and it dawns on me that everyone living on this section of coast is part of one large family.

There's also an unusual synchronicity, or serendipity, at play here. It's as if a kind of force, or an undercurrent, is constantly orchestrating coincidences. Often, when the name of someone I should speak to comes up during the course of my research, that same individual suddenly appears unbidden, and turns out to be connected to some other obscure story I'm pursuing, mentioned earlier by someone else. Or if a location comes up in relation to a Sasquatch report, I will hear more about that same place again and again in the following days, entirely by chance.

At first I considered these incidents to be random, isolated events of chance made more likely by the small size of the community. But now I think otherwise. Their frequency is uncanny. The connections that recur are often too vague and obscure to be coincidence. Also, Bella Bella is not that small. Despite all the people milling about in town, I still see and meet, on a weekly basis, only a small fraction of the overall population. By the time I leave I still will not have met most of the town's residents. I seldom experience this kind of profound connectivity back home in the grind of the city.

This is underscored when I order lunch at Alexa's Diner—Bella Bella's only eatery—from a young server who is one of Alvina's granddaughters. As I wait, I look through the window and watch as a funeral procession moves slowly by, led by a man and woman holding a wooden cross. A pickup truck follows, carrying a coffin and pallbearers. Crowds of mourners trail behind, heading in the direction of the government dock.

I spot Alvina coming out of the variety store that shares space with the diner. I call her over, and she sits down beside me, taking a quick break from her errands.

"What's happening outside?" I ask.

"A young woman from the community died during a heart operation the other day. She's being taken to Pole Island, where we have our graveyard."

"The town seemed more crowded today. It must be people here for the funeral."

"Not all of them," she says. "There's also a big three-day potlatch being put on by one of our chiefs in a few days. So the guests are starting to arrive."

"A potlatch?" I'd heard the word before.

"It's a gift-giving feast, a celebration of culture," she explains, "put on by families on the coast to mark births, deaths, adoptions, and weddings—that sort of thing. It's also a kind of economic system, where wealth, actual material items, will be distributed to the community, and where family business gets done. Potlatches are a big deal around here. Originally, in our culture, prestige and status didn't come from who accumulated the most wealth but came from who *gave away* the most. The potlatch host is the one doing the giving."

Alvina tells me the potlatch is being held in honor of the chief's mother, who had died a short time ago. I ask her if I can attend.

"Everyone's invited," she says, before giving me a penetrating look. "Maybe a chance for you to take a break from all your Sasquatch snooping and learn something different about us for a change."

For three consecutive days, Bella Bella is taken over by the feast, which draws many spectators to the bleachers and floor of the town's gymnasium. I arrive during a break on the first day, just moments before the organizers lock the doors for what they say will be a sacred observance.

Singers and musicians, sitting around a long, polished cedar log, begin to stir. An eerie whistling of reed instruments rises like the distant hooting of faraway steam locomotives. Shakers come alive, rattling along with the rumbling and prattling of drums that follow in their wake.

The murmuring audience goes silent.

Then heavy drums and wooden mallets on cedar explode in thunderous unison. The harmony of chanting male voices fills the gymnasium. A line of four men, Heiltsuk elders, dressed in black and wearing red cloaks with animal motifs etched in sequins, emerges from behind a large drapery with an illustration of a thunderbird grappling with a whale. The men's cloaks jingle with copper as they march piously, methodically, and with heavy hearts toward a denouement, enrapturing the audience. A large, towering young man holding a rattle—the master of ceremonies—leads them.

A guest sitting beside me, a woman from Quadra Island, tells me that the audience is hugely important in a potlatch, as its members not only bear witness to the proceedings but also are an indication of the importance and influence of the family holding it. The larger the audience, the more powerful and prestigious the family.

Canada banned the ceremony in 1884 as part of its policy of assimilating indigenous people and alienating them from their cultures. Potlatch materials were confiscated from their owners and scattered among museums and private collections. Indigenous people caught with potlatch regalia, or practicing the tradition, were imprisoned. But the potlatch merely went underground, where it was practiced clandestinely for three generations before the law was struck quietly from the codes in 1951 (but not officially repealed). Because of this needless persecution, an air of secrecy and sensitivity pervades the tradition to this day.

Events in this potlatch run rapid-fire, back to back, each day between morning and midnight: Sacred mourning hymns for the deceased. The distribution of gifts. Origin stories. The bestowal of formal Heiltsuk names—once owned by others who had since died—upon new honorees. There is the "showing of the copper," in which the potlatch host's family members sing while parading a large shield of hammered copper as evidence of their rights and privileges.*

The centerpiece drama common to most Northwest potlatches is also one of the most sacred. The *Hamatsa*, also known as the redcedar-bark dance or the cannibal dance, takes numerous forms and reenacts the story of the meeting and spiritual combat between a Heiltsuk ancestor and the man-eating cannibal spirit of the north, the *Baxbakwalanuksiwe*, whose earthly representatives, four enormous birds, fight to take the soul of the ancestor.

But the most poignant and moving event at this potlatch, to me, is the masked dance of the deceased. Here the spirit of the woman who has died—for whom the potlatch is held—returns to the material world one last time to say good-bye to family and friends before taking her final place in the abode of the ancestors.

---

* The copper shield is a symbol of wealth and is also considered a living entity.

The four chiefs and the master of ceremonies cross the gymnasium floor, disappearing behind a door. The chanting stops, but the drums and shakers rattle on, getting louder and louder, stoking the attendants' anticipation. After a long time, the door finally opens. The master of ceremonies is the first to step out, shaking his rattle. The drumming and singing again erupt. All eyes fall upon a masked woman who appears behind him: the spirit of the deceased. She is small and frail, wearing a black cape, moccasins, and a kerchief that covers her hair. Behind her is another young man rattling a shaker. Trailing them all are the four elders.

The audience falls into a reverie. The chief hosting the potlatch and his family standing on the sidelines are beside themselves with awe and grief. The spirit treads ever so slowly over the floor. The palms of her hands are held close to her chest. She is shaking to the sound of the rattles, taking tiny steps, while stopping to bend her knees every so often. As she moves, she is constantly looking at the audience. At one point she turns in my direction and gives me a gawking, open-eyed glance, one etched with wisdom, surprise, and sorrow. The living expression of emotion jolts me. I sense that she can see right through me—and through all of us. I'm overcome with sadness for the family members, who wipe away tears.

The deceased continues her journey, shuffling across the floor, peering curiously and nostalgically, drawing in the last drafts of her old life before reaching the room from which she emerged. She turns to look over her shoulder, one last time, before taking her final step across the threshold.

After days of immersion in deep traditions with powerful metaphors and connections to other realms that seem alive and ever present, I feel odd returning to the question of the Sasquatch. The idea of an immaterial, preternatural Sasquatch of spirit makes more sense to me now, while more conventional notions of Bigfoot seem awkward and simplistic. Yet, as more reports reach me of what sounds like a flesh-and-blood forest animal, my mind slowly readjusts.

I'd hoped to have a better sense by now of where I stood on this curious issue of ape-men. But all I have is a muddle of compelling reports barely held in check by some less convincing doubts. Running through it all is a desire for the monster stories to be true. Every day I find myself secretly hoping to see a Sasquatch. I envision the creatures staring at me from every thicket and around each tree-lined corner.

I decide to go to the much-talked-about Old Town area, the site of numerous Sasquatch reports, on McLoughlin Lake, a couple of miles south of Bella. Though long abandoned as a settlement, the vicinity is home to a fish-packing plant, the BC Ferries dock, and a salmon hatchery.

Instead of plodding along the paved road to Old Town, I take the scenic route, walking the rocky shoreline from Bella Bella at low tide. For the next two hours I skip across an intertidal obstacle course of moss- and barnacle-covered boulders piled with driftwood. When the shoreline is impassable, I take detours into the woods and follow game trails that run parallel to the coast. At one point I pass a few century-old Heiltsuk graves, their stones faded and covered in moss. I can still make out names and dates.

I emerge at the fish-packing plant, a facility bleating with the ruckus of forklifts and conveyor belts and peopled by workers in rubbery suits and yellow dish-washing gloves. I push on down the road to the salmon hatchery at the edge of the woods. I duck behind the main building and find the forest trail, which runs alongside a gurgling creek leading to McLoughlin Lake. Some tricky footwork over collapsed sections of a wooden bridge and a trudge through a thicket of trees and berry bushes bring me to the end of the trail at the southern edge of the lake.

I've heard this place is not frequently visited, yet I find myself standing next to three young people—two men and a woman. They are indigenous, in their early twenties, and look like students, wearing jeans, sneakers, and small backpacks. They all sip leisurely from cans of Kokanee beer, taking in the brush-hemmed views of the lake.

They tell me they're visiting from the nearby village of Klemtu, before asking who I am. I give them the annotated spiel about my travels and book project without mentioning Bigfoot.

"I hope you don't write that you met a bunch of Indians drinking by the lake," one of them says jokingly. We all laugh.

Then one of the young men asks whether he should try making a Sasquatch call.

My ears prick up. I ask him why he'd want to.

"Because," he says, "someone posted photos of Bigfoot tracks from this lake on Facebook yesterday. Maybe they're here somewhere."

My heart skips a beat. "Did the person write where they were?"

"No, but the photo was in mud. Probably on the shore somewhere."

If this was true, the tracks would probably still be visible. "Have any of you looked for them?" I ask.

The three shake their heads.

I tell them I'm going to scan the shoreline. To our left, high, forested banks meander back to the head of the creek. I turn right into the bushes, toward the flat, muddy shore. I arrive at the water and walk parallel to it, examining the banks carefully. At first I see nothing but twigs and the tracks of birds and deer in the mud. Later I pass what look like children's footprints in a wide muddy bank. Rocks, large tree roots, and high banks force me to climb up into the muskeg to skirt those obstacles, and I soon find myself on the other side of the tiny bay. It becomes a feverish wild-goose chase, and again I start to feel silly. There are no Bigfoot tracks here. I turn around.

I tell the visitors from Klemtu I found nothing corresponding with giant tracks. One of them suggests that maybe the small footprints I saw belong to a juvenile Sasquatch—a comment I dismiss. But I ask, before leaving, if they remember the name of the person who posted the Facebook photos, and I'm told it's a young woman with the first name Beth.

Back at Alvina's, I pull up the woman's Facebook page. The privacy settings are lax, and I start to shuffle through the deck of selfies and food shots on her wall. I finally come to some photos of human-looking footprints in the mud, and the woman's caption above them: "Bigfoot lil' feet."

In response to a question in the comments section, she says the tracks were found at Old Town's lake. I realize the tracks may have been the small ones that I attributed to kids playing in the mud.

When I ask Alvina if she knows Beth and where to find her, she scrunches her face into a look of annoyance.

"Why do you keep asking me if I know people around here?" she says. "I know everyone in this town."

I tell Alvina about the tracks, and she remarks that finding human footprints there is odd. Not many people go up the trail, she says, and it's almost unheard of for people to walk around in the mud—or wade in the water. "No one ever goes swimming in that lake," she adds. "A lot of people are afraid of that place. It's an old village site."

Alvina picks up the phone and dials Beth's number for me. There's no answer. She leaves a message on my behalf.

I decide in the meantime to head back to the lake to take another look with camera in hand. When I get there, I find a flurry of small, bare footprints, about eight or nine inches long, that meander along the muddy shoreline. The area looks completely undisturbed, except for a few sets of shoe prints nearby, including my own from when I'd walked by earlier. One of the shoe prints belongs to a child and is smaller than the barefoot tracks in question.

My first reaction again is to regard the bare prints as made by human children. But as I look closer at them, I begin to wonder.

I discern two distinct sets of footprints. They originate from separate areas on the edges of the mud and come together before going forward into the shallow water. They reappear together in the mud again to the left, moving toward firmer ground and the bush.

One set of tracks is wider, and looks almost like a Birkenstock sandal with toes attached to it. The other is unusually long and narrow. The big toe is a smidgen apart from the four others.

I also notice a green apple sitting on a log behind me onshore.

I take a few photos of the tracks before heading back to try to piece together the story.

Days later, I catch up with Beth and her boyfriend, Carl, a young couple in their mid-twenties. Beth is a stay-at-home mom, and Carl works as a gas-station attendant at the government dock.

I speak to both of them separately about the day they and their young nephew went up to McLoughlin Lake to go fishing for cutthroat trout. They had cast their lines at the end of the trail (where I stood with the people from Klemtu) but got no bites. So they decided to try a different spot, and walked into the bushes farther along the shore until they came to the muddy banks and the collection of small barefoot tracks. They had seen no other footprints, tracks, or disturbances in the area indicating that other people had been there. (It was their shoe prints I'd seen in the mud.)

They had been astonished by the small prints. Echoing Alvina, they say that not many people go to the lake—and even fewer wander into the bushes there. In all their time in Bella they'd never heard of anyone wading or swimming in the water.

And when they looked closer, as I had, the tracks had appeared odd to them. "They didn't have arches," Carl says. "I've seen arches on my footprints at the beach. These ones were flat-footed. One set of tracks was really narrow. And the heels on the other set seemed wider than normal."

Knowing the long history of Sasquatch sightings near the lake, the group worried that a Bigfoot mother with kids might be lurking somewhere nearby and decided to get out of the area. But before doing so, they left a green apple on the log as a friendly offering.

I still think, mostly, that human children made the footprints during an anomalous jaunt through the bush and mud, and that Beth and Carl, already believers in Sasquatch, are wrongly attributing them to the animals.

But the tracks *are* odd-looking—especially the long, narrow set. Could they be tracks of juvenile *Thla'thla*s? The more I think about it, the more attractive this idea becomes.

The stories of monsters, the fairy-tale landscapes, and the novelty of travel mix to form an intoxicating cocktail. With each story I come across, I find myself more seduced by the mystery. The thrill of the chase is a high. And I want something to show for it. I'm falling prey to the addiction that has ensnared Sasquatch hunters and investigators like quicksand, condemning them to states of obsession that have at times consumed entire lives—sometimes at the expense of marriages and livelihoods.

Hoping to get insight into the tracks at Old Town, I email my photos and a précis of the situation to John Bindernagel in Courtenay. He promptly writes back:

Hi John,

Many thanks for the photos and commentary.

I find these tracks interesting. I can see that the big-name Sasquatch researchers, guys like Jeff Meldrum and Cliff Barackman, would not be very interested in these as I've tried similar ones on them before.

On their own, these photos would be a hard sell as Sasquatch tracks— since even the more common larger broader ones are routinely rejected. I guess I would put them on my metaphorical shelf for now, awaiting evidence which more closely approximates to Sasquatch tracks as we think we know them.

I recently spent a week in western Alberta being pressured by another researcher to agree that night bird calls we heard in the field were not actually northern Saw-whet owl calls, but Sasquatch whistles; that fallen saplings hung up in other trees were not natural deadfall but Sasquatch-related; and that indistinct impressions in the moss were Sasquatch tracks.

So I am feeling worn down and a bit depressed as I wish to affirm evidence but am not always able to do so.

Sorry not to be more helpful.

Thanks and all the best,

John

Later that day, Alvina tells me she's received a phone call from someone working at the Heiltsuk government offices, asking about me.

"They want you to go down there tomorrow," she says. "They wanna talk to you."

"Talk to me?" I ask, concerned. "About what?"

"Dunno," she says unconvincingly, disappearing around the corner and heading down the stairs.

When I arrive at the offices the next day, I'm told to take a seat at a large conference table and wait. All around are posters and charts showing the locations of old village sites and various ongoing research projects. I am told that the office is the natural- and cultural-resources arm of the Heiltsuk government.

Twenty minutes later I'm greeted by three people, a man and two women, and am politely asked to step inside a small office. I recognize the man as the older gentleman who had hosted the potlatch. I don't know the two people with him: a younger woman and an older lady.

We take a seat in the cramped office. Each of my hosts, with pen unsheathed and notebook at the ready, has a look of displeasure bordering on grimness. I feel cornered and quickly realize something's hugely amiss. I have the awkward, uncomfortable sense that I've done something wrong. There is a long pause, before the gentleman, seated next to me, kicks off the proceeding.

"I heard you were taking notes and photos at my potlatch," he says, with a deepening frown, eyes cast downward. The two others look sternly at me.

"I did take some pictures," I say. "A lot of people did."

"There were parts of the potlatch that we asked people not to photograph or film," the man continues. "And I'm worried you captured those. People came to me concerned, asking who you were. I didn't know what to tell them. It was humiliating."

I feel a stab of commiseration and a pang of anxiety. In the minutes that follow, they demand to know who I am and what I'm doing here—although it's hard to believe they don't already know. Maybe they also think I'm an oil company or government informant. I tell them I'm visiting the coast to work on a travel memoir, but this brief explanation changes nothing. The older woman chimes in.

"A project like yours needs our official approval," she says, eyeing me suspiciously. "There are still a lot of stereotypes and discrimination, and we can't have people like you coming here and giving whatever impressions suit you."

I ask what she means.

"A man once came here on an assignment for a magazine. He wrote about the eagles in the trees and described our territory as 'the land that time forgot'—or some nonsense. It was silly and insulting. From our perspective, this place is the center of the universe—and not someplace forgotten by time."

"You just show up from out of nowhere," the man adds. "You come to my potlatch without introducing yourself to me, or asking permission for the things you're doing."

I remember introducing myself to the master of ceremonies at the potlatch on the first day but hadn't thought to approach the host himself. When I put myself in his shoes, I see how that would be upsetting.

I apologize, saying that I didn't mean to cause any anxiety or show any disrespect by my actions. I add that I abided by the photo ban and took pictures only during permitted moments, as others were doing.

"Those people were photographing their friends and family members," he replies. "You don't know them and have no business filming them."

The younger woman, who hasn't spoken yet, chimes in: "And what about that notebook of yours? Why are you always scribbling in it?"

"I'm a writer. I use it to record thoughts and research."

There's a tense silence. I let myself breathe before again acknowledging my misstep. I say that the outcome surely couldn't be as grave as they're making out. Are they not being a bit heavy-handed, I ask?

My words set the older woman off. "Listen, you: You think you know what you're doing. But you have absolutely no idea. Zero clue. Even the approaches of trained anthropologists are problematic. Just because you have the best intentions, and you think you know what you're doing, doesn't mean you're going about things in the right way."

They watch me closely. The older woman, who is now leading the charge, continues more calmly:

"At the end of the day, we don't know you, and gaining our trust takes time," she says. "Just look at our involvement as a kind of process of reeducating you."

"*Reeducating?*" I say.

"Yes, you—and others like you—need to be reeducated," she says leaning forward.

Though I understand the suspicion of my hosts, and the general public's unconcern and lack of knowledge about indigenous issues in Canada, all of this strikes me as harsh for a misstep.

I decide to relate some of my own experiences, so they can understand where I'm coming from. I tell them that, as a person of Middle Eastern descent, I'm well aware of racism, cross-cultural conflict, and misunderstanding—because I see it almost every day. Like them, I say, my ancestors were on the receiving end of violent waves of colonial imperialism going very far back. Ottoman Turk occupiers executed my great-grandfather with a sword, lopping his head off during a genocide perpetrated in World War I. Then came the Brits and the French, the Israelis, the Russians, and the Americans, I go on, with their bombs, the redrawing of borders, oil theft, cluster munitions, and depleted uranium. I may have inherited blue eyes from twelfth-century European crusaders, but I'm no white-man supporter of the status quo or of governmental exploitation.

At the end of my brief monologue, the mood in the room lightens. A glint of interest and recognition overlaps with expiring frowns.

"Well," the older woman says, cutting through the remaining tension. "Sometimes we just need to get everything out into the open and have these somewhat awkward and unpleasant discussions. It's all a learning process, you know."

The gentleman gives me a commiserating look. "If you could come by tomorrow and show me the photos you took just to make sure they're OK, my family and I would really appreciate it."

"Absolutely. Done."

Suddenly, it's as if nothing had happened.

"So, tell us. What's going on in Cairo?" the older woman asks, referring to yet another postrevolutionary upheaval in the news. "Our deepest sympathies for the difficult situation there."

Although the meeting ended well enough, the brief display of anger leaves me a bit shell-shocked and with the impression that I'm now under more scrutiny than ever. Part of me wants to pick up and leave Bella Bella and forget everything.

That evening I go for a walk to the water reservoir behind town to get my mind off things. The sun has set and a sky filled with swirls of wispy cirrus clouds is backlit by the receding yellow-orange glare.

As I walk the road to the reservoir, an old Heiltsuk man approaches from the other direction. The wizened senior, wearing a baseball cap, is slightly hunched over, his face animated in thought. I hear the sound of laughter in the distance ahead of me. I stop to greet him.

"There's kids playing up there by the dam," he says, turning back to look. "Kinda worried one of them animals will get them."

"What animals?" I ask.

"Bears," he says. "Or maybe Sasquatches."

"Sasquatches?"

"Yeah. You can hear 'em sometimes screaming from the mountain behind the reservoir. They take that back trail over there into town and look into people's houses—like a peeping Tom—looking at women."

The man and I part, and I look around, wondering whether someone is playing a joke on me. As I crunch along the gravel road it dawns on me how surreal things have become. For a moment I feel lost, without bearings, set upon a fruitless, meandering trajectory in search of rumors and visions.

By the time I return to Alvina's, a thick fog has rolled in, turning the star-filled crispness of night into an impenetrable soupy bog. I crawl into bed, and as I lie there, the coastal ferry, alerting all to its presence, blasts its powerful horn. For half a minute, the horn's long echo resounds through the deep labyrinth of valleys and channels, an emptiness that seems to stretch forever.

I have set myself on an impossible mission, a fool's quest, I think to myself.

5

KOEYE
(KVAI)

We begin to see in them the possibility of a consciousness quite different from our own, of a being that may be very close to us in hominid origins, but that may have evolved in mysterious ways. We imagine an animal that somehow has understood the world more deeply than we have, and that thus inhabits it more comfortably and freely, while eluding our self-involved attempts to capture it.

—David Rains Wallace, *The Klamath Knot*

Several weeks of molasses-slow island life are broken by the rumbling of a trio of 330-horsepower Volvo engines. Our boat pulls out of the government dock, bathed in fog and sun. After taxiing, the engines rev in a frothy explosion of sea, and we're thrown back in our seats as though in a jet plane during takeoff. We roar south through Lama Passage.

I'm on a sea bus packed with provisions and two dozen people, heading to a youth camp at the mouth of the Koeye River, some forty miles south on the mainland coast. The camp is run by the Qqs Project Society, a Heiltsuk cultural and environmental nonprofit.*

---

* *Qqs* (pronounced *Kucks*) means "eyes" in the Heiltsuk language, evoking the idea of watchfulness and stewardship over the land—as well as the opening of the eyes that comes with learning.

Since 1997, the organization has hosted a series of weeklong summer camps at Koeye, where grade-school kids from Bella Bella are taught a mix of science and traditional culture. The camp programs engender both learning and a sense of belonging, and have led to a generation of healthier, more resilient children—and to a ripple effect of community renewal.

Koeye (pronounced *Kway* and meaning "bird sitting on water") is considered a kind of Eden by the area's First Nations. The river valley, a protected conservancy, is one of the most intact ancient forest ecosystems on the British Columbia coast, hosting a mind-boggling array of flora and fauna, including a healthy population of grizzly bears and every denomination of salmon. Several villages with thousands of years of history were once located at various points between the mouth of the river and the remote inland lake from which the Koeye flows. It is a sacred geography so pristine and brimming with cultural and historical significance that it has fallen at the center of a territorial dispute with the neighboring Wuikinuxv First Nation.

Although I haven't visited the area before, I had the good fortune to fly directly over the Koeye valley at the end of my previous trip to the Great Bear. As I looked out the window of the plane, I noticed an area that seemed to vibrate at a frequency different from everything else around it. The juxtaposition between Koeye and the surrounding forest was almost as stark as that between Vancouver Island and the Great Bear itself. Not only did the river valley look like a bed of thick moss, it glowed with a mesmerizing, otherworldly fluorescent green that I'd never before seen. The estuary, upstream from the river's mouth, swirled in patterns a few shades lighter in color than the conifers at its edges.

I'd first heard about Koeye on that same trip, in the context of its connection with a recent Sasquatch encounter that had caused panic at the youth camp. Three of the camp's teenage counselors had claimed to see a giant, broad-shouldered humanoid watching them in the light of the full moon, just eighty feet from their cabin. The creature stood on two legs and stared at them, transfixed, for almost a minute. When they realized it wasn't a bear, the teenagers became terrified. One of them ran into the cabin and emerged with bear bangers—cartridges that issue an explosive sound—which he fired to scare the animal away. Rather than turn tail, the creature stood its ground and continued to stare. It watched them for several more seconds before it casually turned around and sauntered down the hill, the sound of its footsteps echoing behind it. Prior incidents had also occurred at the camp, going back years, involving howls, tree knocks, and loud stomping late at night.

As the sea bus reaches the southern end of Lama Passage between Denny and Hunter Islands, we veer into the wider waters of Fisher Channel. Up ahead, the massive and enigmatic King Island, with its mist-drizzled horizon of lonesome peaks, looms in silhouette. We turn south into the channel toward the mainland, passing a handful of commercial fishing boats along the way. Half an hour later, we arrive at the edge of a small bay with a crescent-shaped golden beach flanked by lichen-draped conifers. The fog has completely cleared. The mouth of the Koeye looks as resplendent from the sea as it did from the air.

I walk up to the boat's cockpit to get a better look out the front windows. The pilot is sitting on his high, cushioned captain's chair.

"There she is," he says, steering the boat carefully into the bay. "Ever see a beach that pretty this far north?"

As we draw up to the floating pier, the ten restless kids on the boat begin to raise a loud ruckus.

Our first day at Koeye is spent setting up camp. The kids and a few of the counselors stay in cabins located in the old growth behind the beach where the river meets the ocean. The rest of the staff members occupy cabins or tents in and around the main lodge area, which is perched atop an escarpment with a commanding view over the bay. The Heiltsuk ceremonial big house sits on the driftwood-strewn beach between the lodge and the kids' camp.

On arrival, I'm given a small one-person tent and told to pitch it among those of various staff members. A large campfire ringed with benches is lit and will be kept alive for the whole week. One of the co-owners of Qqs, Marge Housty, organizes the nearly round-the-clock operations of the cookhouse with her staff. Marge's husband, Larry Jorgensen, a pensive and bespectacled man in a baseball cap, delegates tasks and is clearly the linchpin of the operation.

I remember seeing Larry and Marge shortly after I arrived in Bella Bella about four weeks ago. They had been sitting outside the burned-down band store, grief-stricken, staring unblinkingly at the partially collapsed building before them. For them, the tragedy carried the weight of two disasters. Just a few years earlier, the lodge at Koeye camp had also been burned down, this time by a troubled night watchman. Since then, a huge effort had been put into rebuilding the camp facilities—and now their offices.

Many of the activities of this camp session are run by staffers from the Raincoast Conservation Foundation—a grassroots collective of local scientists and environmentalists working to protect the coastal ecosystem of British Columbia. They'll be arriving soon in their flagship research vessel, *Achiever*, a sixty-six-foot steel-hulled sloop. In addition to learning about birds and fish along the river, the young campers will be taken out on the *Achiever* to explore the adjacent coast.

After pitching my tent, I follow a short trail leading down from the lodge—walking past two large Great Pyrenees guard dogs patrolling the periphery of the camp—through the forest to the sandy beach below. I reach the Heiltsuk big house, decorated in Northwest native motifs. Piles of driftwood, some of it like polished art sculptures, lie beside languid strands of bullwhip kelp beneath the towering conifers. Halfway to the end of the beach, I come across a large sign posted at the edge of the trees proclaiming Koeye to be part of Heiltsuk territory.

In the 1990s, an exclusive sportfishing lodge had occupied the mouth of the Koeye. For the Heiltsuk, it was a deeply insulting project, made more heinous by its staff's attempts to keep nonpaying guests—including the Heiltsuk themselves—out of the area. Incensed, the Heiltsuk mounted numerous protests against the lodge. With time, the business went bankrupt. The property was then purchased, with donor money, by an NGO called Ecotrust and then given to the Heiltsuk, who transformed the facilities into a summer camp. The sign is partly a declaration of that earlier victory.

I reach the end of the beach, where the river meets the ocean, and enter the forest through a gap in the trees. I come across the cluster of cabins where the kids are staying, set in a small clearing surrounded by thick, moss-covered forest. The campers are away, and the forest is eerily calm.

A tall teenager wearing a T-shirt, jeans, and a black woolen cap exits one of the cabins holding a broom and dustpan. He walks over to me and introduces himself as Rob Duncan, one of the camp counselors. Alvina, it turns out, is his grandmother.

"You're the Sasquatch man!" he says, breaking into a smile. "My nan told me about you. She mentioned you were coming to Koeye. I thought: 'He's going to the right place.'"

"I heard about what happened here last year," I say, referring to the late-night Bigfoot encounter.

"Yeah. Tip of the iceberg," he says.

Rob tells me he's just returned from two months' camping a couple of miles up the Koeye, counting salmon at a traditional fish weir on the river. He says he heard screams there that he can't explain. When I ask if he's sure it wasn't cougars or wolves, he tells me he's positive. He'd heard the same screaming the previous summer, up close. He and other staffers were setting up camp that week in preparation for the kids' arrival.

"We were sleeping in the cabins," he says. "I woke up a little after two a.m. The camp dogs had followed us down that night, which they don't usually do. They were barking a lot. I figured that's just what they did: they're here to scare away wildlife. They kept barking, and I was just trying to ignore them and fall back asleep.

"Then out of nowhere came this roar-like scream. It was loud and echoed all through the valley. It petrified me. My heart started pounding. I didn't know what to think. The dogs were still barking and I convinced myself it was just an auditory illusion—that maybe the dogs were somehow throwing their voices. I was in denial.

"I calmed myself down and tried to go back to sleep. But then twenty minutes later I heard it again. But instead of one scream, I heard five. They came one after another:

"*Ruuooooaaaaaaaaaaaaaahhhhh!*

"*Ruuooooaaaaaaaaaaaaaaaaaaaaahhhh!*

"There was no wind, and no surf breaking on the beach. It was totally quiet, and the screams were just echoing everywhere."

I ask Rob if anyone else heard the screams that night. He shakes his head and tells me that the other camp staff members were sound asleep.

"Are those the only experiences you've had?"

"No. There's another thing that happens around here," Rob adds. "The term we have for it is 'wood on wood.' Sometimes at night, you can hear the sound of a large stick being struck against the side of a tree. It can be one hit, two, or even five. It's like a really loud smack: *Tchshh! Tchshh!* This has been going on since the camp started fifteen years ago."

"So, you believe in these animals, then?"

"Now I do. We used to hear stories about the *Thla'thla* as children. I always thought it was just a way to scare kids to keep them from misbehaving. But when I got older I learned that there was some truth to these creatures. My great-uncle told me once that the *Thla'thla* do what they do deliberately to torment you. They taunt people who don't live their lives correctly. Some of us think they may be drawn to negativity."

"Why is that?"

"The word *Heiltsuk*—the name of our people—translates to 'those who live and speak in a proper manner.'"

"So, you're saying that Sasquatches help keep your people on the right path?"

"Yeah, something like that," he says. "I know it sounds crazy to outsiders, but I know a lot of family members who've had experiences. Most of those people have credibility linked to their names and would never make up stories like that. Believe me when I say the Sasquatch is here. It's always around."

Our expanding paleoanthropological knowledge tells us that modern humans coexisted with other hominins in prehistory. As recently as thirty thousand years ago, *Homo sapiens* may have overlapped with as many as half a dozen other related species. Neanderthals and Deniso-vans are among the better-known examples. Might there remain an existing overlap between humans and an unclassified bipedal primate?

The possibility that a relict hominoid species might have survived in remote areas to this day bumps up against the feasibility of its continuing to avoid official detection in the modern world. Anyone who has expressed skepticism about Sasquatches has focused on this point—that it's too far-fetched for them to have remained hidden in a world that has been fully mapped, and explored, and is now under the watchful eye of every technological gizmo.

But is it really that far-fetched?

An American professor of anatomy and anthropology at Idaho State University, Jeff Meldrum, in his book *Sasquatch: Legend Meets Science*, reminds us that new species not previously detected are still being regularly classified by science. The saola—a rare, forest-dwelling bovine—was first photographed in a remote moun-tainous region in Vietnam in 1999. The Riwoche, a horse breed found in northeastern Tibet, was initially observed by nonlocals in an equally far-flung region in 1995. The kipunji monkey of Tan-zania, first seen by scientists in 2003 and considered Africa's rarest monkey, was once believed to be a myth—a spirit animal of the indigenous people of the country's southern highlands. Those are just three of the many, albeit smaller creatures that are "classified" every year. Perhaps it is because Bigfoots are said to be extraordi-narily evasive that they haven't been officially found yet.

How far-fetched (or not) we deem the Sasquatch might also hinge on our perception of space. Bigfoots may be unbelievable to so many people simply because most of us are disconnected from the true depths and expanses of the earth and its wild areas. We simply may not be able to conceive of Sasquatch habitat. Two-dimensional maps completely downplay the surface area that exists in three-dimensional terms, especially where mountains are concerned. Few, if any, seasoned travelers or explorers think the planet has been comprehensively probed. I find it is mostly those living in and around big cities, with little or no experience with or appreciation for remote, unpopulated areas, who most often declare, "But the world has been explored!" Their limited urban or suburban existence has deeply conditioned them to this view.

Modernity and technology have further eroded our ability to judge space. Cars, trains, and planes make it possible for us to cover huge distances in very little time, rendering the spaces we travel through inconsequential by comparison. Whereas, for example, a medieval religious pilgrim from Morocco would have needed several months filled with hardships and ordeals to travel overland to Mecca on the Arabian Peninsula, today it takes only several uneventful hours to get there by plane (a form of teleportation by comparison). When you or I fleetingly fly over, or even drive through, a large wilderness area, we experience almost nothing of its real depths or dimensions, compared with someone who covers that distance on foot. Even hikers experience only the immediate environs of their narrow trajectory: a mere sliver of a wide expanse.

In March 2014, I was working as a TV newswriter when Malaysia Airlines flight 370 mysteriously disappeared off the radar shortly after takeoff from Kuala Lumpur. Several days after the tragedy, when neither the plane nor any of its wreckage was found, the newsroom, like much of the astonished world, was shocked and bewildered.* "How could a commercial airliner simply vanish?" the newsmongers asked in the story meetings, as if Harry Houdini or aliens had a hand in it. But no one had conceived of the idea that the airliner had possibly, or probably, wound up in the middle

---

* The plane (or its wreckage) still has not been found, despite all the technology on board and on land.

of the Indian Ocean—an immense body of water. Even when we learned later that indeed that was where the plane most likely had crashed, it still didn't occur to anyone that maybe the plane had come down fully, or largely, intact—and thus couldn't easily be found, especially if it sank underwater. Many of us know oceans only as bodies of water we leapfrog during airplane flights. Any sense of scale is conditioned out of us.

A similar conditioning occurs when we watch TV or a movie or read a children's storybook that depicts someone moving through a forest. Fictional characters in forests are often shown traveling unimpeded along a more or less easily navigable trail or through wide-open spaces between trees. Our frequent exposure to these backdrops in the media makes them seem normal. Though some forests may look like that, the reality is that much backcountry wilderness is dense, overgrown, and obstacle-littered, with little visibility and sometimes rent with cliffs, gorges, gullies, and canyons. It's hard for humans to travel through in the best of times. A friend who works on a remote stretch of the British Columbia coast once tried to hike up a creek bed to a mountaintop. It took him eight hours to cover just one mile. He gave up and turned back. Many of the areas I have seen are no less impenetrable.

If the Sasquatch exists, perhaps the reason it hasn't yet been discovered in the eyes of the establishment boils down to the creature's reported determination to avoid people in those vast and difficult terrains to which it has adapted. Being a rare and mostly nocturnal animal would only make it that much more difficult to find.*

---

* Biologists remind us that Sasquatches would require a minimum population in any given area in order to procreate and survive. The infrequency of reported encounters and of trace evidence, and the fact that not one of these animals has been produced after decades, suggests to them that the creatures don't exist. Sasqualogists disagree, saying that Bigfoot populations in many areas are sufficient to ensure their continued survival. Most Sasquatch encounters with humans, they add, go unreported, indicating there are many more of the creatures than is believed.

That evening we all loiter impatiently around the cookhouse in the soft light of dusk, waiting to swoop down on the dinner in its final stages of tending. The campfire crackles and pops, drawing in camp staffers clutching mugs of hot tea. Down in the bay is a scene of perfect tranquillity: the curving beach and its unflinching bodyguard of hemlocks and cedars bask in the honey-tinted rays of the setting sun.

The crew of *Achiever*, the Raincoast Conservation Foundation's research vessel, has arrived. The captain, Brian Falconer, a tall man in his mid- to late fifties, is surrounded by several younger members of his crew. They stand in a row, almost at attention, decked out in colorful, top-of-the-line North Face and Patagonia fashions and gum boots. The young Heiltsuk campers arrive in single file after spending half the day on the river and are served dinner first.

Conversations about the day's events bloom, but I'm encumbered by my own thoughts. Since embarking on this trip, I've been trying to keep myself open to all possibilities and explanations regarding the existence of the Sasquatch. The effort has felt largely forced, and I've found myself again and again seduced into comfortable awe by the accounts I've heard. But new questions are bubbling up.

I wonder whether the frightening Sasquatch stories First Nations people hear as children have an influence on what they see, and I ponder the role of belief and suggestion in all of this. Everyone I've spoken to so far has mentioned growing up with those tales. Even Mary Brown had said that, in the midst of the Sasquatch encounter with the group of girls she had led to the cabin in Roscoe, she panicked when she remembered those childhood stories. Granted, plenty of nonindigenous people who have claimed to have seen the creatures were not raised on those tales, but perhaps a similar triggering mechanism is in play in some of those cases.

Similarly, I wonder about Rob Duncan's idea—that troubled people tend to see the creatures—and whether their sightings are in some way related to their state of distress. Clark Hans, who I went hiking with during my previous visit to Bella Coola, had claimed to have seen a Sasquatch on a bluff and had crossed an icy estuary in terror, later to be hospitalized for anxiety. Could he have been a victim of his own life stresses, or was his breakdown caused by something he really saw? Perhaps that something was a misidentification. For a long time I've wondered whether the loud, ambient stomping noises my friend and I heard during that winter hike on the edges of Nelson, which I took to be a Sasquatch, were just a mental distortion of some other sound.

All of this touches upon specific areas of psychology and neurology: perception, cognition, and belief. The way each of us experiences the world—an objective reality outside us—is dependent upon certain mental mechanisms, as well as our proclivities, predispositions, and biases. Understanding those factors must be crucial to properly grasping an issue like this. Up until now I have been scrutinizing the empirical arguments for and against the existence of the Sasquatch, without much success. That approach alone, I'm beginning to see, is going to get me only so far.

That night a thick fog rolls in, and a heavy silence takes hold at Koeye. Not ready for sleep, I park myself beside the campfire. The young campers are gone, ensconced in their cabin hideaways upriver. The lodge area stirs with a handful of nocturnal souls shuffling around with their head lamps on. The hypnotic flames draw a few of them in. Some are smoking cigarettes; others, like myself, cling tightly to steaming mugs. People mostly keep a silent vigil, lost in their thoughts on the drowsy edges of sleep. Occasionally, mechanical clanking or whirring sounds rising from the fishing boats parked in the protective bay break the silence.

"Damn gillnetters," mutters a large, imposing man in a deep, resonant voice. William Housty, known to his friends as House, is the son of camp owners Marge and Larry. He's one of the chief ecological researchers at Qqs, specializing in bears and salmon, and is a repository of Heiltsuk cultural knowledge. William was the master of ceremonies at the potlatch in Bella Bella. I watch as he pokes at the fire with a long stick.

"Those boats come up here and take whatever fish we have and then hightail it back south," he grumbles. "They won't even sell them to our fish plant."

"The long arm of capitalism," I say, offering my drowsy, half-witted commiseration.

"We hold them responsible for a lot of hardship around here."

"Do you mean because of overfishing?" I ask.

"Yeah," he says, with a tired look of disgust, turning to the fire and prodding it with a couple of tough jabs. "In the old days you'd get two million chum salmon up here. The water would be full of them—as far as the eye could see. Now in a really bad year it's closer to a few thousand. And yet the boats keep coming. This whole ecosystem, which relies on those salmon, is taking a beating."

The drop in salmon numbers is something I've been hearing a lot about since arriving on the coast. Salmon have complex life cycles; the factors affecting their survival are many and varied, and overfishing is deemed to be one of them. For decades, British Columbia's commercial fishermen have been pillaging these waters, selling their bounty to large, politically connected companies that distribute and sell to the retail market. In more recent years, the Canadian government has imposed restrictions on the areas that can be commercially fished, the amounts of catch that can be taken, and the number of boats permitted to take part. But people here still complain that those decisions—made by desk-bound bureaucrats with little local knowledge working thousands of miles away—are ineffective. Warming ocean and river waters and the proliferation of Atlantic salmon farms (which spread disease) on the British Columbia coast are also believed to have affected the life of local species. The drop in the number of migrating wild salmon has been drastic. "In the old days," elders on the coast say, "you could walk across the backs of salmon in the river, so many there were."

Larry shuffles out of the darkness holding onto a VHF radio receiver. He approaches the cookhouse and calls out for Marge. When she steps onto the deck, he tells her he's concerned about a group of three young staff members who had canoed upriver after dinner to camp at the fish weir. They haven't radioed in, he says, and they aren't responding to his calls.

I remember seeing the three, led by a young university undergrad from Victoria named Audrey, leave late after dinner just as dusk was setting in. They postponed their departure to coincide with high tide, without which, especially in the recent period of drought, they wouldn't be able to travel far upstream. I knew it was a few hours' journey paddling and hiking to the weir, and it occurred to me that they were leaving very late.

After deliberating with his wife, Larry brings the radio receiver up to his face: "*Achiever*, this is Koeye Lodge."

Everyone at the campfire is watching, silent. After a moment, Captain Brian Falconer's relaxed voice crackles out of the radio speaker.

"*Achiever* here. Go ahead."

"Hi, *Achiever*. Three of our staff went up to the weir in a canoe after dinner. They aren't responding to our calls. I'm worried something's happened. Any chance you could go upriver and look for them?"

"Yup. Not a problem."

"Thanks, Brian." Larry then radios to his daughter, Jess Housty, one of the directors at Qqs, and asks her to accompany the captain. Within minutes the sound of a boat engine in the bay growls to life. *Achiever*'s inflatable Zodiac—a small, motorized raft dubbed *Achiever Mobile*—drones away up the mist-draped Koeye.

Larry and Marge, now jolted alert by worry, keep attempting to make contact with the women. A VHF receiver in the cookhouse beside the fire broadcasts their static-frazzled radio calls—all met with a silence as deep and boundless as the night around us. The calls keep going out. After a few minutes, from out of nowhere, a woman's anxious voice explodes out of the VHF.

"We're on the trail near the weir! But there's bears all around us! Come quick!" It's Audrey. There's a breathless desperation in her voice, bordering on panic.

"We'll be there soon," Captain Brian replies calmly. "Hang in."

Many more minutes pass without radio exchanges. A sinking feeling comes over me as the scenario carries forward without an update. I find myself trying to fill in gaps in the script as my mind grapples with the idea of being stranded in the thick, fog-filled rain forest in the blackness of night.

The radio crackles alive again with more of Audrey's desperate pleas. "*Where are you guys?*"

"Just hold on, we're almost there," Brian responds, this time with more strain in his voice.

"Come as soon as you can! *Pleeeeease!*" Audrey cries, sounding on the verge of tears.

The radio goes dead again, this time for a while. Then Larry's voice comes over the VHF.

"*Achiever Mobile*, this is Koeye Lodge. What's the situation?"

A female's calm, exacting voice crackles back in reply: "Koeye Lodge, this is Jess. We found them. We're on our way back."

As the tension dissipates, I look around the dimming campfire and realize I'm the only one left. I turn on my head lamp and wander to my tent. Thirty minutes later, I'm still awake when Jess and the three women arrive back at camp. They are silent, but I sense gravity and exhaustion in their footfalls. Almost in unison, the zippers of their tents go up and then back down. A brief shuffling sound follows as they tussle with their sleeping bags. Then dead silence.

The next morning, the same thick fog from the night before sits heavily over a placid, glassy Pacific. In all directions, two tones of gray are spliced by the empty horizon. Five young campers, a few members of the camp staff, and I are aboard Raincoast's sailboat *Achiever*, which is plying the fog-besotted waters of Fitz Hugh Sound. The Raincoast crew is giving a demonstration of its marine mammal surveying operations in the waters around Koeye. We will be observing and documenting pods of whales shuttling up and down the coast.

Captain Brian Falconer is at the helm, moving between the ship's wheel and a slew of technological gadgetry that guards the hatch and entrance to the galley and cabin below. At his side is his first mate, Nick, a scruffy, twentysomething sailor. A young researcher named Megan is above us on a whale-watching platform, scanning the horizon with binoculars. She will be taking photos of the whales' flukes, which, we're told, are as distinctive as fingerprints, allowing individuals to be identified and tracked.

As the morning wears away, so does the fog, which burns off in layers, ushering in gradual sunlight. In the widening gaps of visibility we see a BC Ferries boat heading north in the distance. Closer to us, a tugboat pulls a barge laden with shipping containers in the opposite direction. So far no whales have been sighted, but it is only a matter of time, we are told. These waters are teeming with them.

Just then everyone's attention turns to port. We look over and see a large, dark body, thirty feet away, break the surface of the water beneath a cloud of spray. It's a humpback. As it curves out and back into the water, it drags up a huge barnacle-encrusted fluke, which glistens in a beam of sunlight. In a ballet-like denouement, the tail stands vertical and drops straight down into the water like the end of a sinking ship.

This is the opening act of an afternoon filled with humpback encounters. When the fog fully lifts we see them everywhere, often by way of their geyser-like spouts—misty exhalations drifting in clustered plumes over the ocean. We give chase, crisscrossing sections of Fitz Hugh Sound to reach them.

Roughly the size of a school bus, and weighing up to forty tons, the humpback is among the most regularly observed whales in the wild. The animals are curious, easily approachable, and given to sudden acrobatic performances, all of which makes them perfect for viewing and also made them a favorite of hunters in the past. The whales were butchered worldwide for their oil and meat between the seventeenth and twentieth centuries. They came to the brink of extinction but have made a strong comeback since a hunting moratorium was put in place in the 1960s to protect them.

A certain mystique surrounds these migratory creatures because of their vocalizations. Humpback songs, a complex litany of howls, moans, and cries made largely by males, are little understood by scientists. A typical song can last up to twenty minutes, is often repeated for hours on end, and can be heard underwater up to twenty miles away. All whales in a given region tend to sing the same songs, which constantly change and evolve.

For hours we watch these giants, and they observe us. Between their lumbering yet graceful displays of aquatic ballet, the whales vanish underwater, sometimes for many minutes at a time, often reappearing much farther away than expected. In some cases, they vanish outright. In one encounter, a whale surfaces so close to the boat we can almost reach out and touch it. In that instant, the animal lingers above the surface, watching us with its dark, glistening eyes, before playfully blasting us with spray from its blowhole and vanishing into the murky depths. The plume is acrid-smelling, like rotting fish.

I park myself beside Jess Housty. At twenty-seven, she is the youngest member of the Heiltsuk tribal council, the local governing body of twelve elected officials in Bella Bella. In addition to being a councillor, Jess is the communications director at Qqs, an environmental and First Nations activist, and a writer, poet, fundraiser, occasional teacher, public speaker, and collector of traditional tales. She can, as well, identify all manner of local flora and fauna, and find and prepare medicinal herbs. In speaking with her, one gets the sense of engaging with an uncannily natural diplomat; she is shrewd, clever, reserved, poised, and extremely articulate. Jess says she considers her work at the camp—teaching Heiltsuk stewardship and culture to kids and adults—to be among the most meaningful of her many roles.

"Creating opportunities for everybody to be out interacting with our landscape is, I think, the most important part of our work," she says. "People want to feel connected. There's an overwhelming sense of gratitude for the productivity of the place we live in, how much we rely on it, and how obligated we feel, for that reason, to take care of it."

Because of her knowledge and time in the field, I am eager to find out from her what she knows about the Sasquatch.

"On one level they're supernatural and sacred beings that we interact with," she explains to me. "In stories they gave us great gifts and brought knowledge to our people. Sometimes we had adversarial relationships with them; sometimes we had very close dealings. They also appear in children's fables meant to teach basic human values in the same way that Grimms' fairy tales or Aesop's fables do. So they had a storytelling function as well."

"Do you have any stories you could share?"

"I do. But I can't tell them because they have owners."

"Owners?" I ask, confused.

"In our culture, individuals and families own stories. They're a kind of property. Like when someone writes a book and owns the copyright. To tell other people's stories, you need to get permission from them first."

I shift gears, telling her about my discussion with Rob Duncan and his idea that the creatures appear before people in crisis or with serious personal issues.

"I was raised with the understanding that if you saw them, and you were afraid, it was a sign of some sort of mental imbalance. That there was something inside you that needed to be corrected if you saw them and responded with fear."

"So the creatures are a kind of mirror to your state?" I ask.

"Absolutely. A psychological mirror, I guess. But they're also just physical creatures. I've had multiple experiences of being out on the land and encountering things that weren't bears, wolves, or cougars. It's not something that you're afraid of when it happens. They're there and part of the same landscape that we're a part of."

"So, you've seen them."

Jess nods. She and an ex-boyfriend, she says, saw one a few years ago at the reservoir behind Bella Bella. The creature was crouched down in the water, scooping or dredging something from the bottom of the pond. She stayed to watch as her incredulous boyfriend ran off to get a camera and binoculars from the car, but by the time he came back the animal had walked into the bush.

Coincidentally, her story is one I'd heard, secondhand, during my previous trip to the area. I mention that and tell her about seeing the small but strange footprints found by Carl and Beth at Old Town.

"Well," she says, giving a smile, "that's something a lot of people outside of here don't know: These creatures are not all big. There are small ones too."

"Young Sasquatches," I say.

"Not necessarily. I mean a different variety of being altogether."

A smaller species of Bigfoot living side by side with the larger species? At first the idea smacks me as too strange, but then I see the irony: if I am allowing for the possibility of one, then why not others? I also remember the theory among some Sasqualogists that there may be a variety of related Bigfoot creatures in North America—and not just one species.

"Do you find all of this incredible?" Jess asks, seeing my expression.

"Where I come from it's a bit outside the norm."

Jess grins sympathetically. "The reaction of outsiders interests me. I didn't grow up thinking that these animals were much different from the others living here," she says. "It wasn't until I was eight or nine years old that I realized the subject was exotic to people. I honestly found that funny. What fascinated others seemed, to me, totally normal and part of everyday life here."

For a moment I put myself in Jess's shoes and see the whole gaggle of obsessed Bigfoot hunters and researchers—including myself—in something of an absurd light. Our psychology mirrored back at us.

"You mentioned the sightings serving a psychological function," I say. "What did you take away from your encounter at the reservoir?"

She thinks for a moment and then smiles. "I guess I realized I couldn't trust a man who runs off leaving a woman at the first sight of a monster."

By afternoon, the last tinges of gray have given way to a perfectly blue sky and a sea that looks more Mediterranean than Pacific. The vanishing mists expose an armada of about a dozen commercial fishing boats—gillnetters. The vessels are out fishing for salmon in a two-day window. They cluster at the mouths of rivers, the way a cat sits at a mouse hole, ready for ambush. The fish too are out. All morning we've seen pinks jumping out of the water, at times taking to the air in rapid-fire leaps.

We enter the Hakai Pass, leading to the open ocean. Brian Falconer tells us he's heard reports of sea otters off Calvert Island and wants to investigate. We push through the pass, toward the farthest edges of the outside coast. The shores on either side of us are low-lying, rocky, and windswept, the trees stunted and bent over. Large, frenzied gulls fly hither and thither like bats through air heavy with spray thrown up by waves crashing into the rocks. I shudder at the exposed Pacific, its looming, terrifying expanse. *Achiever* begins to seesaw on huge swells coming in from the open water. Boiling, frothing tumults, they roll in succession as if heralding the approach of some unseen titan. Strong winds and storms make the waters beyond the pass some of the most dangerous in the world;

the routes for the proposed supertankers would take them through those very same areas.

Brian became a conservationist after years of working as a bush pilot for logging companies and running his own sportfishing lodge. Those industries, which make money by extracting resources—trees and fish—brought him up close to the negative impact they had on the environment. He opted instead to run ecotours for fifteen years on a converted halibut ship turned schooner called *Maple Leaf.* Brian then joined Raincoast in 2005 to head up its marine operations division. Since then, he has traveled up and down the coast, doing ecological research critical to the quest to move public opinion against pipelines and tankers.

I ask him why he and others like him are so driven to stop every bit of industrial development on this coast.

"Because there's nothing like this left anywhere in the world," he says. "This is a fabulously intact, working ecosystem that's evolved over centuries in complete harmony. I've sailed in oceans all over the world—everywhere I go, the hands of humans have erased these kinds of places. They're gone. And people don't realize it. People get used to where they live as being a place of great nature. Some people think that Stanley Park in Vancouver is the most magnificent wilderness on the planet. And in reality it's a ridiculously, highly modified urban park. They've never seen or experienced anything like this."

I agree with Brian. But I also wonder at what point any position, regardless of its necessity or merit, strays into dogma, including matters to do with the environment, conservation, science—anything. I ask Brian if there aren't shades of gray in these issues, or plausible scenarios for compromise.

Brian shakes his head. "Not with something as precious and rare as this. Look at this place. Once you've been here—seen it, felt it, touched it—your life's changed forever. It's that special."

I tell him about my connection with the Sasquatch, and ask what he thinks of the issue.

"I like to believe in things for which there's hard evidence," he says, with an enigmatic smile. "I'm not quite sure how you deal with the fact that nothing's been found. On the other hand, you have some really compelling stories from people around here whose expertise and knowledge are almost second to none."

"So, I take it you've seen nothing of these animals in your time on the coast."

He shakes his head. "Sorry to disappoint."

"No theories on what might be going on?"

"Well, this is a place of mysteries. And there are still a few. Do you know who Vitus Bering was?"

"An explorer of the North Pacific, I think."

"Yes. A Danish sailor in the employ of the Russians. He traveled to the coast of Alaska, among other places. Georg Steller, a German naturalist, accompanied Bering on that expedition. Steller became famous by classifying lots of animals that took his name: Steller's jay, Steller's sea lion. He also wrote about another aquatic mammal, which he saw and called a 'sea ape,' whose description never quite matched any other creature that was later corroborated. Steller was not talking about any of the seals or otters he classified and knew well. These sea apes were some other species. Now, I'm not saying it was necessarily a Sasquatch. But it just goes to show some things fall through the cracks. Take these humpbacks we saw earlier. Believe it or not, we just don't know how they find food. They don't echolocate. And then there are their songs: the mystery of how humpbacks arrive singing the same song from all over the coast—from places too distant to hear one another's vocalizations. How do they communicate over such long distances?"

We're back in Fitz Hugh Sound. The ocean is again calm, and the sun, now lower on the horizon, casts a soft, warm light over the mainland shore, which has begun to accumulate patches of fog. As we approach Koeye, we near the cluster of gillnetters, which are starting to pull in their catches for the day. Their nets teem with salmon, whose writhing silver bodies glisten.

"You watch these guys and all their hard work," Brian says, "and you can't help feeling respect for them—and for the longevity of a tradition. But at the same time, there's an impact from all of this. It's huge, and it involves more than they'll ever know."

Nick, the first mate, approaches Brian and tells him there's another humpback close by that's behaving erratically. It's coming to the surface, he says, thrashing, and then sinking back into the water. Brian's face drops. He turns the boat in the direction of Nick's last sighting of the animal.

"I think we've got a whale caught in a fishing net," he says gravely. "On the way to Koeye a few days ago, we saw two other humpbacks that had been caught in nets. This whale may be one of them."

Sure enough, the huge, knobby head of a humpback tightly draped in netting bursts out of the water to port. It lets out a powerful exhalation from its blowhole. Everyone looks on in horror as it lurches and struggles, falling sideways on the surface before sinking resignedly into the water again.

Brian surrenders the helm to Nick and heads to the bow. The whale stays close to the boat. At one point the creature surfaces to within six feet of the vessel and lets out a shrill scream. We can see the gill net draped tightly over the whale's wet, glistening head, trapping its mouth shut. That indescribable sound, a kind of painful screech, echoes in my mind.

Brian says the scream is a distress signal. He shakes his head and clenches his fist. "Damn it! Too many fishing boats!"

Brian continues to shout out orders to Nick, who's steering the boat, as the whale bobs in and out of the water around us. I approach him and ask if anything can be done. He shakes his head.

"Not now," he says. "The whale is panicked. It's too dangerous to go near it. Maybe later when it gets tired someone might be able to get close enough to cut or remove the net. The important thing is not to lose sight of the whale. It's already beginning to drift with the current. If it escapes our view, it'll flounder for a few more days and then probably die of exhaustion."

Brian gets on the VHF and reports the whale to the Department of Fisheries and Oceans (DFO) field station on Denny Island. Its staffers respond, saying they're dispatching a speedboat to the scene.

Jess reminds Brian that it's getting late and that the kids have to return to camp. Brian asks Nick and Megan to track the whale in the Zodiac until the fisheries people arrive. He instructs them to bring extra gas and provisions.

"We'll come back and get you after dropping the kids off," Brian says to them. "If the fog gets heavy, and we can't find you, follow the shoreline back. Do not go into deep water."

News of the entangled humpback has spread back to camp. Larry Jorgensen, with whom I haven't spoken much until now, tells me how many times he'd found himself in the very same situation in the past.

"Back in the day we used to jump into the water like heroes to try and save those whales," he says, "but it seldom worked." He too complains about the number of fishing boats, and says that the DFO is to blame for not having a better response capability—and for not equipping and training local communities to disentangle whales.*

---

* There is only one DFO official in all of British Columbia, based in Vancouver, who is authorized to disentangle whales.

At dusk we hear that *Achiever* and its crew have arrived safely back—and that Nick and Megan lost sight of the whale in the choppy waters of the sound. Neither they nor the DFO people were able to relocate it.

No sooner has word gotten out of their return than another drama fills the evening's growing void. Audrey and her small team of researchers have gone back up the Koeye to spend the night at the fish weir so they can get an early start on mapping work the next day. She radios to the camp in a panic, saying there is crashing in the bushes and loud vocalizations all around them. In a repeat of the other night, Larry requests *Achiever Mobile* to fetch the women. This time it's a lightning-quick extraction. When they arrive back at camp, I watch as a shell-shocked Audrey, holding back tears, tells someone: "I've never heard a noise like that in my entire life. It was like a roaring scream that went on and on and on. I can't even describe it. It was so horrible."

Koeye's guard dogs bark up a storm at the edge of camp the entire night.

I'm invited to join William Housty, Jess's older, thirty-two-year-old brother, in long-line fishing for halibut out in the sound. Jess and others tell me that William, more than anyone else, is the man to speak to among the Heiltsuk about traditional culture. He also knows, I am told, about Sasquatch.

On a morning as thick with fog as any I've seen on the coast, we depart in William's twenty-seven-foot converted aluminum herring skiff. Three Heiltsuk teenagers are with us. Within moments of turning north out of the bay, we're lost in a mist-choked void of gray punctuated by phantom intimations of evergreen. The ocean is remarkably, almost frighteningly still, like a tepid, vaporous River Styx. A squadron of mergansers flits into view. The ducks race their reflections inches above the water before vanishing back into the ether. William maneuvers slowly, methodically, to avoid colliding with driftwood.

Though generally a man of few words, William is among the most active and vocal figures on the coast, a storyteller, a repository of culture, and a leader in the science of conservation, in charge of keeping track of the territory's salmon and bear populations. He often spends his summers at Koeye counting the area's fish and managing a bear DNA collection project, for which grizzly and black bear hairs are extracted from barbed-wire traps and analyzed to track the animals' health and movements. In 2014, William made international headlines after publishing a Heiltsuk study about Koeye's grizzlies, in which he wrote that the animals travel along ancient multigenerational ruts in the ground he called "bear highways," stepping into the same track impressions over and over again.

At six and a half feet tall, William is big, burly, and imposing. During my time with the Heiltsuk, I've seen him jovial and playful as well as critical and brusque—speaking out against meddlesome outsiders, politicians, and industrial interests. He's proud of his culture, unencumbered by fear, and speaks his mind without mincing words.

By the time we arrive at our fishing spot, the sunlight has started to drill through the fog. William kills the engines and goes to the front of the boat, where he and two others prepare the longline, tying a weight to one end that will sink the line to the bottom of the ocean. Attached to the other end is a floating buoy, which will allow William to return later and find the line. William sits on an upturned bucket beside two containers holding about a hundred big, baited hooks, and begins attaching them along the length of the line. One of his assistants, holding the weighted end, slowly releases the line into the water.

"Halibut love salmon," William says in his deep voice, engrossed in the work. "But I've thrown in some octopus this time, which they love even more."

"This must be something most men learn to do growing up here," I say.

"Everything we do has been passed down from our elders," he says, adding another hook to the line. "Both the old knowledge and the new. My own grandfather taught me a lot."

"Is that why you have so much respect for them in your culture?"

"We take care of our elders because they're our link to the past. They're the ones that can validate information and reaffirm knowledge. They're the source of strength for everything that we do. So you look after them."

William gets up to untangle the line behind him. As the fog thins into sinewy streaks, I begin to see the ruins of the abandoned fishing port and cannery town of Namu in the distance. It's also the location of a Heiltsuk village site that dates back at least eleven thousand years.

"So, you're here to find out about the Sasquatch?" William says, redirecting my attention. "I hope you're not here to make fun of us."

"No, that's not my intention. I'm trying to understand the whole thing better. And to come to terms with a childhood interest in it."

"Our culture really reveres the Sasquatch because it's a reminder that at one point in time, we were living in the same way that Sasquatches are living. It's also a reminder of our connection to the land and everything that exists in our territory. It's not something to be afraid of. It's something that teaches you things."

I ask him about the idea that seeing one might be a reflection of a personal crisis.

"This is more the case when someone sees a *Bukwus*—not a Sasquatch."

"But I thought *Bukwus* was just another coastal indigenous name for Sasquatch."

"Some nations on the coast call Sasquatch *Bukwus*. For us Heiltsuk, the *Bukwus* is the little woodsman. A small man, which is really a form of evil. If people are really struggling in life and are imbalanced, they tend to be the ones more likely to see a *Bukwus*. But for us, they're two completely different things."

Is this another reference to the smaller footprints I saw at Old Town? I mention them to William, and he tells me that if the tracks were in fact *Bukwus* prints, my seeing them may be indication of some inner turmoil in my own life. He looks at me with a grin while attaching another hook.

"Have you ever had any encounters with these animals?" I ask him.

"Oh yeah. One of them took place when I used to run the kids' camp at Koeye. It was a really foggy night. We had a big camp that week, so our cabins were totally full. Two of the staff members slept outside under a big cedar shelter whose roof is ten feet off the ground. They were in a tent underneath it.

"That night the guys in the tent were woken up at around three a.m. by something moving outside. They thought it was a bear, so they climbed on top of the shelter. They couldn't see it, but they could hear whatever it was moving beneath them. It was messing with the tent.

"Once it went away, they jumped down and ran into our cabin and told us what happened. Everyone was freaked out. But then we all calmed down and went back to sleep. About an hour later, one of the kids in our cabin, hearing a noise, woke us up, and we could hear it walking beside the cabin, dragging its hand along the outside walls. You could hear it stepping on twigs and branches. It would also tap its nails—or a stick—on the walls. It was right there—nothing but a two-by-six between us and the Sasquatch."

"What about someone playing a practical joke?" I ask. "That sort of thing happens a lot at camp."

"That's what we thought at first: that it was someone fooling around. So we banged back against the wall telling him to fuck off. But it kept happening. Finally I said, 'I'm going to go see what it is.' So I picked up a big stick I had with me and went outside to the other side of the cabin. I flipped the outside light on. Through the fog and darkness I could see someone step behind one of the big trees near the cabin. All I heard after that was the crunch-crunch-crunch of footsteps running into the distance.

"In the morning we saw its tracks on the beach. It left footprints fourteen or fifteen inches long and had a deformation, like a big bunion, on its left foot."

"Wow."

"It was weird because during that one summer we were able to communicate with it," he says. "Almost every night at around midnight the boys would go to a tree near the cabin and hit the trunk really hard with a stick. You'd listen and hear the same sound come back. Then we'd do it again: *Whack!* The next time the sound would return a little bit closer. That whole summer it was lingering around."

"Skeptics would say you're seeing and hearing what you want to see or hear."

"We have those sorts of people here too. They'll say, 'Ah, that's bullshit. They don't exist. There's nothing out there.' But some things just can't be explained. I used to do electrofishing for a logging company when I first finished school. One day in late November we were dropped off in a helicopter twenty-five miles inland along a creek. There was a white guy working with me. It was really dark, rainy, and cold. We were following the creek downhill, when it forked, going around this little island. He went down one side; I went down the other. I got to the bottom before he did and reached this patch of snow and gravel by the riverbed. I found humanlike tracks there, sixteen or seventeen inches long, that went through the snow, into the river, and back up the other side. When that guy made it down I showed him, and he was in total denial—he wouldn't believe it. He was shaking his head, saying: 'Nope. There's no way. It doesn't exist.' I said to him: 'You tell me who was up here with feet that big walking around with no shoes on, buddy! We just got dropped off in a helicopter, for God's sake! No one's out here wandering around barefoot!'"

"So why do you think no one's been able to find or catch one?" I ask him.

"They're intelligent," he says. "They're just like you and me. They're smart about how they act and where they go."

"Smarter than the humans looking for them?"

William laughs. "A lot smarter. Which isn't saying much. Those people that go running around in the bush trying to catch them aren't smart. They're being disrespectful. Over here we don't go looking for them. If you see a Sasquatch out on the land, it's meant to tell you something. You were supposed to see it. You don't go looking for it just for the sake of seeing it. If you do, you'll never find them." William holds my gaze for emphasis.

"It's just like in life: when you try too hard to find something, you can't. But then as soon as you stop looking, stop trying, you become more likely to find it. That's exactly how it is with the Sasquatch."

Characters and personalities are legion at Koeye. But the protagonist, the unrivaled character, the one so deceivingly simple to overlook is the river itself.

Koeye Lodge and the camp are perched at the river's mouth— where its waters meet the sea. That final section of the seven-mile-long waterway is different from the river farther upstream. Concealed at arm's length, beyond the camp, past a hard and virtually invisible bend in the river, are a broad, grassy open swath, usually referred to in and of itself as "the Koeye estuary," and the legendary river's less-visited upper reaches.

There is no overland trail leading from the camp to the estuary. To get there requires a boat. And even then, traveling is subject to the on-again, off-again nature of the tides. If the tide is not high enough, especially in times of little or no rain, gravel bars and exposed riverbed will obstruct the way.

Because of that, the unseen Koeye is spoken of as if it were another locale: far-flung, a place apart, taking on nearly mythic connotations. When it is mentioned, its beauty is invariably cited and spoken of with reverence. In a sense, the farthest reaches of the river are its most sacred. There's a trail through the old growth that starts beyond the estuary and leads past the salmon weir (where Audrey and her associates were rescued), continuing all the way up to the lake from which the river flows. It's a daylong trek to get there, requiring an overnight stay. Few people have made the journey to the lake, and stories about the area always seem to be second- or thirdhand.

An air of profound mystery hangs over the river, ironically, since the Koeye is not a long or treacherous waterway. Yet the awe it

evokes locally—as powerful as that of the world's great rivers—
derives from its deeper, intangible qualities.

My micro-journey up the Koeye comes on our last full day at camp
on a balmy, cloud-filled afternoon. We leave on *Achiever*'s Zodiac as
soon as the tide is high enough to allow us entry into the hidden
estuary. Five members of the ship's crew and I are piled into the raft,
which tows two canoes and one kayak carrying Captain Brian. First
mate Nick commands the vessel. In silence, we drone past radiant
conifers, the camp cabins, and the mudflats that lie beyond.

Everyone is excited. Only Brian and one other crew member
have been up the river before. For the rest of us, the trip represents a
kind of initiation in our quests to unfurl the mysteries of this coast.

We reach the farthest point upriver that I've been to, where the
Koeye seems to vanish or end but in fact furtively bends right and
bottlenecks into a narrowing, tree-lined corridor. Nick slows the
boat as we enter the channel, its banks thick with brush. The sput-
tering sound of the engine fades away and is replaced by another
kind of noise—the sounds of the forest itself: the din of the river,
the satisfied croaking of ravens, the rumblings of the breeze.

The shoreline, louder than anything else, is a boisterous, anar-
chical arrangement of life. Muscle-bound spruces and cedars with
lichen beards several feet long loom above clusters of rocks caked
in fluorescent-green moss. Snags, deadfalls, and pieces of driftwood, some covered in fungi, also tangle at the water's edge. These
poetic, cacophonous scenes create otherworldly reflections in the
water, like Rorschach blots, that glow and pulsate. Along the hor-
izontal axes of those fractal reflections, I see haunting, alien faces
wearing transcendent expressions. Whole stretches of shoreline

resemble totem poles of the spirit, and I am convinced this vision of the natural world served as the inspiration for the indigenous pole-carving tradition.

I turn to look at the others to register their reactions, but I can make no eye contact. My fellow travelers—some sitting, others standing—are frozen in incredulity, struck by their own worlds of wonder. It is a spectacle within a spectacle. I gaze down into the clear, shallow water below the boat and am startled by battalions of young Dungeness crabs clambering over one another in panic as the Zodiac sails above them.

The dimness of the cloistered stretch of river lifts when we enter an almost blinding opening at the end of the corridor: the upper Koeye estuary. Here the river valley widens into a grassy expanse, a great hall, hemmed in by distant mountain slopes topped by cloud. We've traveled only a few miles, but it feels as if we've crossed into a separate world.

In the estuary, we cut Captain Brian loose in his kayak to paddle around on his own. Two Raincoast researchers, Nate and Kyle, hell-bent on seeing a grizzly, park themselves with their camera equipment in the tall grass beside the Zodiac. The rest of us—Nick, Megan, Leah (*Achiever*'s cook), and I—paddle farther upriver in the pair of canoes. We get as far upstream as we can until the river becomes a trickle and our vessels hit gravel. We pull the boats ashore and explore the river valley on foot, stepping into monochrome-green patches of old growth filled with astonishingly tall cedars and ten-foot-tall berry bushes. We linger for hours, like children, each exploring our own little corner of the moss-covered immensity.

It is a giant's domain.

On our way back down the river, our hushed tones and silent gawking are replaced by lively conversation. Nate and Kyle, who had staked out the estuary for grizzlies, tell us, crestfallen, that they haven't seen a single bear.

We pick up Brian in his kayak. This time he rides with us in the Zodiac. He is beaming with happiness. "It's just magnificent here," he says.

Leah looks at Brian with an exaggerated childlike frown. "But we're leaving so soon," she says.

"Don't worry," Brian says, patting her in consolation. "We'll be back soon to hunt for bears."

I do a double take. *Hunt for bears?* Since when do environmentalists hunt bears? I look around but no one else reacts to the strange comment until a moment later, when Nate turns to Brian with a clownish expression.

"I hear your aim sucks," he says. Everyone bursts out laughing.

The inside jokes go straight over my head. I ask Brian what he meant by the comment about hunting.

He explains that it's still legal to hunt grizzly bears in British Columbia, and that in an attempt to stop the hunt in this area, Raincoast had bought the local bear-hunt guiding license—a permit —usually held by an outfitter. By owning the license, Raincoast prevents outfitters from guiding hunters, thereby bringing partial protection to the bears.

"But here's the catch," he says. "Under regulations, the holder of the license is obligated to offer hunting in the area every year—or give up the license. So we do the hunting that's required. We bring people in to hunt. They buy grizzly tags from us, and our own guide outfitter comes down. We just, well . . . we haven't been successful," he concludes, with a guileful smile.

"Who used to own these licenses before?" I ask.

"A man in Bella Coola named Leonard Ellis," Brian says. "He bought up the licenses for a bunch of adjacent guide territories in an attempt to create a kind of hunting empire. At the time we started lobbying the government to end the hunt, Leonard experienced financial trouble with his business. So we bought his guide territories from him. He's now making a living by running bear-viewing tours."

It's another serendipitous reference: I had come across Ellis while on my first trip to the area. I had rented one of his cabins in Bella Coola for a few nights, during which he'd mentioned the controversial nature of the bear hunt on the coast.

"Look! Over there!" Nate yells, pointing toward the trees. "Mama bear and cubs!"

We all reflexively reach for our cameras. On the edge of the water is a sow trailed by two of her young. We begin snapping photos. Nick steers the Zodiac closer. The bears weave through the thick brush at the water's edge—headed toward camp.

Brian pulls out his radio receiver and informs the lodge of the bears' movements. A flurry of VHF activity follows between people at camp as word spreads. We trail the bears slowly, until the animals, probably sensing us, vanish into the woods.

Everyone is elated, looking at camera display screens. Nate looks like someone who's just won the lottery.

"The whole week I've been trying to see a bear," he says, amazed. "And now, close to the last minute of the very last day, just as I'd given up, a bear suddenly appears."

Brian radiates a knowing smile and places a hand on Nate's shoulder. "That's how it happens."

Later that evening, I head to the ocean down a short path that leads from the edge of the lodge. The barnacle-covered rocks of the intertidal zone are exposed in a vivid display of textures and colors. In the distance, the western sky is bathed in a fiery, post-sunset light, silhouetting the adjacent islands of Fitz Hugh Sound.

It has been an intense week. It feels as though a month has elapsed since I arrived at Koeye—and many more months since the start of this journey.

The one thing that has caught me off guard, more than anything else, is the unbridled power of nature in this area—and its ability to wreak havoc upon the senses and emotions. It's an exceedingly charged place. Exposure to these most beautiful and pristine faces of the Great Bear means allowing oneself to be bombarded by awe-generating stimuli. And like any positive stimulus, these can act in the manner of a drug whose pleasures generate cravings, culminating in a kind of addiction. During my day up the Koeye, and even now, amid this brilliant miracle of the intertidal zone with its pools of red sea urchins and colonies of painted starfish, I can feel my emotions well up. But excessive emotion can also lead to self-certainty and absolutism. I can see why those who are at the front lines of protecting these incredible places are invariably so vehement in their mission, so focused and unyielding—and also so successful.

Where the Sasquatch is concerned, things remain less clear. Weighing the Bigfoot data seems to produce the same trap as a pros-and-cons list. Often the information just accumulates on both sides without being really convincing one way or the other.

If the animals do exist and are indeed intelligent, nocturnal, elusive, fast-moving, sensitive, and adaptive to their environments—as well as wary of humans—we have the starting point for an explanation as to why they remain unclassified. This explanation makes even more sense when we add the impact of our own biases—especially those of us in a largely urban-minded world that is unaware of the extent of reports, unappreciative of the vast and remote habitat, and unfamiliar with what might pass as evidence, such as tracks. Add to that a closed-minded scientific establishment and the derisory media, and you might have a situation in which the truth remains deeply hidden. The creature's rarity, due in part to its natural elusiveness, is increased exponentially by our own false assumptions.

It all sounds good and possible—alluring even. But in the end, it's just a hypothesis.

As I walk along the rocks, taking care to avoid the anemones and mussels, a quote I'd once read and committed to memory pops into mind: *Learn to be as analytical about things of which you are credulous as you are of those which you criticize.*

What if there really, truly, is no Sasquatch? What other explanations can we offer?

Throughout this trip, and even before it, a series of questions has increasingly nagged at me: What is the role of belief and perception in all of this? What about our eyes and our brains? Aren't our experiences the culmination of sensory inputs, filtered and then interpreted? We make loads of cognitive mistakes in other mundane areas of life—isn't that reason to explore the mechanics of perception here? What can psychology tell us, if anything? Hardened skeptics and debunkers pay these types of arguments lip service but never really fully, or properly, unfurl them.

Even if the Sasquatch does exist, and there's enough to suggest that it might, some understanding of how we perceive—and misperceive—reality may shed light on some, or even many, eyewitness accounts.

As I climb the trail back up toward the lodge, I have a commanding view of the sound and the sunset. Far off in the distance, on the water, something catches my eye. It looks like a sailboat—sometimes one, at other times more than one. It appears just on the surface of the water before disappearing, like some phantom ship. I squint my eyes a little, focus, and keep watching. A little farther down the sound, I see it again: a form that I can only conclude is a sailboat. It takes me a moment, but then I finally realize what I'm looking at: plumes of whale exhaust appearing and disappearing in the distance!

It's a beautiful and deeply moving sight—and a fitting end to my stay at Koeye. But when the sentimentality settles, I find another message in that magical spectacle:

Things are often not what they seem.

PART III

6

WUIKINUXV

A father said to his double-seeing son: "Son, you see two instead of one."
"How can that be?" the boy replied. "If I did, there would be four
moons up there in the place of two."

—Hakim Sanai of Ghazni, in Idries Shah's *Caravan of Dreams*

"That is a very dangerous lake, Mulla," said a local fisherman,
"and people who swim in it are always found at the bottom."
"That's all right, friend," said Mulla Nasrudin, "I'll keep well
away from the bottom."

—Idries Shah, *Learning How to Learn*

I travel by floatplane to the village of Wuikinuxv (*Wee*-kin-no)—a
First Nation community of roughly forty people located at the
head of Rivers Inlet on the mainland coast, sixty miles southeast
of Bella Bella. It's no more than a row of homes situated along a
rough gravel road that runs beside the two-and-a-half-mile-long
Wanukv River, which empties into the Pacific. From the air, the
village appears so diminutive it makes Bella seem like a sprawling
metropolis.

Just behind the town lies Owikeno Lake—a thirty-mile-long
body of fresh water ringed by high mountains and fed by dozens of

rivers and creeks. Epic in size, the lake was once the site of numerous indigenous settlements before the twin blows of disease and
population amalgamation under colonial rule cleared its shores of
inhabitants starting in the late nineteenth century. The area is noted
for its Sasquatch lore, which people attribute, in part, to the lake's
acting as a kind of travel corridor between neighboring regions
within the Great Bear Rainforest.

Wuikinuxv is difficult to get to. Located far to the side of the
Inside Passage route, it is completely bypassed by the ferry. The
only way to get here is by boat or by chartering a floatplane from
Vancouver Island. I made inquiries prior to my trip to Koeye about
catching a boat ride from Heiltsuk territory to Wuikinuxv. The
feedback from the Heiltsuk, usually friendly and helpful, ranged
from shrugged shoulders to flat-out refusal. It became apparent that
there is no regular traffic between the two communities. Similarly,
when I reached out to contacts in Wuikinuxv to hire a boat pickup
from nearby Koeye, no one responded.

At first I made little of this awkwardness. But then I started hearing murmurs of a falling-out between the two nations.

"You should be careful when you go there," warned one Bella
teenager at Koeye who learned I was leaving for Rivers Inlet in a
few days.

"Be careful of what?" I asked, unable to imagine what would
constitute a danger there.

"The Wuikinuxv. They're still angry," she said.

"Angry about what?" I pressed.

"Being conquered."

I'm staying at Grizzly's Den, a bed-and-breakfast located on the eastern end of the Wuikinuxv strip. It's a comfortable two-story home. A flag showing the profile of an indigenous warrior on top of a Canadian maple leaf stands in the front yard. My host is Lena Collins, a petite, middle-aged woman of mixed Wuikinuxv and Heiltsuk ancestry. There is a youthful vigor about Lena, who loves to dialogue. From the moment she picks me up at the floatplane dock, I am flooded with information and trivia about the town: the lack of cell-phone service, the absence of a proper grocery store, the packs of rowdy street dogs that patrol the gravel road. When we reach her home, I finally manage to squeeze in a question, asking if she does anything else apart from running the seasonal B and B.

"Ha!" she snickers, unpacking a crate full of food that arrived on the plane. "You've obviously never been to a place this small before. Everybody's got a million jobs here. You should be asking me: *What don't you do?* Let's see," she says, before counting on her fingers. "I work at the band office. I'm a language and culture teacher at the school. I'm also the custodian there—that translates to glorified janitor. I pick up people and goods that come in on the plane. They call that position the 'band van driver.' And I happen to be the volunteer fire chief. That was a job I was tricked into doing. Oh, and I'm also a mom."

Then our chat turns to politics. Lena complains that the people in power in the village aren't doing enough to better the community. That segues into a long digression about the conflict I'd heard about earlier. The Wuikinuxv and the Heiltsuk, she tells me, are locked in a complicated dispute, part of it territorial, involving, among other places, Koeye, which was once populated by villages from both nations.

"I hope that's resolved soon," I say, deciding to steer the con-versation away from the thorny subject of tribal politics. "Do you know why I'm here?"

Lena looks at me in shock. "Oh, I'm sorry! I haven't even asked about you yet. When you called you mentioned you were working on a book, right?"

I explain that I'm collecting stories related to Sasquatch and ask if she has seen or heard anything.

"No, not me," she says. "I think it's been quiet around here lately with regard to that. But I know people you could talk to."

She fires off several names, which I scribble into my notebook.

"I'm really sorry for going off on that tirade just now," she says. "I'm a bit worn down by everything. In spite of the difficulties, we really are a great nation. We just keep getting the short end of the stick. And not just politically."

Like other parts of British Columbia, Rivers Inlet and Owikeno Lake used to be blessed with bountiful salmon runs. In years gone by, every salmon species returned in droves in the autumn to spawn in the area's many connecting rivers, streams, and lakes. Foremost among them was the sockeye, in numbers up to three million strong. The homecoming of this keystone species, a grand gesture of nature's benefaction, made the region's waters crimson with hurtling bodies. The Rivers Inlet salmon run was once among the largest and most dramatic in the province.

But by the 1970s, after decades of unchecked commercial exploita-tion, the numbers of these fish, so crucial to the well-being of the ecosystem, began a dramatic decline. It was a trend seen across the Pacific Northwest coast. Overharvesting by commercial and sport

fisheries, combined with damage to habitat caused by the introduction of clear-cut logging, was thought to have had a negative impact
on the salmon runs. By the 1990s, sockeye salmon were returning
to the area in just the tens of thousands. It was barely enough fish
to provide Wuikinuxv's residents with their main winter sustenance.
Those foreboding signs were mitigated only by the knowledge that
salmon runs had declined and rebounded naturally in the past.

But in 1999, something inconceivable happened: the legendary
Rivers Inlet salmon run collapsed. For the first time in the town's
memory, sockeye salmon, a mainstay of the diet and culture of the
local people, stopped turning up in fishing nets. Roughly thirty-six
hundred salmon, about 0.1 percent of historic levels, returned to
the Rivers Inlet ecosystem that year.

"It was devastating to walk by the river knowing there was no
fish," Lena tells me. "Because that's part of who we are—and what
we look forward to. But that was only part of the problem. We knew
that if we weren't going to get any fish—neither would the bears."

Local grizzly and black bears congregate at rivers and streams
in the late summer and early fall to gorge themselves on spawning
salmon. During the several-week feeding frenzy, an adult bear will
consume many dozens of fish, to get the fat reserves it needs to
survive the winter hibernation. Because of the historically bountiful salmon runs, and the huge size of some of the fish, Owikeno's
grizzlies had a reputation as some of the largest on the coast. To say
that bears once thrived here is an understatement.

Every year, the animals passed through the village to access feeding spots along the Wanukv River. But in the autumn of 1999,
when the salmon didn't return, hungry grizzlies invaded the town.
In a last-ditch effort to find food, around two dozen weak and dis-
oriented bears, some with cubs, took up residence in and around
Wuikinuxv. Some foraged for scraps at the town's garbage dump.

Others ventured close to homes, digging through people's front yards. At first, residents tolerated the invasion. But as the weeks went on, the bears became bolder and more unpredictable, sleeping on people's porches and trying to break through doors and windows.

Lena, living in another home in Wuikinuxv at the time, had one starving grizzly sow with cubs in her yard. "One day," she recalls, "one of the cubs came right up to my window—and I looked into its eyes. It was a powerful moment. I felt I was looking into the face of a family member, and not being able to do anything to help. We had nothing to give them."

When the bears started breaking into trailers and threatening people, the decision was made to put them down. By early winter, sixteen grizzlies had been shot dead. One black bear, among the many that had wandered through town on the heels of grizzlies, was also put down, bringing the total to seventeen bears. Locals say they're certain many more bears starved in the forests during the winter months.

The ecological chain of events resulting from the salmon die-off—a symptom, in part, of a rapidly changing habitat—ran deeper than even the residents of Wuikinuxv initially suspected. Only in retrospect did a few locals realize that the bald eagles had gone missing that autumn. Like the bears, they had always been plentiful around Wuikinuxv during salmon season, perched on conifers by the dozen, their white heads gleaming like ornaments on a Christmas tree.

Take any street in small-town North America and transplant it into an impossibly rugged terrain that smacks of some northwest coast version of Jurassic Park and you'll have Wuikinuxv. The physical village—a collection of homes set on spacious plots of unfenced,

overgrown land along a gravel road—nestles in the shores of the
Wanukv River, with the slopes of craggy mountains towering over
it. The nation's school, government building, and cultural big house
cluster at its center. The main road continues past the town in both
directions through thick, brushy rain forest before dead-ending at
Wuikinuxv's two points of arrival and departure: the government
dock at the head of Rivers Inlet at one end and the airstrip and an
abandoned logging depot on Owikeno Lake at the other.

Wuikinuxv is small to begin with, but the vast scale of the surroundings and the difficulties of life shrink the village even further.
The skyline of towering conifers across the river is dwarfed by rocky
bluffs, which serve as the bases of mountains that rise ever higher,
toward the white, glaciated alpine zone. As Lena had mentioned,
there are no fully stocked stores here. All provisions are ordered in
advance and either flown in by plane or delivered by sea barge.
Telephone landlines arrived here only in 2000, and service remains
temperamental. The Internet is also unreliable, and mobile-phone
service is nonexistent. As a result, people still prefer to communicate with one another by way of VHF radio, the simplest and most
dependable technology. As no power lines reach Wuikinuxv, electricity for the community has to come from a large diesel generator,
droning day and night behind the homes. The village school has
nine students, who fall into grade levels ranging from kindergarten
to twelfth grade. They all attend class in the same room, share the
same teacher, and hang out with one another at recess.

From the perspective of my boisterous city existence, Wuikinuxv
is eerily quiet—like a town abandoned. The muffled sound of a
child's laugh or the distant howling of a dog only amplifies the feeling of solitude, as does the area's signature feature: a blustery wind
coming in off the inlet. It blows almost incessantly, effervescently,
rattling the chimes hanging on Lena's porch. There is a wise and

knowing quality to the wind, a rhythmic push and pull that make it sound as if it is speaking in tongues. When the wind is paired with the heart-stopping red and orange sunsets that cast the mountains in dark silhouette, the majesty of it all can be overwhelming. I understand why, in spite of the remoteness and the sacrifices needed to keep a community and nation alive, people continue live here.

For days, I pace up and down the road, visiting with Wuikinuxv's residents. Armed with a casual referral from Lena, overcoming my natural hesitancy, I make impromptu appearances at people's front doors and in their garages and backyards. I'm more than welcomed. Maybe it's due in part to the isolation and the novelty of a new face, but people are warm and open in the extreme.

I discover there are few, if any, recent Sasquatch reports from the village itself. There were reports decades back, however, and more than one of them involved a white-haired Sasquatch often seen at the edge of Owikeno Lake. But no one claims to have seen it personally. More recent reports involve incidents at lakeside cabins near the mouths of creeks in the middle of the night. They're hauntingly similar to the stories I heard in Koeye.

In Wuikinuxv, as well as the territory of the Kwakwaka'wakw people farther south, Sasquatch is known as *Dzonoqua* (pronounced *Joon*-ah-*kwah*)—the wild cannibal woman of the woods. The hairy and unruly giantess, a malevolent being of the highest order, is nearly identical to the Heiltsuk *Thla'thla* in appearance and behavior. Many old masks and pole carvings of the *Dzonoqua* depict her with a wide-open mouth, pursed lips, and deep-set eyes.*

---

* The German American cultural anthropologist Franz Boas (1858–1942), who spent forty years traveling through northwest coast communities and documenting traditional tales, wrote of the creatures: "The Dzonoq!wa have black bodies; eyes wide open, but set so deep in the head that they cannot see well. They are twice the size of a man. They are described as giants, and as stout. Their hands are hairy. Generally, the Dzonoq!wa who appears in the story is a female. She has large hanging breasts. She is so strong that she can tear down

Discussions with villagers, who view the creatures in somewhat more folkloric terms than the Heiltsuk do, don't last long and often taper off into politics. Again I'm assailed with complaints, similar to Lena's, about the current state of the reserve, its uncertain future, and the indifference of its leaders. I am told the details of an alleged Heiltsuk slave raid and massacre near Wuikinuxv in 1848—an episode that continues to be a thorn in the side of relations between the two nations. The incident, referred to locally as the "slaughter Illahie," is named after the entrance to ocean narrows near the mouth of Rivers Inlet, where the Wuikinuxv claim the Heiltsuk ambushed them in their canoes after inviting them to a potlatch.

But of all the stories, the one that stands out for me is about an obscure valley that runs into Owikeno Lake. I hear about it for the first time while speaking with Dennis Hanuse, Lena's next-door neighbor. The topic comes up in a discussion about old Bigfoot reports from local loggers.

"There was another logging camp on the lake that was reporting some really strange stuff," Hanuse says. "It happened in a place called the Hoodoo Valley."

"The *what* valley?" I ask, not sure that I'd heard correctly.

"*Hoo-doo*. It's a short valley up the lake, on the north side, several miles out. More than one logging company went in there back in the 1950s and '60s. All of them went broke. The last crew that went in left suddenly, scared shitless."

I ask if he'd seen or met the loggers.

He shakes his head. "I was just a kid. But the older folks said the men got on their boats, tore into the village, and flew straight out. They were as pale as ghosts. Their equipment is still up there."

---

trees. The Dzonoq!wa can travel underground. When speaking . . . [her] voice is so loud it makes the roof boards shake" See Boas, Franz. *Bella Bella Tales*. Boston: American Folklore Society, vol. 25, 1932, pp. 142–45.

"Did anyone here know these guys personally?"

"Doubt it. They were mostly strangers. When they left, they just flew back to Vancouver, or Victoria, or wherever they came from. I don't think anyone recalls who they were."

I wonder if the story is Sasquatch-related, and I ask Dennis. He shrugs his shoulders. "Dunno," he says. "We don't really go up there. Two white guys later went into the valley not long afterward to retrieve the equipment. But they didn't stay. They said it was too scary."

I press Dennis for names, hoping for even a sliver of a lead.

"If you ask around, someone might know."

I jot the words *Hoodoo Valley* into my notebook, underscoring them with two lines. It's as hokey and ominous a name for a valley as could be.

"Have you met Johnny Johnson yet?" Dennis asks.

I shake my head.

"He's famous around here. He survived a bad grizzly attack a couple of years ago. His dad knew the lake and that area well. Talk to him. I think he has a Sasquatch story of his own."

Since my time in Koeye, I've been thinking more and more about the role our minds play in mediating what we see and believe—and how these processes work. Contrary to our assumptions, humans don't perceive the world in the way we think we do. The manner in which we register our surroundings is at best convoluted. That may sound strange. After all, when we look at things around us—the environments, people, and situations—we feel that what we see is a comprehensive picture of things. But it's not. There's a huge gap in the education we receive in school about how our minds work.

To discover the real nature of how we make sense of reality is to realize that each of us is, in a way, fumbling around blindly.

We know that our brains sketch only the most basic impressions of the outside world—mental models containing only the information most relevant to our survival. The late American psychologist Robert Ornstein, known for his pioneering research on the hemispherical specializations of the brain, wrote numerous books about consciousness and perception. He explains that, contrary to what we think, we experience reality not as it actually is—but as a simplified model. The reason for this? Reality is far too complex. Infinitely complex in fact. If our minds tried to process everything around us, we'd be hopelessly overwhelmed. We'd get lost in labyrinths within labyrinths of stimuli, unable to find food, safety, shelter, or mates. Our species would quickly die out. As a result, our minds evolved to construct a deeply simplified version of all that surrounds us: a virtual reality made up of only the important information—perhaps a trillionth of the possible external stimuli. And we make do with that.

"Our experience of the world assembles in a fleeting instant," Ornstein writes in *The Evolution of Consciousness*, "with no time for thinking but just enough for producing a best guess of the world."[13]

Our mental habits are subject to the same shortcuts. Much of our thinking, for instance, involves the use of assumptions, which are wrong as often as they are right. We confidently form opinions and draw conclusions about subjects and events of which we have little or no knowledge. All of this came about as a survival strategy. Our prehistoric ancestors had no time to gather all data methodically and work through the various possibilities of a situation. If they did they might have become a meal for a tiger or been impaled by an enemy's spear.

So we evolved the habit of jumping to conclusions. The price of this inherited shortcut reflex, valuable as it can be, is frequent inaccuracy in our perceptions. And no matter how often we are proved wrong, we just aren't clued into it, *because our self-image is subject to this same modeling.* Of all the simplifications the mind creates, the most powerful and convincing is the illusion that we are psychologically consistent—that our perceptions are complete and reliable. It's the ultimate hoodwink.

How many of us know, for instance, that our memories are affected by the same generalizations and are notoriously poor? Memory, we know, is at best a rough, dreamlike reconstruction of select details skewed by interpretation. Our memories are constantly being reworked, changed, and subjected to new suggestions in the present. Humans as eyewitnesses have been described as "in the disaster class." Individual eyewitness testimonies, for instance, are unreliable and are responsible for many of the wrongful legal convictions in the United States. Experiments in which subjects are told to watch something and are tested afterward show that people hardly ever know what they have seen.[14]

Apart from the issue of memory, we tend to fool ourselves into thinking we are younger, and better looking, than we actually are and that we have more friends and will live longer than we actually do. If something has not happened to us, we tend to delude ourselves into thinking it never will happen. If we have a positive or negative experience, we trick ourselves into thinking it will infallibly recur. The fact alone that most of us are unaware of these facts—part of a much larger body of knowledge about how we tick—is a serious indictment of our perceptual abilities.*

The most obvious implication for my investigation of the Sasquatch is that the accuracy of our perceptions and recollections is

---

* A BBC Two television presenter hoaxed viewers in 1969 by saying he had obtained film clips of a famous 1920s comedian known as "The Great Pismo." When he showed the fraudulent clips of Pismo to people, and/or asked them about the performer, many remembered him, sometimes vividly.

unreliable. We cut too many corners in seeing and drawing conclusions about what we see. In at least some cases, what people take to be a Sasquatch, or signs of one, are likely nothing of the sort.

On Denny Island weeks before, I had come across what I was convinced was a large Sasquatch track. It wasn't enormous, but it was larger than my size-ten foot and looked a lot like the classic Bigfoot tracks you see on the Internet and in books. But as I examined the track more closely, I was shocked to see that it was actually composed of different overlapping prints. The toes were actually tracks of a wolf that had stepped right at the top of an old boot print, making it look like a Sasquatch track. My mind had played a trick on me.

Hardened skeptics and debunkers rightfully remind us that these sorts of tricks happen. But seldom do they tell us exactly how the tricks work. The mechanics of misperception, however, are now coming to light.

In their book *Human Givens*, Irish psychologist Joe Griffin and English author Ivan Tyrrell describe the human brain as a "metaphorical pattern-matching organ." We see, or otherwise discern something, they say, when the brain matches up stimuli in the outside world to templates—patterns—which we've inherited genetically and/or collected since birth. Infants, for instance, can distinguish human faces and will recognize the smiles of their caregivers, often smiling in return. This is a "pattern match." As infants we have genetically inherited the innate pattern, or template, for the human face and its emotions. When that pattern is matched to the same, or a similar enough, pattern in the external world, the baby will "see" and experience a flash of consciousness. The same process occurs with other patterns, which we all pick up throughout life—patterns for every conceivable object, idea, or circumstance. Everything we can see is by way of patterns we've acquired in our mental storehouse that find their matches in the outside world.

But here's the kicker: because our templates exist as metaphors (and not literal blueprints precise down to the last detail) and because our minds already oversimplify reality, our pattern matches are subject to considerable error. Our brains, operating on a best-guess basis, tend automatically to match things that come close enough to the patterns we hold. This creates "pattern mismatches." We easily confuse one thing for another. When a few people in Bella Bella took me for a Big Oil or government spy, they were matching a pattern at the forefront of their minds to something seemingly approximate. One form of pattern mismatching, known as pareidolia, happens when we see faces or the shapes of animals in clouds, rock formations, or stucco. It's the reason spelling mistakes in our writing can often be invisible to us even while we're proofreading: we see the words we had intended to write.

More than 90 percent of reported unidentified flying object (UFO) incidents, when scrutinized or looked at again in light of new information, have been shown to have mundane explanations: satellites, weather events, meteors, stars, planets, conventional aircraft, flocks of large birds reflecting light, balloons, hoaxes. In other words, the sightings are pattern mismatches. In fact, the UFO phenomenon arose only after the idea of aliens and extraterrestrials—a pattern—took hold in the collective mind by way of the first media reports about alleged spacecraft. The different physical descriptions of space-ships and aliens recounted by eyewitnesses often followed the first visual prototypes described or illustrated initially in science-fiction writing, art, movies, and TV shows—not the other way around. It's an example of life imitating art.

This knowledge is useful regardless of one's position on Bigfoot; it at least will explain some spurious reports of the Sasquatch: flashes of fur in the bush, odd sounds, impressions in the dirt, and misidentifications of bears standing in the distance. Pattern matching may

also account for the apparent universality of the wild-man arche-
types that have existed across numerous cultures. After all, our earlier
ancestors coexisted with other primate beings, including perhaps
Gigantopithecus itself.* It would not be surprising if the patterns of
these Bigfoot-like beings reside in our collective consciousness and
memory.

But can we say that perceptual mistakes alone dismiss the Sasquatch phenomenon? How could lengthier sightings at close range
by multiple witnesses, like that of Mary Brown, be explained with
this knowledge? Wouldn't bears, with their long snout, upright
ears, and short legs, be hard to misidentify at close range? Similarly, what should I make of the many reports I've collected so
far that begin with the eyewitnesses thinking they were seeing a
bear, only to be shocked when an apparent humanoid stood up,
looked at them, and walked or ran away, sometimes in view for
hundreds of yards?

I call Johnny Johnson later that day and am invited to his home, a
few doors down from Lena's. I'm greeted by a smiling man with a
shaved head, wearing a brown T-shirt with cut-off sleeves. We climb
a flight of stairs to his sparsely decorated living room and sit on his
couch. I give him the spiel about what I'm up to. He looks at me
penetratingly, almost sadly.

"Did you make it down to Koeye?" he asks.

I nod.

---

* "In recent years *Gigantopithecus* and *Homo erectus* fossils have been found together at a site
in Vietnam and another in China, evidence that the giant ape and humans coexisted," Michael
McLeod reports, in *The Anatomy of a Beast: Obsession and Myth on the Trail of Bigfoot*, Berkeley:
University of California Press, 2009, p. 161.

"It's beautiful, isn't it?"

"Beyond words."

"My family, the Johnson family, are from Koeye," he says, with a flicker of pride. "From the south side of the river."

With Johnny I feel I'm in the presence of a close friend, even a family member. He's fifty-three, gentle, and hospitable. But he's also intimidating: solidly built, with faded tattoos on his shoulders and forearms and large scars on his head, back, and arms. Johnny, I had been told, had survived a terrible grizzly bear attack a few years ago.

When I ask what he does for a living, he tells me that he assists archaeologists excavating old village sites along the coast. He says he hasn't worked much recently, owing to his health.

"You heard what happened to me, right?" he asks.

"I have. Are those scars from the attack?"

He nods self-consciously.

Johnny's brush with death took place in the summer of 2011. He was out picking salmonberries by the side of the road on the edge of town one day. Earlier that morning, the village dogs had been harassing a grizzly sow and her cubs, which had wandered into the community. Johnny had waited for things to quiet down before going into the bush. Soon after he began gathering berries, he was struck by a force so powerful it threw him into the air. When he sat up, he saw a huge grizzly coming directly at him.

"She was mad," he says. "I put my arms up to block her. But half of my forearm went into her mouth. She chomped on me and then tried to get into my stomach. I almost popped out both my shoulders trying to keep her back."

Johnny says his memory of the attack is hazy and fragmented, but he's certain that it unfolded in waves. After each assault, the bear ran out onto the road, where the village dogs were barking madly. Johnny realized the dogs had returned and were attacking the cubs, and the sow was simultaneously trying to fend them off. Every time he tried to take advantage of those intervals to escape, the bear was on him again. At one point the grizzly bit into his leg.

"I remember thinking: 'If she breaks my leg, I'm not making it home.' And I'm not one of these guys who like to quit."

In desperation, Johnny jabbed her in the eye with his finger. The bear roared in pain, slapped him in the head, and then broke off the attack to go fight the dogs that were harassing her cubs.

Johnny took advantage of that pause to make a final attempt to save himself. He began rolling his body, trying to get as far away as he could, until he reached a nearby creek bed. Before he could get any farther, he heard the heavy panting of the sow. Soon she was in view again, growling, gnashing her teeth, and frothing at the mouth. She charged at full speed.

"The last thing I remember was kicking up my feet and cata-pulting her with my legs," he says. "But the strain was so great that I blacked out."

When Johnny regained consciousness, it was dark. He was covered with a pile of tree branches a foot high. The bear had buried him until she could return later to feed on him. His final memory before waking up in the Royal Jubilee Hospital in Victoria ten days later was clambering to his feet and stumbling down the road into town in the pitch black of night. Although he has no recollection of it now, Johnny made it a mile to a neighbor's place and used his first-aid training, which he learned as a logger, to instruct the gathering crowd of villagers on how to keep him alive until the air ambulance arrived.

Johnny spent two months in the hospital. He'd suffered serious bite and claw injuries on his head, neck, back, torso, and thighs. The doctors told him one of the claw marks had missed his spinal cord by just a millimeter.

I ask Johnny what happened to the bear.

"The game wardens got her," he says. "But it was a year later. And after she chased a kid in the village—and also me."

"What?"

He nods.

"She ran after me by the band office. I escaped by climbing into one of the trucks parked there. She knew who I was, too. I could see it in her eyes. She remembered me from my smell."

Johnny tilts his neck to one side and winces, then massages it with his hand.

"I felt relieved when they got her. I didn't have to look over my shoulder anymore. But when they shot her I felt physically sick. I felt bad. I don't hate her for what she did. Bears are just animals. They don't have the rational thoughts we do."

Johnny tells me he has to leave to go fishing with a friend visiting from out of town. I quickly ask him what he knows about Sasquatches—and the so-called Hoodoo Valley.

"I don't know much about the place," he says, gathering his gear. "Only that loggers got spooked in there—and left. It was a long time ago. People here stay away from that place."

"And Bigfoots?"

"One story," he says. "I was staying a few nights at a cabin on the lake, at a place called Kwap. It's an old village site. About five miles down, on the north side. Near Hoodoo. We were doing work at the lake. This was about twenty years ago. We were sleeping one night, and then all of a sudden we heard this deafening banging on the walls: *Boom! Boom! Boom!* It went all the way around the cabin. It felt like the cabin was gonna fall apart. It kept pounding on and off for about ten minutes. We had a couple of bear dogs with us, sleeping outside. They were 120 pounds each. When we finally opened the door to find out what was going on, the dogs bolted into the cabin. They didn't bark once. It was definitely not a bear."

"What happened next?"

"Nothing. The banging just stopped."

"So you didn't actually see the culprit. But you're assuming it was a Sasquatch?"

"Bears don't walk around cabins banging on walls. Besides, my dad and uncle had seen a Sasquatch around the same time, bathing in the creek behind that same cabin."

"And the cabin's still there?"

"It is. But nobody's been there for ten years now. People are afraid of the place. Some students didn't believe my story until they went on a camping trip there. The next morning they were back here with their tails between their legs. But they weren't as lucky as we were. They lost one of their dogs."

"Lost?"

"Their dog chased after whatever was bothering them. It never came back."

There's a long pause. Johnny throws me a serious yet commiserating look that seems to say: *Have you got your fill of stories yet?* He cuts the silence by saying he has to leave.

"Wait," I say, getting up. "Is there any way I can get to these places?"

"Where?" he says, exasperated.

"Hoodoo. The cabin."

He chuckles sarcastically. "If you can find anyone here willing to go with you to Hoodoo, or that cabin, I'll give you everything I own."

"What about you? Could you take me?"

Johnny makes a cringing face and shakes his head. "I'm not going out there. I've been through enough."

"Can you suggest anyone?"

Johnny thinks a moment. "Do you know Alex Chartrand Jr.?"

"No."

"He's one of our Guardian Watchmen. He patrols our territorial waters. I heard him say he's going out that way in a few days. You can ask him to guide you into Hoodoo."

"What's the chance he'll agree?"

Johnny gives me a deadpan look. "About zero."

Despite my continued attempts to remain neutral and objective, I still find myself being yanked back into that comfort zone of credulity—as if tied to it by bungee cord. Every time I hear a new yarn, something clicks inside me. I'm especially enraptured by the old rumor of the Hoodoo Valley. How is it that I—though I've neither seen Sasquatches nor come across my own hard evidence of any—am so easily swayed by arguments of their existence? And why does part of me stubbornly refuse to budge from that position?

I'm not alone. There are perhaps millions like me who have read the Sasquatch books and watched the Bigfoot TV shows—none of us have ever seen the creatures, but we are certain they exist. And no amount of contradictory information, no assemblage of reasonable doubts, can change that.

How can that be? One likely answer, I discover, boils down to one thing: our need to remain sane.

Our brains construct simplified versions of reality, helping us to see just enough of what we need to survive, but those simplifications apply not only to our sensory world. They also affect our understanding of events. The narratives and stories we use to explain the world are also caricatures. It's what we call our "worldview."

We spend our early lives building mental models of how the world works, using our education, experiences, predispositions, and intuition as brick and mortar. How and why do certain things happen in the world? What is possible, and what is impossible? Because we don't have access to all information—no human can be all-knowing—our ideas are always a best guess. We fill in the many blanks with our hunches, opinions, and assumptions. Any new information that conforms with our ideas, our worldview, is easily incorporated.

In his book *Brain and Culture*, Yale psychiatry professor Bruce Wexler tells us that up until adulthood our brain is exquisitely skilled at building its models. But once that task is complete, the brain is far less skilled at changing them. Most adult brain activity from that point forward, he writes, is "devoted to making the environment conform to established structures."[15] In other words: we work to set our views in stone. We all have our own internal models for what's going on in the world. These models can be seemingly reasonable or outlandish in their assumptions. We might believe that oil companies, Freemasons, or Zionists rule the planet. We may allot blame for the problems in society to white men, immigrants, or liberals. The perceived rights and wrongs in any given conflict—such as those that underscore the Wuikinuxv's grievances against the Heiltsuk, and vice versa—also constitute a mental model. For most of us, sooner or later, these cobbled positions become rigid, fixed, inviolable.

So what happens when we eventually come across information that contradicts our simplified narratives?

"One option," writes Indian neuroscientist V. S. Ramachandran in *Phantoms in the Brain*, "is to revise your story and create a new model about the world and about yourself. The problem," he adds, "is that if you did this for every little piece of threatening information, your behavior would soon become chaotic and unstable. You would go mad."[16]

Our tendency is to look away when our hard-won and cherished narratives are faced with information that undermines them and the way we live.

Investigative journalist Will Storr says our brain adores our models and "guards them like a bitter curmudgeon." It reworks them only when absolutely necessary. "Your brain," he writes in *The Heretics*, "is surprisingly reluctant to change its mind. Rather than going through the difficulties involved in rearranging itself to reflect truth, it often prefers to fool you. So it distorts. It forgets. It projects. It lies."[17]

Similarly, Jonathan Haidt, author of *The Righteous Mind*, argues that our intuitive reflexes are the basis for much of what we believe, and that those reflexes seek rationalization. Reasoning, he says, "evolved not to help us find truth but to help us engage in arguments, persuasion, and manipulation in the context of discussions with other people." The good reasoner, he adds, is really good at one thing: "Finding evidence to support the position he or she already holds, usually for intuitive reasons."[18]

There is a term to describe the mental discomfort that arises when we hold two pieces of contradictory knowledge at the same time: *cognitive dissonance*. Instead of going back to the drawing board or recomputing in the face of new information, we resort to chicanery. We reject, ignore, rationalize, or distort the new data, becoming even more hardened in our position. We cherry-pick, find additional evidence, and reinterpret facts that support our position—a process known as *confirmation bias*. In more extreme cases, in which political power or wealth is at stake, we simply marginalize, penalize, cast away, or kill the messengers responsible for the dissonant information. Turkish journalists who write critically of their regime are labeled "terrorists" and thrown into jail. Environmentalists who loudly protest deforestation in certain Latin American countries are often killed by police or thugs hired by logging companies.

This devotion to what we think we know and what we think should be runs deep. Margaret Heffernan, author of *Willful Blindness*, says that at the root is a fundamental preference in our lives for what is known and familiar to us, whether real or imaginary. Anything that falls outside that—the unknown, the dissonant, the alien—is seen as an enemy. "Embedded within our self-definition, we build relationships, institutions, cities, systems, and cultures that, in reaffirming our values, blind us to alternatives," she writes. "This is where our willful blindness originates: in the innate human desire for familiarity, for likeness, that is fundamental to the ways our minds work."*

This is partly why many members of the ever-growing congregation of Bigfooters, never having seen a creature for themselves, push aside the dissonance caused by the fact that a Sasquatch body has never been presented. Even John Bindernagel and his Bigfoot-positive scientist colleagues, who are not pure "believers" because their arguments stem from professional assessment of the Sasquatch data, are still working with their own cherished models of reality. Their emotions and intuitions are fully engaged. Their minds are no less like Storr's "bitter curmudgeon," defending their models to the end.

All of this also applies to debunkers or conservative scientists. The desire to discredit or deliberately disbelieve, whether rightly or wrongly, is also a mental posture. Because science operates within the convenient circle of what fits with its preconceptions—which is anathema to what science is supposed to be about—it has rejected the work of Bindernagel and his colleagues outright.

---

* Heffernan also writes: "People are very resistant to changing what they know how to do, what they have expertise in and certainly what they have economic investment in." Heffernan, Margaret. *Willful Blindness: Why We Ignore the Obvious at Our Peril*. London: Bloomsbury, 2012, p. 51.

Alex, the Guardian Watchman, it turns out, is hard to find. He's never at his place. When I ask Lena about him, she tells me he has no phone and that he uses only the radio. I try calling out to him on the VHF channel, but I get no response save for some unintelligible, static-filled chatter coming from the sportfishing camps out in the inlet.

While at Lena's I find myself restless and unable to stay put. I decide to walk to a place called "the reload"—the old logging depot at the edge of Owikeno Lake. Lena advises me not to make the hour-long walk. A huge grizzly, she says, was seen earlier on this side of town. She tells me to take her pickup instead and throws me the keys with a smile.

I drive along the heavily potholed gravel road through a stretch of forest that separates the village from the lake. The approach is dark and a touch ominous: a landscape of silhouetted, mossy trees, streaked with sunbeams, towering above huge spiderlike ferns. I drive out of the forest and into a wide clearing strewn with old logs and rusting equipment. Before me are the azure waters of Owikeno Lake, a long, flooded alpine valley stretching far into the distance. About a dozen seals are sunning themselves, lazily, on a log boom a few feet offshore.

Once I step out of the pickup I hear voices from behind a pile of timber and the sound of an engine starting. Then I see a motorboat drone away from the edge of the reload toward the distant reaches of the lake. That's followed by laughter and a dog yelping. I walk over to the other side of the woodpile and find a man and two women, all in their forties, sitting on logs around a small fire. A tiny, rodent-like dog with puffy brown fur is running around them, barking madly. Parked behind them is a truck. All three are holding cans of Budweiser beer, and they stare at me as if I were an apparition.

"You're that guy from New York who's staying at Lena's," exclaims the man, who's dressed in a T-shirt and jeans. The two women pull at their cigarettes and stare at me with fascination.

"Toronto," I say.

"Same thing," he replies. The women chuckle. "I'm Alex," he says, breaking into a smile and extending his hand.

"Alex Chartrand?" I say, shaking it, taken aback by the coincidence.

"Yup, Junior. Alex Senior is my dad."

I mention the referral from Johnny Johnson—and my interest in exploring the lake and the Hoodoo Valley. The women's faces drop at the mention of Sasquatches and the valley. Alex nods, straight-faced.

"I heard that you were asking about that," he says. "Want a beer?" He reaches into a box beside him and fishes out a warm can, handing it to me. "I'm one of the Guardian Watchmen in the village," he adds. "Many of the communities on this coast have watchmen. We patrol our waters. Keep an eye on our resources, on the environment. Tomorrow we're going out on the lake looking for poachers."

"*Poachers?*" My imagination instantly conjures up ragtag groups of men in pickup trucks stalking elephants and rhinos in the Serengeti with AK-47s.

"Bear hunters," he says, clarifying. "We've banned them here. But they still try to slip in." I remember the discussion with Captain Brian in Koeye.

"Could I tag along?"

"Sure, but we won't be going into any of those places you mention," he says, closing the door on discussion about the Hoodoo Valley.

But I press him. "Can you at least tell me something about the Hoodoo Valley? About what happened there?"

Alex tells me he neither has been there nor knows more about the place than anyone else. I can see he doesn't want to talk about it. The two women avert their eyes when he speaks. When I ask about Sasquatch he's more forthcoming. He says that once, while spending four days camping alone on the south end of the lake, he came across a huge humanoid footprint beside a creek.

"It was pretty unnerving. I was in the bush purifying myself for a *Hamatsa* dance I was going to perform at a potlatch. So I couldn't leave. And I could barely defend myself. The only things I had with me were my sleeping bag, a tent, an ax, lighter, knife, and a water bottle," he says.

"What did you do?"

"I stayed put," he says. "Those were the rules. I wasn't allowed to go upriver, or follow any noises in the bush, because it could be a *Dzonoqua*—whose track I probably saw—trying to lure me," he says. "Or even the Little People."

I do a double take. "The Little People?"

"Yup."

Alex tells me there are smaller Sasquatch-type creatures inhabiting the valleys around the lake. He describes the same beings I was told about in Bella Bella and Koeye after I mentioned the small tracks I saw in the mud at Old Town. As I did with the others, I ask Alex if the small creatures aren't just juvenile Sasquatches.

He shakes his head. "They're a separate race. They even sound different. I heard their laughter behind my tent at night while on that same outing."

The women follow the conversation, spellbound, clutching their cigarettes, the long ashes dangling precariously from the tips. One of them, itching to say more, interjects: "You gonna tell him *what else* happened to you out there?"

Alex shoots her a stern look as if she has relinquished a secret. Everyone goes quiet.

I down the rest of my beer and stand up.

"Hold on," Alex says, getting up with me. He waves me over to his pickup. I look into the back when we get there and see that it's filled with a dozen large salmon. "A buddy of mine just came over with these."

"What kind are they?"

"Sockeye," he says, smiling from ear to ear. Alex grabs one and hands it to me. I hook my fingers into its gills. The heavy fish reaches down to my knees. It's the first time anyone has casually given me a whole fish. I stand there for a moment, awkwardly, wondering what to do next. The women begin to chuckle.

"Go ahead," Alex says. "Throw it in the back of Lena's truck."

I look at him quizzically.

"It's a gift," he says. "Go back and eat it."

Alex's mention of voices and laughing in the woods reminds me of extended periods I'd spent alone in the forest and the desert, hiking and camping, when I'd experienced similar phenomena.

In the 1950s, the head of McGill University's school of psychology in Montreal conducted a series of experiments on paid student volunteers. The goal was to study the effects of isolation on the mind. The experiments were funded by the CIA, which wanted to know more about the role that isolation played in the brainwashing of American prisoners of war held captive by the Chinese during the Korean War. The volunteers were isolated in soundproof cubicles and cut off from all meaningful human contact for up to a week.

Researchers deprived them of stimuli, reducing what they could feel, see, hear, and touch, by making them wear opaque visors and cotton gloves. Air-conditioning units were made to hum continuously in order to mask any sounds that might reach them from the hallway. A few hours into the experiment, the volunteers became deeply restless and started to crave stimulation. Most began to talk and sing to themselves to break the monotony. Soon the test subjects began to experience things that weren't there. This began with nonspecific objects, like points of light and abstract shapes, that then turned into dreamlike scenes replete with dogs, babies, squirrels, and, in one case, eyeglasses marching down a street. Some volunteers heard music and singing, or felt that they were being poked and prodded.

In 2008, British professor Ian Robbins, head of trauma psychology at Saint George's Hospital in London, conducted a similar experiment in conjunction with the BBC program *Horizon*. Six people were left in a bomb shelter for forty-eight hours under very similar conditions. All subjects experienced pronounced visual and auditory phenomena.

From these sorts of experiments researchers have determined that when humans experience prolonged social isolation they are susceptible to hallucinating. If there's a dearth of sensory information reaching the brain—an organ that normally processes a huge amount of data to construct our reality—it tries to make up for those scant signals, and the patterns they evoke, by concocting extra ones of its own.

Charging an eyewitness, who is certain to have experienced *something*, with having had a "hallucination" can be tantamount to an insult. The word is heavily loaded and wrongly implies a flawed capacity. Yet, I wonder whether some of the more dramatic Bigfoot encounters might be related to the effects of prolonged isolation in the wilderness.

The story of Albert Ostman, the Swedish Canadian prospector who claimed he had been kidnapped and held captive by a family of Sasquatches near Toba Inlet in 1924, stands out. He had been wandering in the woods alone for three whole weeks before he was allegedly abducted in his sleeping bag.

Mary Brown of Bella Bella, who was part of the group sighting at the cabin in Roscoe Inlet, related another secondhand Sasquatch report concerning a different forest cabin that, to my mind, also fits the isolation hypothesis. This one involved a troubled Heiltsuk youth who spent weeks in rehabilitative isolation at the cabin and claimed the building had been attacked by a Bigfoot.* Yet, interestingly, over the course of my researches, I hear of other incidents from campers involving a Sasquatch assailing that very same cabin.

When Lena asks how my Hoodoo Valley research is going, I tell her, resignedly, that the trail has gone cold.

"Have you spoken with Frank Hanuse yet?" she asks.

I had spoken with Frank—a Wuikinuxv elder and elected councillor—several days back about Sasquatches and the Rivers Inlet sockeye collapse. But that had been before I'd heard about the Hoodoo Valley from his brother Dennis.

"Talk to him again," Lena urges. "Frank's full of stories, and he knows everything happening around here." Lena dials his number and hands me the phone. After several rings, the lively, good-humored

---

* See Addendum 1 for Mary's interesting, verbatim account of that incident.

man answers in his trademark cowboy-like drawl. After a bit of small talk, I tell Frank that I'm trying to find out more about the loggers who fled the Hoodoo Valley and ask whether he knows anything about that episode.

"Know anything? Of course I do!" he says, laughing at the seeming silliness of my question. "I was alive back then. I heard the whole story, which goes back generations, from the old chiefs at the time."

Frank says the elders told him that sometime in the 1800s, the villages dotting the lake experienced a period of what he terms "bad luck." It was a combination, he says, of bad weather, poor fish runs, and freak accidents. Malevolent spirits were blamed for the misfortunes. So the heads of all the villages organized an emergency meeting and performed a ceremony to cleanse the village sites of the evil.

"So, what's the connection to Hoodoo?" I ask, wondering whether I had missed something.

"Well, you can't just get rid of bad energy. It doesn't just disappear. You have to *move it* somewhere. See where I'm coming from?"

It takes me a few seconds to realize what Frank is saying: the evil spirits were cast away by the village chiefs—*into* the Hoodoo Valley.

"Bingo, kid."

"But why there?" I ask.

"Because it's a good-for-nothing valley. Not too deep. Water barely runs there. And so the elders thought it was a perfect place. No one would have any reason to go in there in the future—except for those poor loggers who all ended up being plagued by mishaps. That's why they fled the place. All those companies went bankrupt in the end."

"And the name 'Hoodoo'—is that the name of the creek?"

"No. The white guys just called it that."

"Why?"

"*Why this and why that!* Because it's bad 'hoodoo,' man—that's why! Maybe 'hoodoo' sounds like 'voodoo'—so they called it that. How should I know?"

"That's crazy," I say.

"If you don't believe me, go and spend the night up there yourself."

"I can't! No one will take me there."

"You know why, kid? Because no one here in their right mind goes up there. And come to think of it, neither should you!"

The next day, the engines of the Guardian Watchmen patrol boat sputter to life as the sun lifts itself above the Coast Mountains. It hovers like a beacon directly in line with the long axis of the lake, turning the water a dazzling gold.

Alex unties the boat and sits in the pilot's chair, and we roar eastward into the blinding morning. Seated beside Alex is his Guardian Watchman colleague and copilot, Archie—a ginger-haired thirty-something from Vancouver Island who is married to a woman in the village.

Alex inserts his iPhone into a yellow waterproof boom box beside him, and we are bathed in the deep bass rhythms of a rap song. Alex and Archie light up smokes, and their dialogue and laughter are drowned out by the deafening music and growling engines. We're thrown up and down in wind-whipped swells in rhythm with the thumping baritone poetry and the occasional sound of gunshots. Water drenches the windshield, obscuring the view of mountains ahead, silhouetted in the glaring light.

We are heading east, hugging the lake's south shore, but my gaze is glued to the distant north shore. I'm wondering which of the valleys we're passing is the Hoodoo. Surrendering to my momentary obsession, I ask Alex, yelling above the music, where the valley is, but he shrugs his shoulders and says he can't tell from here.

Our plan is to circumnavigate the lake, looking for bear hunters. Though the trophy hunting of bears in British Columbia remains legal and is backed by an influential hunting lobby, some First Nations in the province have come out strongly against the practice. They say killing grizzlies for trophies is an antiquated, unethical, and inhumane practice that erodes their ecosystems. In 2012, Coastal First Nations, an alliance of nine indigenous nations on British Columbia's central and northern coast, and including the Wuikinuxv, banned the hunt in their territories, all situated in or near the Great Bear Rainforest.*

When I asked Alex earlier what authority and means he has to enforce the ban, he curtly answered, "Tribal law."

"What do you do when you find hunters?"

"We politely ask them to leave. And offer to escort them out."

"But what if they won't go?" I asked. "You can't just arrest them."

"We'll follow them around. Make a lot of noise. Mess up their hunt. Scare the bears away so they can't get a shot."

"And hope," I add, "that a group of alpha males carrying guns in the woods won't get pissed off enough to turn them on you."

A disconcerted look comes over Alex's face. "Something like that."

The lighthearted sense of adventure with which we've embarked evaporates after we pass the first and second narrows at the far end of the lake. Here Alex cuts the engines and we bob in silence near an abandoned logging camp at the mouth of the Sheemahant River. The mood turns militaristic. Alex and Archie pull out a pair of

---

* Other First Nations in British Columbia, including the Nisga'a and the Tahltan, oppose bans on the grizzly hunt, largely for economic reasons.

binoculars. They pass it back and forth and murmur to each other quietly like tense army generals at the front line. Straight ahead, onshore, are a few white trailer-like buildings. The lake is still.

I crouch down next to Alex. "Why the cloak-and-dagger?" I ask.

"It's hard to tell from here, but that's a really big camp," he says, handing me the binoculars. "Lots of buildings. Old vehicle trails. Even an airstrip in the back. They logged the shit out of this area in the seventies. So, it's like a small town. A group of hunters could easily hide in there."

I look through the binoculars and see no movement among the trailers and trees. "Who would know about a place this hidden and remote?" I ask.

"Anyone," Alex says. "It's easy to find on marine charts or Google Earth. All you need is a floatplane, or chopper, and you can get anywhere in this country."

"We have a few hunters around here who might be tempted," Archie says, taking the binoculars from me. "One of them, a guy named Leonard Ellis, lives in Bella Coola." It's the same man Captain Brian Falconer had mentioned in Koeye, whom I'd met the previous year.

"You mean the former grizzly hunter who now does bear tours?" I ask.

"Yeah, you should go and write about *that guy*. Forget the Sasquatch."

This second reference to Ellis piques my interest. I'd had no idea he was so well known. I make a mental note to seek him out when I get back to Bella Coola.

We restart the engines and crawl slowly up to a long pier at the edge of the abandoned camp. We moor and get off the boat. Alex has put on a Guardian Watchman jacket and cap, both emblazoned with native insignia. He's holding a 12-gauge shotgun, which has materialized out of nowhere, and has a big knife strapped to his waist. Archie hands me a Velcro belt holding a container of bear spray.

"Just in case," he says.

We enter the abandoned camp, cautious but determined, like narcotics officers on a raid. No one speaks. We weave around the sides of several large, decaying Alcan trailers set in a wide clearing with sprawling weeds and berry bushes.

Inside the musty-smelling trailers everything seems to have been left just as it was when the loggers were in residence: old teak furniture, a small, bulbous black-and-white turn-dial TV with its antennae up (how did they get *any* signal out here?), faded fashion magazines featuring Farrah Fawcett–haired women in bell-bottoms, and a beautiful retro silk-screen print of an alpine scene.

I break off from the others and enter the largest trailer—the living quarters. It's no more than a long hallway lined with bedrooms. Each is a hollow shell containing broken bed frames, filthy mattresses, and collapsing wardrobe closets. Scrawled on each room's door in colored marker is the name or nickname of its former occupant:

Pin Ball Jason
Davey and the Grinders
Crazy Ray's Palace: No fags, fruits, or fat chicks
Boom-Boom Man

And on the very last door, to room number 34, scrawled in big, bold caps:

BIGFOOT

Finding no intruders at the camp, we push up the Sheemahant valley. With even greater trepidation we follow an old track out. It's lined with tall alders concealing a thick, dark forest. At first our hike is easy going. The path, an old dirt road, is covered in moss, short grass, and fallen leaves. But the farther we go the more overgrown it becomes, the weeds reaching up to our knees and even our thighs at times. Our legs become so drenched in morning dew it's as if we'd waded waist-deep into a lake.

Alex is holding his shotgun nervously across his chest with both hands. The added worry now is bears. And after we see two huge grizzly tracks, the anxiety becomes infectious. Archie walks ahead issuing a rebel yell to ward off any bears. Between howls, no one speaks. The only sound is from our footfalls—and from our breathing, which dispenses small clouds of vapor in the shaded morning cold. Although the area we're in has been heavily altered by humans, it feels deeper in the bush than anywhere else I've been on this trip.

"It's kinda like walking those city blocks, back home, eh?" Alex says, trying to lighten the mood. I make an effort to imagine Toronto and its sobering blue-gray concrete grid, but I'm unable to. It feels farther away than any real place possibly could.

"I can't imagine going home," I tell him.

"You know what it is about the city that's the real buzzkill?" Alex asks.

I laugh. "Take your pick," I say.

Alex stops in his tracks and looks at me seriously. His eyes widen. "It's *the noise.*"

We reach the overgrown airstrip, no more than a long, rectangular clearing in the forest. There is a fork in the trail. Archie and Alex argue about which branch to take.

But suddenly they're interrupted by the droning of a small plane in the distance. We all stop and cock our ears. Alex and Archie listen intently, meticulously, trying to discern clues in the sound. They glance at each other, volleying questions back and forth with their eyes: What kind of plane? How far? Is it coming or going? Is it headed for the lake?

But just as the droning gets loud enough to arouse real suspicion, the sound crests and trails away in the soft rustling of alder leaves.

By midafternoon we're sitting on the pier at the abandoned logging camp eating our lunches and preparing to leave. The weather has become stiflingly hot. Alex and Archie take off their wet shoes and socks and lay them on the pier to dry while they stuff themselves with sandwiches.

I strip down to a T-shirt and marvel at the fact that in my several weeks of rain-forest travel, it hasn't rained once. Drier, warmer weather has become the norm on the coast in summertime. But this is something different—more like a drought.

Alex finishes eating and begins to unload his shotgun. He places several slugs and shells on the pier, in a line next to him. I stare at them in morbid fascination. I tell him that I know nothing about guns or hunting, having lived all of my life in one city or another.

Alex and Archie exchange grins before Alex turns to me. "Wanna try shooting it?" he says.

I'm gripped by an involuntary fear and hesitation. His invitation has the tinge of something taboo. "No. It's all right," I find myself saying, in spite of an intense desire to say yes.

The two throw me looks bordering on disbelief, as if to say: *Who would turn down the chance to fire a shotgun for the first time?*

"It's easy," Alex says. "Plus, if you're going to be wandering around these parts, it's something you need to learn."

The decision has been made to initiate me. Alex picks up a shell and grabs the gun before standing up. Both he and Archie have a look of impatient relish on their faces, as if they're about to play a joke on me. I stand up without protest.

"This is bird shot, but it'll still have a kick," Alex says, inserting the shell, loading it, and then handing the gun to me. I take it awkwardly, adjusting my grip to its heavy weight.

"The safety's off," Alex says, backing up. "Go ahead."

"Where should I point it?" I ask, thinking aloud.

"Away from us," Archie says.

Alex gestures toward the water. "Shoot into the lake."

I see an old tree stump sticking out of the water, about eighty feet from the side of the pier, and take aim.

"That's good," Alex says, approaching and readjusting my grip. "Now hold it like this."

All skittishness evaporates as my attention is directed outward, focused on the target. I adjust my aim and pull the trigger.

After what feels like not much more than a microsecond, there's a peal of thunder and an incredible shock wave . . .

The late Argentinean writer Jorge Luis Borges wrote a fantastically surreal story called *The Aleph*. It's about a tiny orb, the Aleph, which when gazed at allows the observer to see the entire universe from every conceivable angle. The main character describes the moment he peers into it: time stops and in a split second he bears witness to everything that ever existed—and would ever exist—from all visual perspectives, all at once.

No metaphor is exact. But the experience of firing the shotgun feels like Borges's description of looking into the Aleph. In that instant, a universe of impressions washes over me. Every shooting I've ever seen in a film or TV show or read about in a book, from handguns to artillery, is reexperienced, from the perspective of both the shooter and the shot. It's a profound and debilitating shock. In that moment I understand what it's like to be on the giving and receiving ends of a deadly projectile weapon. I feel a mishmash of contradictory emotions: the ego-amplifying elation of power merging with disgust. And all of this unfolds within a split second.

The top of the stump and the water around it explode. A gruesome, diabolical thunder runs amok across the lake and mountains, reverberating, repeatedly, back and forth.

"I think you hit it," Alex says, taking the shotgun out of my hands and patting me on my shoulder. "You all right?"

"I feel a bit jolted."

"That's how it always is the first time," he says. "And that was just bird shot. The slug's got a lot more kick."

"What's the difference between the two?" I ask.

"We carry the slugs to use against bears—in worst-case scenarios. It's really rare, but if a grizzly is coming at you, and it's going to kill you, the slug will usually stop it in its tracks."

That hypothetical scene plays out in my mind. An all-consuming chill runs down my spine, and I quickly shake the thought.

The ride home along the lake's north shore is a blur. I'm tired. I barely notice the two cabins, sites of alleged Sasquatch attacks, that we pass at different creek mouths.

We barrel again toward the sun, now hanging over the western end of the lake, and pass high precipices of dark, shiny granite with small trees growing in their clefts.

We approach a narrow valley whose entrance is elevated above the water. Alex and Archie slow the boat down and in unison crane their necks and look up at the slope leading to it from the water.

Contorted trees, deciduous and coniferous, tangle at its entrance. The men, skittish, speak into each other's ears, look at me, and then throttle the boat's engines.

Acting on a hunch, I tap Alex on the shoulder. He turns and looks at me as if caught in a secret act. I jerk my thumb backward, from where we just came.

"*Hoo-doo?*" I yell, over the sound of the engines.

He stares at me for a moment and then nods, conceding. I see he wants to say more, but the engines are deafening. It has been a long day. His eyes implore me to leave it alone, to let it go.

I nod. We both turn away. And neither of us mentions it again.*

---

* There's a remarkable epilogue to my attempts to find out about the strange events surrounding the so-called Hoodoo Valley—proof that all stories find their ending. See Addendum 2.

7

Ocean Falls
(Laiq)

Sasquatch is a fulsome liminal symbol, containing fundamental paradoxes of being and non-being, mind and matter, life and death. It straddles and incorporates boundaries that we consider absolute, that are fundamentally required by our system of rationality. To the extent that it is as it appears to be—a being of the mind which leaves footprints in the earth—Sasquatch remains absolutely inexplicable, a genuine mystery.

—Marjorie M. Halpin, *Manlike Monsters on Trial*

Tales of haunted valleys. Hairy mini-men with a bad attitude. Shaggy colossi shaking log cabins to their foundations. James Bond–style speedboat adventures. Bear politics. Environmental wars. At most I had been expecting just a handful of Sasquatch reports. Instead the floodgates had opened, sweeping me along in the deluge. There is simply too much to digest at once.

I book myself a spot on the *Queen of Chilliwack*, a three-hundred-foot passenger ferry that carries me, slowly, methodically, and soberly, to the next precinct of this adventure. I forgo the action-hero dramatics of floatplane and speedboat, opting for something calmer, less kinetic. I need an interval of perspective.

My next stop is the all but abandoned pulp and paper mill community of Ocean Falls, located in Heiltsuk territory at the head
of Cousins Inlet. The ferry journey, beginning in Bella Bella, is a
circuitous, full-day affair, first heading north along the Inside Passage
route to the village of Klemtu, in Kitasoo/Xai'xais territory, before
doubling back and then turning east through the upper channels
of the inlet system toward Ocean Falls.

Earlier, in Bella Bella, snide remarks had followed any mention
I made of taking the ferry. The government-run ferry monopoly
is widely considered overpriced and inefficient, the product of an
inept bureaucracy. Though many locals depend on its services, it's
reviled with the intensity of an oppressed people's hatred for their
dictator. But I have a fondness for ferries. Having spent my early
travel years plying every possible ferry route in the Mediterranean,
often sleeping on the deck, I learned to appreciate their austerity and
patient plodding. The slow-rolling vistas and the sense of impending
arrival set to the smell of oily grime on metal, sea breeze, and engine
exhaust can, strangely, have an almost soothing effect.

The *Queen of Chilliwack* feels, in that sense, familiar as it plows leisurely through the forest-lined arteries of ocean. On the front deck,
a few dozen tourists lean over the railings, gazing toward the rugged
slopes of Swindle and Dowager Islands. I find myself thinking about
Leonard Ellis, the former bear hunter turned bear-viewing guide
from Bella Coola. Though he offers no obvious connection with
the Sasquatch, I'm eager to visit this controversial mountain man
again. The more I hear of him, the more I envision an antihero, a
kind of Clint Eastwood cowboy.

While waiting to catch the *Chilliwack* in Bella Bella, I brought
up Ellis with Ian McAllister at Pacific Wild. Ian, who has butted
heads with Ellis many times over the latter's bear and wolf hunts,

described him as a hard—but also charismatic—man. That second
quality chimed more with my memory of him.

"He's a skilled predator who's bagged a lot of animals," Ian said.
He took a moment to mull his next words, before deciding to say
nothing else.

The *Queen of Chilliwack* docks in Klemtu's bay shortly after noon
to a litany of metallic screeches and clanging noises. The hamlet of
450 people, a cluster of homes set in a few rows, hugs the curving
bay beneath a pair of scruffy conical hills. I go ashore for the afternoon and find many of Klemtu's residents, whole families, crowded
outside the boat. For a moment, I think they're a welcoming committee for someone important getting off the boat. The Kitasoo/
Xai'xais have a reputation for being the friendliest First Nation
community on the coast. But then residents impatiently board the
ship. I learn that the townsfolk gather weekly to have lunch in the
ferry's cafeteria.

This is my second visit to Klemtu. I had come here by floatplane as part of my magazine assignment the year before. At the
time, Klemtu, like other nearby communities, was experiencing
a surge in reported Sasquatch activity. Kitasoo/Xai'xais territory
has a long history of reports, with documented cases going back
to the 1930s—long before the words *Bigfoot* and *Sasquatch* became
commonplace. Residents here claim some of the creatures live on
the shores of Kitasoo Lake, nestled in a bowl in the mountains just
above the community, which serves as the town's water reservoir.
Sasquatch sightings over the decades have always come in periodic
waves. During my previous visit, the creatures were showing themselves again after years of inactivity.

In the few hours I have in Klemtu I visit the Spirit Bear Lodge—a
world-class ecotourist bear-viewing resort, owned and run by the

Kitasoo, that has completely revitalized the community. While there, I run into Charlie Mason—a jovial storyteller and hereditary chief. I ask him about Bigfoot activity in the village. He tells me the earlier spike in incidents has already dropped off.

"How do you account for that?" I ask him.

Mason shrugs his shoulders. "That's just how it is with them Sasquatch," he says, in his characteristically baritone voice. "You won't see 'em for years, and then suddenly they're back like they never left. Then one day, you realize they're gone again—*poof*—like they were never there to begin with."

There one moment, gone the next.

Is this the cunning of some unknown being? Or the shenanigans of the most complex piece of machinery in the known universe—the human mind?

I've lost track of time. The long blast of the *Queen of Chilliwack*'s horn, signaling its imminent departure, yanks me away from Klemtu's relative normalcy—a state that will prove to be short-lived.

The *Chilliwack* pushes on into the advancing dusk. I am standing on deck, alone, as we backtrack through Heiltsuk territory, crawling through the channels and passes dividing jigsaw slabs of land. As we go from Return Channel to Fisher Channel, the mountains, with their heads above the clouds, transform into shadowy presences. At midnight a distant light appears through the sea of blackness at the head of Cousins Inlet. The *Chilliwack*'s intercom announces our impending arrival in Ocean Falls. I gather my things and queue up with an older couple from Oregon at the ship's exit. As the ferry pulls up to the illuminated pier another message comes over the intercom warning passengers disembarking with their cars not to drive while talking on their cell phones, or they may incur a hefty fine.

Two ferry employees walk by as the message is broadcast. One of them laughs at the announcement.

"What's so funny?" his colleague asks.

"That message. There's no cell-phone reception in town. No cars are getting off the boat here. And you wouldn't be able to find a policeman in this place if your life depended on it."

Blessed with a charming name, Ocean Falls is an outlier, a place neither here nor there. The carcass of a once thriving pulp and paper mill metropolis, today's village of two dozen people is beyond description. How does one define a locale that is at once a ghost town, a squatters' camp, a settlers' outpost, and a safe haven for misfits and runaways, situated somewhere between lost and forgotten?

It all started with a waterfall.

In the industrial boom of the late nineteenth century, the future site of Ocean Falls—the location of an old Heiltsuk village—was earmarked for its potential to generate hydroelectricity. The crystalline waters of a stunning glacial lake (later named Link Lake) that emptied into Cousins Inlet, below it, made the location the perfect spot to situate energy-dependent industry.

Construction on a pulp and paper mill began in 1909, followed later by a dam to power it. Meanwhile, Heiltsuk residents were encouraged to relocate. Soon a hospital, a school, a hotel, and numerous homes and apartment buildings had been built to house and service the people who would run this factory deep in the heart of the northern rain forest. Within a few decades, Ocean Falls, a company-run labor-camp paradise, would swell to five thousand people, becoming the largest pulp mill town in British Columbia.

Archival pictures taken at the town's apogee in the 1950s show row upon row of terraced, barracks-style white homes sitting beneath cumulus-like plumes of vapor spewing from smokestacks ringing the gargantuan mill. At the time, any job in Ocean Falls was considered a plum position. The mill and town, owned first by Pacific Mills, until 1954, and then by Crown Zellerbach, until 1972, provided for every need of the employee. In addition to a decent income, workers received lodging, meals at the mill cafeteria, and a list of social and sporting clubs to choose from. Forest cottages lined the shores of Cousins Inlet and Link Lake for those who wanted to escape the monotonous work grind but didn't have it in them to make the long and tiring pilgrimage to vacation spots in the outside world, and back in again.

As all societies do, Ocean Falls would boast its own milestones and achievements. Its man-made wonder, its Parthenon, was twelve miles of boardwalk that crisscrossed the town. A huge swimming pool produced a pedigree of world-class swimmers. One third of Canada's national team at the 1952 Summer Olympics in Helsinki were swimmers from Ocean Falls. For a period, the town was considered so important that it had its own daily news pages in the *Vancouver Sun*.

Sometime in the 1950s (no one remembers exactly when), the residents of this exurban outpost in the rain forest started referring to themselves as the "Rain People." By some unknowable configuration of air currents, mountain relief, and sea, Ocean Falls was said to get more rain than any other place on the British Columbia coast.* Close to two hundred inches fell annually on average. It is now an accepted though apocryphal theory that the noxious gas

---

* Or perhaps it just seemed that way, given that rainfall wasn't being measured across most of the uninhabited coast.

cloud emanating from the pulp mill and hanging almost permanently over the town created its own weather system, amplifying the rainfall. Whatever the truth, those old downpours remain the stuff of legend. The Rain People emblemized this mythology by adopting as their official mascot and corporate logo a Disneyesque Daffy Duck knockoff holding an umbrella happily over its head. The weather may have been uncooperative, but life for Ocean Fallers couldn't have been better.

And then everything changed.

As in other places on the coast, boom went to bust with little or no warning. By the early 1970s, Ocean Falls' viability became increasingly tenuous. Geographical isolation, obsolete machinery, growing competition, rising overhead, and shrinking markets made Ocean Falls less and less profitable for its owners. In 1973, Crown Zellerbach pulled the plug on the mill's operations. The provincial government stepped in at the last minute and bought Ocean Falls to keep it alive. But persistent fiscal issues dogged the town. By 1980, the community was shuttered for good, consigned to the long list of canneries and sawmills whose lifeless, rotting husks pepper British Columbia's coast.

Today, a dystopian mood has replaced the mill steam hanging over the town. Many of the old derelict buildings left standing—including the four-hundred-room Martin Hotel (once the largest lodging in the province), a few low-rise apartments, the school, and a cluster of homes—have succumbed to the tenacious reclamation program of the rain forest. The aesthetic of abandonment is reminiscent of Chernobyl. Rotted homes covered in lichens and moss. Foliage punching through the buckling pavement of old tennis courts. Forests of berry bushes growing into porches and doorways. A mostly unseen legacy of pollution also adheres to the place. For decades, the pulp mill spewed a cocktail of toxins into the air and water, including dioxins, PCPs, nitrogen oxides, and heavy metals. Crabs and prawns caught in the ocean closest to town are reportedly often deformed. The few fishing enthusiasts in town head far out into the inlet.

To be fair, a spark of life remains within the festering ruins. Since the town was shuttered, a handful of people have come to live here, and they love the place; their numbers triple or quadruple in summer when boaters moor in town for days at a time. A few historic buildings have survived with their dignity intact. And the old hydroelectric dam still generates power—not only for Ocean Falls but for Bella Bella and Denny Island, too.

For all its drawbacks Ocean Falls manages to cling on, sustained by an enduring nostalgia, the beauty of the surrounding mountains, and the promise of an unhurried existence devoid of officialdom's nettlesome interference.

It's appropriate, even poetic, that my first experience of rain in the Great Bear Rainforest on this trip comes on my first full day in Ocean Falls. It lasts only twenty minutes—in marked contrast to the weeklong downpours that took place during the town's golden age. But it's enough to tear me away from my breakfast in the dining room of Darke Waters, the lodge where I'm staying. Through the window, I watch raindrops the size of gum balls lash the asphalt. The mountains and their wraiths of cloud, visible earlier that morning, are blotted out in the bland, impenetrable gray of precipitation.

There are a few others staying at Darke Waters. The Oregon couple from the ferry sit at the back of the dining room. At another table are four rugged-looking middle-aged men in construction gear, laborers from out of town who are in Ocean Falls to make repairs to broken sections of the dam.

Turning pancakes and strips of bacon, maestro-like, in the fully exposed kitchen is Rob Darke—a co-owner of the lodge. A forty-nine-year-old former ski-hill manager from Grande Prairie, Alberta, he has an eighties rocker look and a tendency to cackle at his own jokes.

"We're finally back to some decent weather around here," Rob says, leaving the kitchen with a breakfast plate in his hand to sit at my table. "Terrible with all that sunshine. *Hahahaha!*"

Rob's wife and business partner, Corrina Darke, wipes down a nearby table.

"I'll take the sun any day," Corrina says. "The last thing we need is to get depressed around here."

Corrina, formerly, was a graphic designer with the Grande Prairie *Herald Tribune* newspaper. When she was laid off after thirty years of service, Rob, a fishing fanatic, convinced her to support him in his dream of owning a fishing lodge. Both had grown tired of life in Grande Prairie, a predominantly white, working-class community ridden with crime and recently dubbed "the most dangerous city in Canada." A simple Google search was all it took to find the property, which, to their surprise, had sat idle on the market for several months. The twenty-three-room, two-story European-style chalet had been built in the mid-1940s as a women's dormitory. Following a few other incarnations, the building became a lodge once the mill closed down. It remained one of the most intact structures in town. The Darkes purchased it for just over $100,000.

It's the couple's second season of operation. The lodge is still a work in progress—and running it has come with a steep learning curve. Renovations continue, and there still aren't many guests. But the place is in working order and is slowly accruing charms. Framed nautical charts, old black-and-white photos, and drawings of locomotives hang in the hallways and rooms. Vintage knickknacks looted from the ghost town and placed in the rooms lend the lodge a retro feel.

Suddenly, a bespectacled woman in her sixties saunters into the dining room. She says hello to us, pours herself a coffee, and sits at our table. Corrina introduces her to me as Glenna, before adding proudly: "She's one of the *original* residents of Ocean Falls."

The woman smirks. "I'm the *longest* resident here."

"How long is longest?" I ask.

"Oh, about forty-one years and counting."

Rob gets up. "Her family's been here even longer. She's a kind of encyclopedia about this place."

"John's collecting stories about the Sasquatch," Corrina says to Glenna, excitedly.

"Sas-quatch?" Glenna says, unimpressed. "You mean like . . . Bigfoot? No, if there was anything like that here, I'd have heard about it."

I turn to Corrina. "And you and Rob haven't heard anything."

"Sorry, we've got nothing," she says, shaking her head before turning to look at Rob, who's pouring himself a coffee at the waiters' station. "Well, except for . . ."

"For what?" I ask.

"Ghosts."

Glenna smirks again.

"We haven't actually seen them," Corrina adds, looking a bit embarrassed. "But strange things have been happening here."

Rob sits back down with his coffee. "When we closed after the first season, we left all the room doors in the lodge open," he says. "We came back and found them all closed. And many of them were locked. That's one story."

Corrina runs a hand up and down her bare arm. "Look, I'm getting goose bumps," she says.

"I'm not," Glenna says. "If I can't touch something, I don't believe in it."

Corrina leans over the table toward me. "Did you know that this lodge used to be a hospital?"

Glenna cuts in. "They made this building the new hospital in the 1970s after the old one closed. That driveway leading into the back was for the ambulance."

Corrina's voice tapers to a near whisper. "And behind me where the baking pantry is—that was the *morgue*."

Rob sees me cringe, slaps his leg, and keels over, cackling. Corrina leans back into her chair and nods at me, eyes wide open.

"Well," Glenna says, "maybe you ought to change the topic of your book."

"No, no," Corrina tells her. "All he needs to do is speak to a few more people. Who would you recommend?"

Glenna's face goes stone cold. "No one."

"Come again," I say.

"Nobody here knows anything about this place," she says. "People here invent stories. They make things up as they go along."

"Are you calling the people who live here bullshitters?"

"With the straightest faces you ever saw. It's the gospel truth coming out of their mouths."

"But you don't mean the original residents of Ocean Falls?" I ask her.

"Mister, *I'm* the only person originally from here. The rest are people who came after Ocean Falls was shut down, burned, destroyed. They're the new people. This is their town now. And so their stories are whatever the hell they want."

If I can't touch something, I don't believe in it. Glenna's words echo in my mind. Could it be that what many people are seeing by way of a Sasquatch is not a rare, flesh-and-blood animal but instead some nonphysical, incorporeal entity? An apparition? After all, we know that there is a wider reality than what we can perceive through our specifically tuned senses. And that what's "out there" is so different from what we feel and experience every day that we simply would not believe it if it were presented to us.

Discoveries in the area of quantum physics demonstrate that things are truly *not* what they seem, and that the universe, at the subatomic level anyway, operates far differently from how it is known to most people.

For instance, the world appears to be composed of separate objects with clearly definable boundaries, which we slot into categories of space and time. We evolved to see the world in terms of separate objects partly in order to distinguish the things that could either help or hinder us. But this view is more apparent than real. On a fundamental, subatomic level, nothing is fixed or separate. Objects that appear to us as solid, static, and separable—whether atoms, apples, or asteroids—are in fact made up of transient particles that are continually appearing and disappearing. They occur in no fixed time and space but only show tendencies to exist and occur. There are no objects, only processes—fluid bundles of energy, patterns of relationships, that ebb and flow in an ever-shifting web of interconnectivity. Fundamentally—and in total contradiction to what we know at our scale of day-to-day experience—all things meld into all other things. We just can't see this. It's an almost impossible thing to wrap our minds around.

Experiments conducted by the late Arthur J. Deikman, an American pioneer in the psychology of advanced states of consciousness, reinforced the above ideas. The ability of humans to perceive the full richness of life around them, he said, is constrained by an almost default state of mind he called "action mode" or "survival mode"— one characterized by a focus on objects. Mental postures involving greed, acquisition, consumption, excess logic, analysis, preoccupation with time, and the use of categories and language fall into the survival mode. That mind-set's capacity to appreciate wider reality, he said, was like a hand trying to grasp water by making a fist around it. The closing hand can't retain the liquid.

Deikman also observed experimental subjects in another, complementary mental state he called the "receptive mode"—one characterized by intuition, openness, and an attitude of relaxed allowance. Subjects in that state reported holistic sensory experiences with more vivid details and colors and a blurring of boundaries between physical objects. They also claimed to experience a sense of connectedness to their environment. Deikman wrote that while a person was in the receptive mode, "aspects of reality that were formerly unavailable" and "new dimensions of the total stimulus array" were able to enter his or her awareness. He compared the receptive mode's capacity for appreciating reality to a cupped hand scooping up water. The hand is able to retain the liquid.[19]

The science concurs with what mystics in traditional cultures have always known: that the reality underlying appearances is not accessible to our conventional senses. In Middle Eastern and Islamic cultures, to use one example, groups of mystics known as Sufis have often referred to a hidden reality, of which our world of appearances is but a partial manifestation. According to them, our survival-oriented brain and culturally conditioned mind narrow our vision, thereby preventing us from seeing a much wider reality that functions more holistically. But unlike most contemporary scientists, Sufis have always known that when those constricting mental postures are loosened or relaxed in a certain way, it is possible to get a glimpse, or more, of that bigger picture. This same psychological knowledge was systematized by the Sufis, as well as by mystics in other cultures, adjusted for the local context, and taught as science. The important point is that according to traditional psychologies, even though we are usually cut off from the bigger picture, it is still possible for us to tap into it—even if for most of us it's often just a random flash in the pan.

Might there be a link, in some cases, between the emanations of the unseen universe, its fits and starts, and the things we occasionally feel, see, or experience that are out of the ordinary? Could it be that what some people register as a Sasquatch is a mental signature, a blip, representing an impulse from that reality beyond? A frequency to which the mind is open in certain states and which it interprets, symbolizes, and personifies as a hairy wild person—especially when we're in or near nature?

If a mind that is somehow rendered "receptive" enough comes across a flicker of stimulus for which no innate pattern exists as a match, the brain would naturally search for another pattern that comes close enough under the circumstances: in this case a Sasquatch. This might explain why Bigfoots are most often seen by accident but are never deliberately found or captured. The late scientist and Pulitzer Prize–winning writer René Dubos once wrote: "Man converts all the things that happen to him into symbols, then commonly responds to the symbols as if they were actual external stimuli."[20] Perhaps Bigfoot hunters and investigators are chasing the symbol, the mental representation that is generated in the minds of Bigfoot eyewitnesses—the Sasquatch itself—*after* the fact. When people who see a Bigfoot in a transcendental way then choose to search for the creature afterward, they are really looking to relive, or recapture, a moment of expanded awareness that has long since vanished.

If rare and elusive physical Sasquatches exist, Deikman's ideas still hold. Deliberate sleuthing, investigating, and chasing after the Sasquatch would be "survival mode" activities that narrow our perception—we see less overall as a result. By contrast, people who see or experience Bigfoots by accident (the vast majority) seem to be, more often than not, in a more receptive mode—something that exposure to nature can definitely engender. Even hunting, which is otherwise a survival mode activity, can involve many hours of sitting in tree stands and perhaps getting into a meditative, or receptive, frame of mind. Many hunters report seeing Sasquatches under those very circumstances.

It's just as William Housty said to me at Koeye: as with anything in life, if you try too hard to find something, you'll be hard-pressed to succeed. But as soon as you stop trying, your odds suddenly change.

I meet another member of the Ocean Falls congregation outside the lodge in one of those intermezzos between downpours—intervals characterized by a testy, tepid rain that makes fat polka dots on your clothes but doesn't come down hard enough to drench you outright.

"The name's Darell Becker," the man says, "but I go by the first name Darellbear."

I offer my hand, which he takes in a rock-hard grip.

"The Bundjalung people in Australia gave me that name during a music festival when one of them saw the bear energy in me."

"Bundjalung?"

"Aborigines. They knew I was coming. They said it was a prophecy."

Darellbear looks to be in his mid-fifties. He has a mop of wavy, now rain-drenched, brown hair and striking blue eyes. He is solidly built and wearing a light khaki rain jacket over shorts and sandals. A white crystal hangs around his neck. He comes across as a wizened retired surfer transplanted into the mountains.

"I was in Australia for thirty years playing professional baseball and hockey," he says. "Now I spend the warm months here."

"What do you do?"

"Mostly hang out on my boat and go fishing. But I also sell miracle ointments for knotted muscles, cuts, and abrasions. I call it 'The Goo.'" He reaches into his pocket and pulls out a small jar, handing it to me. "That's the hot Goo," he says. "Great if you have aching hands or an aching neck."

I turn over the red-labeled jar, trying to remember the last time I had aching hands.

"There's cayenne in it. So don't have a piss or touch your dick after using it. Or you'll get a hot rod. Then you'll need the cold Goo to put the fire out—and I'll make a double sale."

I hand the jar back to him.

"So, what brings you to this charming dystopian settlement in the middle of paradise?" he asks.

I tell him about my research.

"The big fellah, huh? Well, I haven't seen anything around town. And no one living here has either, as far as I know."

Darellbear's answer adds to the collection of blank stares and shrugged shoulders I've accumulated in the last few days, seeming to confirm Glenna's claim that the Sasquatches, if they exist, have neither stumbled upon nor ever intended to come to Ocean Falls.

"That's what I've been hearing," I tell him.

"The only Sasquatch stories I know are from the outskirts. A guy I know has a small cabin way behind Mount Baldy over there," he says, pointing to a rounded, rocky peak in the distance. "It's a bush-whack to get in. Super remote, secret spot. One day he found the place broken into. Stuff moved or taken that no bear could get to."

"Thieves?"

"Thieving Sasquatch, more like. Human thieves rob jewelry stores and embezzle from taxpayers. They don't point to an empty spot on the map and then go wandering there hoping to get lucky. A chopper pilot I met once who worked on a logging show in that same area saw snow tracks in the alpine. Massive. Huge stride. Absolute middle of fucking nowhere. Do you know what people told him? They told him: *Maybe it was someone snowshoeing.*" He breaks into a chuckle, shaking his head.

"It could also have been that," I say, without intending to be skeptical.

"Buddy," he says, becoming serious, "take a look around. This is no weekend recreation area. These are big, dangerous mountains around us. Ranges upon ranges of them. Grizzly Adams territory. No one's out wandering or going snowshoeing up there."

The rain's pitter-patter transforms into a steadier shower. We begin to get drenched. Darellbear starts shaking his mop of wet hair and laughing.

"Yeah baby! Now we're talking! *Wooo! Woooooooooooo!*"

I crack a little grin. When I don't join him in his hooting, Darellbear cuts his laughter short and puts a concerned expression on his face.

"People told you about the rain here, right?"

If clock time and calendar time become opaque in the Great Bear Rainforest, they effectively stop dead in Ocean Falls. They're replaced by a suspended animation whose silent symbol is the whorls of vapor rising from the mountains.

Ocean Falls thwarts my expectations. It's upside down in relation to the rest of my journey. For one thing there is rain here, where previously there was none. And it is no normal rain, with a beginning, middle, and end. It starts and stops in whims that are nonsensical, bereft of logic, and without a real prologue or epilogue. When the rain does stop, there is no knowing when it will return. But invariably it soon gathers itself for another discharge at the same moment you watch, marveling, the sun illuminating another rainbow.

In dealing with the rain, there is no planning or waiting things out or consulting the weather report. You just live with the downpour, surrender to it, cavort in it. And forget umbrellas—here they are mauled by the rain, outflanked by it.

As awe-inspiring as the rains have been, they've only slightly resembled the legendary rain-forest torrents of my mind's eye. When I say this to Ocean Fallsers, they chuckle. But then, in a more sober, ominous tone, they inform me that, yes, I have seen nothing yet.

In Ocean Falls, one of the smallest communities in Canada—a place tucked into the back of a maritime cul-de-sac no one's ever heard of, and condemned to crushing isolation as if in a dress rehearsal for the apocalypse—there is a bar. Or it is what one might be tempted to call a bar—but is, by name, a saloon.

Saggo's Saloon, Rob and Corrina tell me, is like no other drinking establishment on the planet. For one, it's open only on Monday, Wednesday, and Friday evenings—and from only four o'clock to seven o'clock at that. Unless, of course, its owner, thirty-six-year-old Bartender Bob, the youngest person in Ocean Falls, is having a bad day and decides to kick everyone out. Or unless the place runs out of beer, in which case everyone will still have to leave. The saloon's burgundy shag rug, from the age of disco, wafts the aroma of cigarette smoke—as smoking is still unofficially permitted there.

The day after my conversation with Darellbear I find the no-frills watering hole—an old brown wooden bungalow located down the road from the lodge. Apart from a small, hard-to-read sign beside the door, there is no indication that the former Standard Oil fuel station is now Ocean Falls' reluctant tavern.

Inside, the place looks and feels like an unmaintained legionnaire's hall from the seventies. Several people, a mix of older men and women, sit at roadhouse-style chairs and tables, the kind you often see in bar brawls in movies.

I find Rob Darke sitting at the bar, which is manned by an uncomfortable-looking man who, I conclude, is the owner, Bartender Bob. The portly and somewhat swarthy gentleman is hunched over the bar, sipping from a straw in a tumbler glass. "Black Magic Woman" plays from an old television set behind him, tuned to one of those cable TV stations that run generic music round the clock. A few old and nearly empty bottles of liquor line the shelf behind him. A shredded dartboard, a sickly pair of mounted antlers, and a derelict billiards table complete the tableau.

"Hey, look who's here!" Rob says.

I take a seat at the bar beside Rob and make eye contact with the bartender, who's wearing a wide smirk on his face: a smile tinged with cynicism and something bordering on contempt. Rob introduces me to Bartender Bob and tells me it's Bob's birthday. I shake the barman's hand, wishing him well.

"Thanks," he says. "Want a beer?" He reaches below the counter and extracts a generic-looking can, placing it on the countertop with a loud thud. The label reads "Lucky Lager." I notice that everyone else in the bar is drinking it. "Five bucks," Bartender Bob says.

"Just put it on my bill," Rob says, and Bartender Bob gives me another questionable look and marks the sale in his notebook.

Saggo's owner remains uneasy and slightly combative with everyone, until a few other locals come into the saloon bearing mood-altering birthday gifts: potato salad, sausage rolls, cashews, and those small liquor bottles you get on airplanes. As the loot accumulates, Bob's temper changes for the better.

An older man with a black eye patch stumbles in. He's wearing a blue T-shirt, ripped around his stomach, with "Christos Glass" written on it.

"How long till last call today, Bob?" the man asks.

"It's my birthday, Tim, so I'll probably keep her open for an extra half hour today."

"Bullshit! Gimme three of whatever you got," he says to Bob, before noticing me and approaching, coming to within inches of my face.

"I know I got an eye patch on right now and it looks like I'm blind," he says, pointing at his patch. "But I'm just getting my eye fixed." With that, he grabs his three cans of Lucky in a fat choke hold and carries them over to a table, where a barnacled old man greets him with a yellow-toothed smile. The old man snatches one of the beers and cracks it open to a hail of protest from Tim.

Rob whispers that the man who stole Tim's beer is "Nearly Normal" Norman Brown, the infamous pot-smoking, opium-eating curator of the Ocean Falls junk museum. "Norm used to date Janice Joplin," Rob adds. "He once cooked and ate a wolf someone had shot."

Bartender Bob leans in. "So I hear you're a journalist and that you worked in the Middle East."

Before I can reply, Tim, who has overheard Bob, swivels in his chair to face us. "He's a terrorist, don't you know."

Tim's words are spoken in such a way that they run perfectly down the middle between seriousness and humor.

"Actually, he's a writer," Rob jabs back.

Tim grins. "And he knows everything about an AK-47 you'd ever want to know!" The whole saloon explodes in laughter.

Bartender Bob taps me on the shoulder and points toward one of the people sitting at Tim's table, a heavyset man with an enormous beer belly. "That guy over there in the baseball hat is Barrie. He spent some time in the Middle East. Hey, Barrie!" Bob shouts to the man, "maybe you and John here have crossed paths."

I ask Barrie where he's been in the Mideast and what took him there.

"Oil work," he says. "I been all over. You name it: Baw-rain. Koo-wait. Eee-rak. Doo-bye. Saw-dee. And Aboo Dabee."

Rob lights up a smoke. "John here's looking for the Sasquatch."

"If you wanna see a Sasquatch around here, have a few more of those beers and take a walk thataway," Tim says, pointing to the door.

More laughter greets the rabble-rouser's comments.

Bartender Bob takes a sip of his cocktail. "You're not going to get much information in here," he tells me.

"I haven't heard *any* reports so far."

"Well, remember there's only a few dozen residents here. The average age is like sixty. Nobody goes into the bush. And everyone's in bed by nine p.m. If there are Sasquatches, people here aren't likely to see them."

"Makes sense. But there's no older reports, either, as far as I can tell."

Bob shrugs his shoulders. "I wish I could help you." He then goes quiet, deliberating for a moment. "Come to think of it, I did see something odd not that long ago. It happened about a year ago. There's a couple of small lakes near town. We call them Twin Lakes. I was out for a long walk one day and reached the farther of the two. When I got there, I found footprints on the beach. Two sets of them—humanlike."

"How big?"

"Well, that's the thing. They were small. Smaller than mine. Kid-size. But they were strange. Funny looking. Splayed toes. Human—but not, somehow."

I quickly try to remember whether I've told Rob, or anyone else, of the small tracks I came across in Bella Bella. I realize I haven't.

"What's the matter?" Bob says, noticing my reaction.

"Nothing," I say, trying to disguise my surprise. "Could it have been kids playing at the lake?"

"Doubt it. This place is deep in the bush. No one goes out there. There's few, if any, kids in town. Almost all the boaters who stop here are retired. And the tracks came right out of the bush at one end of the beach and walked along the sand into more tree cover. There weren't any other footprints alongside them. Totally random."

"How does one get to Twin Lakes?"

"Just follow the logging road out of town. You'll need a four-by-four. Or you could walk, but it's a distance. The road keeps going all the way to a place called Shack Bay, in Roscoe Inlet."

Roscoe. I'm thrown off by how close the inlet is to Ocean Falls. But then I remember that shortcuts abound in the Great Bear—like secret doors in a labyrinth. If you could trudge through valleys and over the mountains in any direction you'd find yourself in another inlet, watershed, or region considered distant if you were to travel by boat.

"They built the road just before Ocean Falls closed," Bob goes on. "When everyone realized how polluted the area had become. They were going to relocate the town to Roscoe."

Shack Bay is near where Mary Brown and her group of young campers say they encountered a Sasquatch—the one that had crawled under their cabin. The connections continue to pile up.

Bob sees the wheels turning in my head. He reaches down and brings up another Lucky Lager, placing it beside me with a wry smile.

"You're lucky today is my birthday," he says. "I'm almost never this talkative."

Ocean Falls was the quintessential company town in its heyday. The community was built, owned, and run entirely by "the corporation." So when its last owners ended operations here, they chose to demolish their property rather than leave it behind for others. Though much of the town had been wiped off the map, some of the largest buildings, perhaps too costly to destroy, were left behind to rot.*

I spend a few days exploring the dilapidated buildings, a kind of macabre tourism that in reality differs little from visiting any other archaeological site. I survey all five floors of the Martin Hotel, a gutted megalith of peeling paint and wallpaper and shredding asbestos, littered with books, papers, broken furniture, and antique machines left behind by earlier waves of looters. The ruins are a kind of sneak preview of the end of the world. All of it leaves me feeling slightly downcast.

I visit the old school, which has imploded and sprouted a grassy field inside the old gymnasium. When I step back outside, Glenna pulls up in her white van. The self-appointed custodian of Ocean Falls' memory offers to give me a personal tour of the town, which starts, at my request, with a perusal of her legendary scrapbook of newspaper clippings. I spend hours at her place poring over the

---

* In 1986 a counterterrorism unit of the Toronto Police came to Ocean Falls to test its weapons and pyrotechnics on the derelict buildings, temporarily making the town look like a smoldering action film set.

yellowing Ocean Falls pages of the *Vancouver Sun*—bound together in one epic volume thicker and heavier than the largest reference atlas. It reads like a parochial community newspaper, filled with minutiae, recording every happening, and teeming with names. Except for a few references to the school football team—called the Ocean Falls Bush Apes—I find nothing referring to sightings of hairy humanoids.

"I told you," Glenna says, with a self-satisfied smirk.

Before I can say anything more, she hands me a blue paperback book, magically produced out of thin air, entitled *Rain People: The Story of Ocean Falls*, by a writer named Bruce Ramsey.

"If any sightings happened here, it would be in this book," she says, tapping the cover, "which of course it's not."

Rain People looks and reads like a high school yearbook, except that it covers the better part of a century. It's filled with old black-and-white photos of the community during various phases of its existence. I'd learn that *Rain People* is as revered in Ocean Falls as the Bible is by Christians. Everyone has a copy of the town's official biography, first published in 1971 and reissued in 1997. It's constantly being referenced and quoted by people around here as if it were holy writ. Apart from a little snippet in the introduction, which Glenna shows me, referring to an indigenous legend concerning a lost tribe of humans who turned wild and hairy, on nearby King Island (a site of many Sasquatch reports), there's no mention of anything related to Bigfoot. I would read the book later and confirm this myself.

I find the dearth of Sasquatch lore here fascinating and peculiar —especially when so much of it exists in nearby communities. There's a similar and even more puzzling absence of reports from the hundred or so non-native residents who live on Denny Island, across from Bella Bella. Perhaps these outlier communities and their lack of reports support the idea that there is no Sasquatch. I wonder whether the wide discrepancy stems from Sasquatch lore being more ingrained in indigenous culture, so that people in some First Nations communities, like all of us, are interpreting their experiences through their preexisting beliefs. Or could it be that aboriginal residents are better equipped, perceptually, to see and feel the animals —if they exist—because of culturally and genetically inherited perceptual templates, and an overall sensitivity to the land?*

Later that day I go for a walk in the Martin valley—where most of the town's residents now live. I'm on a footpath that begins where the residential road ends and leads deep into the forest. The dark, narrow enclosure is peppered with a few old-growth Sitka spruces, dark spires towering over aging, moss-encrusted alders and berry bushes. The sound of rushing water from the nearby Martin River overtakes the pitter-patter of rain on my jacket as I continue along the trail, which becomes more overgrown with each step.

Both walking and nature—separately but especially together—are conducive to thinking, and I find myself turning everything over in my mind. I feel I'm approaching another impasse in my attempt to make sense of this wild-man phenomenon. Of course, the journey remains open-ended. Anything might still happen. But wishful thinking, hoping for a new turn of events, is also dangerous, for it can seduce one into the same trap that has ensnared nearly every other hell-bent Sasqualogist: continuing with the never-ending quest, the journey that never quite bears fruit, whose cost is an ever-deeper,

---

* When I hiked with eyewitness Clark Hans on my previous trip to Bella Coola, I could scarcely believe the details he picked up in the forest that were initially invisible to me. Once he pointed them out, deer rubs on the bark of trees, faint animal impressions in the moss, and banana slugs partly concealed by foliage were all revealed in an instant.

more consuming, obsession. Maybe the rain is bringing on this mood, but the specter of futility is now staring me in the face.

I tell myself the Sasquatch is one of two things:

It's a physical being, an animal, which—through a combination of its intelligence, stealth, evasiveness, rarity, and environment, and our own psychological and cultural filters and blind spots—we are prevented as a society from seeing, identifying, classifying, or otherwise acknowledging. People who see it are simply lucky, in the right place at the right time.

Or Bigfoot is a psychocultural or metaphysical phenomenon. It's a symbol arising from a range of possible experiences, some explainable, some perhaps unexplainable. People who regard Bigfoot as real and who go looking for it, as well as eyewitnesses who become obsessed by it, are chasing a symbol, a mental representation of their own or someone else's experience. That symbol is a "downstream" mental by-product of an experience stemming from known and/or unknown stimuli. Perhaps that's why the Sasquatch can't be found. It doesn't exist as we know other things to physically exist.

Though I've done my best to avoid choosing a contrived position based on false certainty, I still find myself caught between the either/or poles: "It exists" versus "It doesn't exist." Even if I bridge these explanations by saying, "It may be a bit of both," that is still a superficial synthesis—a fusion of somewhat foregone conclusions. Using logic and deductive reasoning to choose between possible explanations doesn't translate to a fuller, more robust knowledge.

The walking trail fades ahead of me in a commotion of tall weeds and berry bushes. The narrow, mist-drizzled valley carries me gently upward in an ever-increasing tangle of wildness that feels deeply forbidden. The way ahead seems ungraspable, unfathomable even, and I stop in my tracks, a preamble to turning back. I stare into that defile of seemingly infinite chaos, marveling at its depth, inaccessibility, and paradoxical subtlety. And then a thought hits me: maybe the Sasquatch hasn't been found, indeed can't be found, because it resides *in the place most difficult for us to find and navigate*. A wilderness of an altogether different sort. A place where people seldom look, or are loath to look: in the subtler shades, the gradations between black and white—the middle ground between "this" and "that," between "It exists" and "It doesn't exist," where the components of truth most often reside.

I arrive back at the lodge and head to the dining area, where the guests are having dinner. It's pizza night. Rob is rolling dough in the kitchen. Country music is playing from a hidden stereo. Corrina, also in the back, sees me, grabs a menu, and shuffles over. She has a big smile on her face.

"You're a popular guy around here," she says teasingly, handing me the menu.

Rob looks up from his dough roller. "You gotta hear this," he says.

"One of the residents," Corrina says, "a guy named Don, came by earlier. He was asking about you—and what we thought of you."

"Of *me*?"

"Yeah, like, what kind of guy you are. We told him we really liked you and felt you're like family."

Rob scurries over, his hands and apron covered in flour.

Corrina continues. "So the guy keeps saying, 'Really? Are you sure?' And we tell him, 'Yeah, he's great.' Then he lets out this huge sigh of relief and says, 'Thank heavens! Now we can stop checking the water supply!'"

Rob breaks into a gut-wrenching cackle. Corrina chuckles with him.

"I don't get it," I say, smiling, infected by the inexplicable humor.

"*Right?*" Corrina says. "So I ask Don why they're checking the water supply and he . . . *hahahahaha* . . . he tells me, 'We thought your guest might have been an *al-Qaeeeeda* terrorist. We figured he was here to poison the reservoir.'"

Rob and Corrina both double over in laughter.

"A terrorist!" Rob squeals, eyes tearing.

The other guests stare at us uncomfortably. Rob is one convulsion shy of collapsing onto the floor. Corrina can't contain her mirth but manages, after a moment, to go on with her story.

"So . . . so I tell Don he's being ridiculous, and that you'd have to be a real genius terrorist to come all the way from the Middle East to Ocean Falls just to kill all two dozen of us—and then get caught while making your big escape on the *Queen of Chilliwack* ferry. Then Don said: 'Well, he was in the Middle East. And he barely told us anything about himself. He only asked questions.' And I'm like, '*Duhhhh!* He's a writer. That's his job!'"

"Who is this Don guy?" I ask.

Robs wipes the tears from his eyes. "Remember Tim? The guy at the saloon the other night with the eye patch who made those jokes? Don is Tim's brother."

Corrina leans in, lowering her voice: "And the two men haven't spoken to each other in about *ten years.*"

"A decade?" I ask. "In a town of two dozen people?"

Corrina nods, with a *Yup, can you believe that shit?* look on her face.

"Just like Cain and Abel," Rob says.

Corrina smiles. "Welcome to Ocean Falls."

The sound of a downpour draws our eyes to the window. Rob takes a few steps over and stares excitedly outside. "Wow, look at it out there."

Corrina raises her order pad and pen, and gives me an ironic look: "So, are you gonna order, something, Mr. Sasquatch Terrorist Man?"

I have a few days left before I move on from Ocean Falls. Though there's been little in the way of Sasquatch reports I feel I'm coming close here to breaking down, or surmounting, a wall in my understanding. Another key kernel of information might propel me further.

The downpour continues for days, drowning out all other noise and obfuscating everything. I suit up in my waterproof gear and step out into dusky air that smells of damp earth and soaked evergreen.

I head in the direction of the Martin valley again, passing the boat-choked marina and the shuttered saloon. Across the shimmering inlet, where I know huge fjords to be, there's nothing but an impenetrable haze. Sheets of water flow down the mountainside beside me, crossing the road at several points and emptying into the sea.

I reach the residential area and approach a small, beat-up bungalow with a Canadian flag and a big picture of Bob Marley in the window. In the driveway is an aging sports car. The driver's door is ajar. As I get closer I see a man dressed in shorts and sandals rummaging through the back seat. Darellbear emerges from the vehicle just as I reach the house. He closes the door, sees me, and breaks into a wide smile.

"Hey, man! What are you doing out in this mess? I got some people over. You wanna join?"

He waves me toward the front door. "Come on. I just grabbed me a couple of the hot Goo for the folks inside," he says, flashing the small jars of salve as we enter.

His place is dimly lit and toasty warm, reeking of must, candle wax, and incense. A Mexican flag and a Harley Davidson banner hang on faded walls above retro furniture, probably surviving pieces from the old Ocean Falls. Dream catchers and pieces of native art abound in the rest of the house.

A young couple, in their early twenties, sit on chairs drinking Lucky Lager. The young man is Lucas, a family friend of Rob and Corrina's, whom I'd met at the lodge. The woman with him is from Victoria and is visiting her parents, who own a summer home in town.

Darellbear hands me a cold beer before taking a seat. He tosses Lucas and the woman the jars of Goo. "That'll stop all the itching and clean up those bug bites right away," he says.

"That's sick," Lucas says, in an exaggerated surfer's drawl, reading the label of the jar and then opening and sniffing it.

"It's powerful stuff," Darellbear says proudly, cracking open a beer.

"This'll be perfect after the hike up to the tunnel," Lucas says to the woman.

"Tunnel?" I say.

"There's a tunnel that connects Martin Lake at the head of this valley here with Link Lake in the next one," Darellbear says. "It's a six-hundred-foot-long hole through the mountain drilled back in the 1920s. It was an engineering feat. They brought in the Chinese to work on that. That's why there's so many opium bottles lying around here." Darellbear nods at the woman: "She'll tell you."

"Yeah, my mom's got two thousand opium bottles," she says, flatly.

"*Opium?*" Lucas says. "Are you kidding me?"

The woman's frown flickers into a brief smile. "She has a big treasure chest full of them. Sake bottles too. She finds them on the water where the bunkhouses used to be. We went and got them appraised. Some lady wants to buy them."

Darellbear asks about my investigations. I tell him I have no real leads apart from the small tracks Bartender Bob saw at the lake, along the old logging road to Roscoe. I add that I plan to go up there and poke around.

Darellbear shakes his head. "Those animals just don't wanna be seen."

"Are you hunting the *Sasquatch*, man?" Lucas says, looking at me wide-eyed. "If you're going up that logging road to Roscoe, I'm coming with you!"

The woman turns to Lucas and stares daggers at him.

"You just got me thinking," Darellbear says. "You know why it's so hard to see a Sasquatch? Because it's not just 'right time' and 'right place'—it's also right *people*. What's the observers' consciousness like? Will *they* be able to see the Sasquatch, if it's there?"

Before Darellbear can say any more the woman groans, rolls her eyes, and stomps out of the room. Lucas, momentarily stunned, looks at the two of us and gets up to go after her. There are muffled sounds in the back. The door opens and then slams shut.

"I guess we freaked her out," Darellbear says, wearing a puzzled expression.

We hear the door open again. A middle-aged man, short, balding, and wearing glasses, suddenly walks into the room carrying two six-packs of Lucky. "Behold," he says, "the last dozen beers in all of Ocean Falls till the barge comes in. Do you know you've got a crying woman outside?"

"Ronny!" Darellbear says, smiling. "Forget that and sit your ass down here. We're having a discussion about the Sasquatch."

"The *Sas-quatch*? Oh boy!"

"Ronny here moved to Ocean Falls from the illustrious city of Winnipeg," Darellbear says to me.

"Yep, I went from the car theft capital of Canada to a place that's got absolutely no car theft whatsoever," Ronny says, taking the empty chair next to me.

"I was just telling John that few people have the right consciousness to see a Sasquatch. You could be the best tracker, the best mountain man, and still not see one. Heck, I'll bet that even our hunter friend Leonard Ellis hasn't seen a Sasquatch either."

"Leonard?" I say.

"That's right."

"You know Leonard Ellis?"

"Do I know Leonard?" Darellbear says, raising his voice, laughing. "Heck, man, we're only sitting in the guy's fucking house!"

"What?"

"Yeah! He used to live here. In this very house! The person I bought it from took it off Leonard when he moved to Bella Coola. What's the matter? Your face is pale."

I tell Darellbear about the coincidental references to Ellis and the serendipitous meetings over the course of my trip.

"Well, of course! What did you expect?"

"What do you mean?"

"Man, you amaze me. Do even you know where you are?" he asks, with his arms outstretched.

I answer with a puzzled expression.

"You're in the Noble Beyond."

"The Noble Beyond?" I repeat, in a tone of deliberate incomprehension.

"That's right. The Great Bear Rainforest, this whole coast, is the Noble Beyond. This is *the* land of serendipity, man. The ultimate landscape of myth, magic, and metaphor. The domain that is the unseen universe. Interconnection and deeper meanings lie around every corner here. It's where your Sasquatch, your coincidences, and a million other possibilities exist. Haven't you ever read Joseph Campbell, or those Don Juan books by Carlos Castaneda?"

Ronny nods knowingly, as if I'm being let in on a secret.

"Heck, let's just call a spade a spade, man," Darellbear says. "This whole business of you, or anyone, *finding* the Sasquatch—that's bullshit. *Exists? Doesn't exist?* You're never going to know. Besides, that's not even the point."

Lucas wanders back into the room and sits down gloomily.

"What happened?" Darellbear asks him.

"It's her last night here. She said she didn't wanna spend it with a couple of old dudes."

"So take your beers and go to her, man! What are you waiting for?"

As Lucas reaches for his cans, the rain outside doubles down.

"Oh yeah!" Darellbear howls, looking out the window next to him and laughing. "Listen to it!"

The rest of us get up and stare out into the drenched blackness.

"God damn," Ronny says, entranced.

"I'll bet it can go on like this for days," Lucas adds, with a touch of concern.

"*Ha!* Are you kidding?" Darellbear says to him. "It can go on like this for the rest of the year! *That's why they call it Ocean Falls, man!* You should see it when it comes down full tilt. When the rain bounces two feet in the air after it's hit the ground. Once you've experienced that, it's game over. The rain's made you its own."

"Made you its own?" I ask.

Darellbear shoots me a serious look. "You become one of us."

The old logging road from Ocean Falls to Roscoe Inlet is a pock-marked, rock-strewn gravel track. A couple of miles in, past a cata-clysmic rockslide of boulders the size of Great Pyramid blocks, the path begins its gradual disappearing act. From here it continues as a fading avenue of weeds that reach higher and thicker with each step.

I'm walking with Lucas and his dog, Gnarly—an energetic white retriever who's constantly ducking into and out of the bush ahead of us. There is an on-and-off pitter-patter of rain. The goal of our micro-journey is to reach Roscoe Inlet. Our plan on the way back is to reconnoiter the two lakes along the road, where Bartender Bob saw the small tracks similar to those I came across at Old Town in Bella Bella.

We push along the path and reach a washout thick with deadfall. We spend what seems like forever crawling both under and over the debris. From that point forward the path is barely visible, continuing through thick second growth choked with blueberry and huckleberry bushes. We plod through the dark, claustrophobic corridor, having to crawl at times, coming across bear prints and what we think are cougar tracks.

"If I saw a Sasquatch and got evidence of it, I'm not sure I'd tell the world," Lucas says, voicing a sentiment I've felt more than a few times. "It would probably put them in danger. That's probably why they hide from people."

Some Sasqualogists take for granted that proving the existence of Bigfoots would result in eventual protection for the species—and the forests they inhabit. But what if the discovery were to have the opposite effect? It's hard to imagine the chain saws and mining machines going silent for the sake of a few remaining wild men. The announcement would be earth-shattering from a scientific point of view and would probably also result in a thousandfold more atten-tion being heaped on the creatures and their habitat from hordes of tourists, government officials, newsmongers, scientists, and hunters.

After much effort, bruised and scuffed, we emerge into a clearing. In front of us is a creek coursing through a dark, spacious, and mossy old-growth forest. To our left, immediately downstream, lies a pulverized wooden bridge—presumably part of the old road we tried to follow and lost. Lying on top of it is an enormous Sitka spruce, one of the largest trees I've ever seen. The tree had somehow fallen over, splitting the bridge in half as if with a karate chop. The trunk is so wide that a small car could drive along it. The almost deliberate precision of the impact is eerie.

Just beyond the bridge, several miles from where we started, there is no sign of the road—not even the faintest whiff or vestige of a track. Lucas, heroically, wants to push on. But we have no maps or navigational equipment—nor sufficient provisions. I make the decision to turn tail rather than risk getting lost in an unfamiliar landscape whose depth, after one wrong turn, could become nothing short of infinite.

On the hike back, we arrive at Ikt Lake—the second body of water along the logging road out of Ocean Falls. We saunter along the sandy shoreline scanning the ground. This is where Bartender Bob claims he saw the unusual, small humanoid tracks. But there is nothing here save loads of goose shit, deer and wolf tracks, and a plague of baby frogs on the move. The rain ended hours ago. Except for the intermittent breaks made on the surface by cutthroats catching bugs, the lake is as still as glass. The sky is in the throes of post-rainfall tumult. Thick foggy vapors rising from the drenched rain forest churn in cottony swirls. This captivating scene, mountains and all, is reflected in the lake.

Lucas and Gnarly, lost in their own investigations, wander farther down the shore, appearing to grow punier in the surrounding gigantism. I quickly tire of searching the ground for tracks and decide there's far greater reward in just sitting and watching the Rorschach-blot reflection of the mountain scene in the water.

And then something strikes me. When I tilt my head, turning the mountainside and its reflection in the lake sideways or vertical, the scene takes on the contours of a head and torso. I keep looking and discern facial features, which materialize in the lighter patches of alders and shrubs beside the lake, where the "head" is. There I see eyes, a fat nose, and lips. The bushiness creates the impression of matted hair. The head rests on no neck. The darker conifers on the higher mountain slope (and their mirror images in the lake) form wide shoulders that jut out from behind the head. Higher yet, the rising slope of the mountain curves to a level ridge, creating the impression of hanging arms. The image is of a humanoid being, bulky, hairy, and muscular. It's somewhat abstract but has an unnerving presence and edge—and a stolid personality. Its power is equal to that I perceived in the ghostly faces I saw in the shoreline reflections while traveling up the Koeye, which I likened to beings on a totem pole.

I'm jolted to the core when I realize that I'm staring into the eyes of what looks to be a Sasquatch—one of my mind's rendering— hewn from the mountain and forest and radiant with the presence of the surrounding wilderness. I'm transfixed and stare at the creature as the mist around it roils.

I'm mindful that I'm seeing what I'm seeing because I want to, that our minds are adept at generating images from our surroundings, especially images that consciously occupy us. But even though I know that this creature is just a mountain and its reflection in the lake, something about the image feels real to me. The image is expressive, its detail convincing. It's saying something, speaking to me. It may as well be real. It doesn't matter that it's literally not.

And this is what changes my entire perspective. For although this symbol is an object lesson in the psychology I've considered, it also reframes that knowledge: rather than thinking of perception as just our senses distorting reality and thereby somehow separating us from nature (implying a kind of error or falsehood), I see now that our creation and interpretation of symbols is also part of our nature—an aspect of nature itself. There's something normal, even essential about this process. Our minds work this way not just because they evolved to do so over time but because these functions help us fulfill a very human need.

I think of all the Bigfoot sightings. Whether they're real, pattern mismatches, or phantasms deriving from an altered state, they must, I realize, all resonate equally in the observer—evoking sentiments that deepen life and make it more enriching. Take the relationship indigenous peoples have to Sasquatches. The attitude of some First Nations peoples yields far more because these people see the animals as a combination of physical being, spirit, story figure, symbol, and teacher. There is a definite takeaway, with manifold social and psychological benefits for both the individual and the community. All that many of the rest of us can seem to muster is the possibility of a physical ape-man and the impoverished, binary either/or debate about its existence.

And perhaps this is what Darellbear, in his idiosyncratic way, was trying to convey the other night: that beyond the obsession with the rational question of whether the Sasquatch physically exists, there is a whole other field of inquiry that is being neglected, an ether of subtler possibilities—his Noble Beyond. What can the Sasquatch and our pursuit of it tell us about *ourselves*, about *our* motives, individually and as a culture, about what we deeply and truly yearn for?

Perhaps I'd find out in Bella Coola.

8

BELLA COOLA
(Q'UMK'UTS')

Long, long ago, there lived a lad who was so poor that all he had for clothing was a rough goat-skin blanket. He was so miserable and friendless that he made up his mind to commit suicide. The ice was breaking in the Bella Coola River at the time, and large cakes were floating down to the sea. The lad leaped out upon one block, then sprang to another, and finally into a clear patch of water. Associates seeking to dissuade him had followed him from one cake of ice to another, but they drew back when he plunged into the cold water.

The youth was not drowned. He found a road under the water which led him to the land of the herring; then, still following the path, he passed in succession the countries of the olachen, the steel-head salmon, the spring salmon, the sockeye salmon, the hump-back salmon, the dog salmon, and lastly the cohoe. Each kind of fish dwelt in its own country, the cohoe salmon, being the last to reach the Bella Coola River, living at the greatest distance from it. Not long after his arrival in the land of the fish, the salmon boat, Noäkxnim, left for Bella Coola and on it the youth returned home. Owing to this experience he became in time both wealthy and famous.

—Traditional Nuxalk tale recounted in T. F. McIlwraith's
The Bella Coola Indians

A thick patch of vapors chokes the high forests of South Bentinck Arm. Snippets of tree-lined mountainside appear teasingly through the clouds.

"The sun's about to punch through," our captain, a tall, heavyset man with curly hair and glasses, says to me. "We'll stop in Green Bay now. Those Dutch ladies are dying to see some bears."

The engines of the forty-two-foot *Nekhani* rumble to life, sending us on a northeasterly course. The water becomes siltier as we approach a bay at the mouth of the Nooseseck River valley on the mainland. When we arrive at the estuary, much of the morning cloud cover has dissipated. The valley glows in hues of gold and green beneath the thinnest swirls of mist.

Four women—two from Vancouver and a pair of older travelers from the Netherlands—and I gather our packs for a hike along the river. The captain, who has put on waders over his jeans, reaches into a nook just above the deck of the boat and pulls out a 12-gauge Defender shotgun—the same weapon I fired with the Guardian Watchmen along Owikeno Lake. As he loads the weapon, his manner becomes militaristic and dramatic, suitable for a Hollywood action film.

The six of us pile into an inflatable rubber dinghy, and the captain paddles us to shore. The Vancouver women and I, wearing gum boots, climb out and wade through the waterlogged edge of the estuary to the high bank. One by one the Dutch women, dressed in hiking shoes, are hoisted piggyback-style by the captain over the shallows. They coo and giggle, like teenagers as the man strains under their weight.

We tie the raft and wander single file, quietly, through an estuary bank thick with high grasses and sedges, following a web of animal trails. Our guide—the captain—surveys the ground ahead of us. He stops and points the muzzle of his gun toward exposed dirt in the grass.

"That's another fresh grizzly dig," he murmurs in a slight drawl, pushing up his glasses and looking around. "They're here all right. They could be anywhere hidden in the grass."

We enter the forest, walking parallel with the river, and push through thorny berry bushes and devil's club. Large bear tracks appear in the soil, leading out of the woods toward the riverbank. We continue bushwhacking and finally emerge onto the wide, rocky bank of the Nooseseck River, which is flowing swiftly down from the upper valley.

"We'll park on these logs and wait," the captain says, leading us to a pile of driftwood on the river's edge. The shallow Nooseseck splashes with salmon battling the current to swim upriver. A few half-eaten fish carcasses lie on the rocks in front of us, evidence of bear activity.

We're interrupted by a rustling in the bushes slightly upstream. We freeze into a perfect tableau, breaths and heartbeats stilled as we look toward the forest edge. But the sounds fade away.

As the afternoon wears on, restlessness takes hold. Our guide urges us not to speak and scare off the bears he's convinced are all around us, just waiting for the right moment to step out. His periodic sighs and grumbles are the only interruptions in what feels like an eternal stretch of present. When the first intimations of dusk appear, our guide stands up and declares that we're throwing in the towel. The Dutch women look crestfallen, but we are all relieved. It has been a long day, and everyone is looking forward to getting back, to a shower, food, and some rest.

As we push back through the bush toward the estuary, I can see that our guide is disappointed. He carries himself languidly, almost spitefully, in protest to the world.

"You saw all those tracks and diggings," he says to me. "They were there. They were *right there*. I just don't get it."

I turn to the man, who's resting his shotgun casually over his shoulder. "They must have heard you were coming, Leonard."

Days earlier, I had arrived in Bella Coola and gone to see Leonard Ellis, the erstwhile bear hunter turned wildlife guide. His guide operation and beautiful cabin complex, called Bella Coola Grizzly Tours, is run from his home and property at the foot of the Coast Mountains, partway up the valley in the community of Hagensborg. I don't know any bear hunters, and before I revisited Leonard, I had expected him to look surly, like a person tinged with madness from his remote wilderness existence. His detractors depict him as difficult and unrelenting, but I found Leonard soft-spoken, polite, and even charming. He was obviously hardened and rough, as a serious woodsman would be, but with a seemingly more malleable interior, a cowboy's drawl, and a cherub's smile.

I'm still not sure what the overriding reason was that led me to Leonard's door again, beyond my attraction to the reputation attached to him. The fact that other people on the coast seemed obsessed with Leonard made him seem larger and more interesting in my eyes. And after spending time with many indigenous residents and environmentalists, becoming familiar with their ideas and values, I was admittedly curious to learn more about people of a different ilk living on this same stretch of coast.

As Leonard led me into his home, I found myself paying close attention to his hunting achievements—which were hard to avoid. All over his house, which felt like a big, disheveled backcountry cabin, were the mounted heads of various prey animals he had culled over the years, mostly ungulates like mountain goats and deer. In his back shed Leonard had stashed away his most prized possessions: two stuffed bears, a grizzly and a black bear, standing side by side on their hind legs, front paws extended, their teeth gnashing. The grizzly was massive, standing around nine feet high; the black bear beside it was shorter, reaching up to the grizzly's shoulders. As I gaped at them in morbid fascination, Leonard told me that he had taken the animals on a road show years earlier.

"Those bears traveled with me to places like Biloxi, Denver, and L.A.," he said. "Heck, maybe ten thousand people have seen them."

Though I knew Leonard was a hunter, it hits me now that he is an outdoorsman par excellence who lives and breathes hunting to the core of his being, and that the qualities engendered by that lifestyle, combined with the commercial aspect of his old hunting business, probably mean that Leonard has more to him than the sugar-and-spice coating of his rugged, backcountry veneer.

My arrival in the Bella Coola valley, the last stop on my trip, comes a year after I completed my first visit to the area. As such, it feels like the closing of a circle. What I'd forgotten, or perhaps never fully realized, was how immense and dramatic the valley is.

The Great Bear Rainforest, from top to bottom, left to right, inside and out, is a rare and wholly resplendent place. But for me its mountainous eastern flank exists on some other plane of mesmerizing beauty. As you move away from the lower-lying islands abutting the open ocean, away from places like Bella Bella and Klemtu, and continue east into the channels and inlets—through ever-larger mainland ranges—the scale of things tilts heavily toward grandeur. Bella Coola, the name for both a town and a region of villages, is situated in this prodigious landscape. It is located at one end of a system of channels and inlets extending more than sixty miles inland from the open ocean—one of the deepest interior reaches of the Pacific in the Americas. This places the seaside community of Bella Coola three quarters of the way inside British Columbia's Coast Mountains. From sea level, the mountains here look colossal, and they become bigger, burlier, and rockier as you ascend the town's fifty-mile-long namesake river valley. That main rift connects with other alpine valleys, each more mysterious than the last.

Regions and ecosystems exist along a continuum. The Great Bear's "outside coast" extends west to the open ocean, while its more mountainous "inside coast" morphs east into the interior. The Bella Coola valley straddles both coastal and interior ecosystems. The area's first peoples, the Nuxalk, have reigned since before recorded time here. It is the place where Scottish explorer Alexander Mackenzie, traveling the final leg of his cross-continental journey along indigenous grease trails, reached the Pacific in 1793.* Residents in the 1950s, fed up with their isolation and empty government promises to create an overland route, mobilized here to build a dirt road over the mountains to the outside world; almost impossibly steep, with terror-inducing switchbacks, it is known simply as "the Hill."

This terrain, sized for giants, is also, appropriately, the chief locus of Sasquatch activity on the British Columbia coast—and perhaps beyond. Access to the ocean, deep impenetrable valleys, and the high alpine zone make the area the best of all worlds for the creatures, some say. Stories of encounters, which are numerous and reach far into the past, have made the town of Bella Coola a byword for Bigfoot activity among aficionados everywhere.

"This is the epicenter of all things Sasquatch," claimed a local man on the ferry, repeating what countless others have told me on this trip. "You needn't have gone anywhere else."

---

* Grease trails were indigenous trade routes running between the northwest coast and the interior, along which fermented oil (i.e., grease) of the sacred *oolichan* (eulachon) fish was traded for other goods.

Leonard tells me he knows little about Sasquatches when I bring it up. We're in his living room watching episodes of old cable-TV hunting programs in which he guest stars. The American-produced shows, often scored to generic banjo music, are meant to promote hunting and gun culture. As Leonard digs through a pile of DVDs, I tell him a few of the stories I've heard so far on my journey. He is attentive at first but then tells me that in his many decades of traipsing through the bush, he has never come across any Sasquatches. But just as we're about to change the subject, he remembers something: he'd heard strange vocalizations a few years before in a place called Eucott Bay, a secluded shore about an hour's boat ride from town. He had been with his girlfriend and three tourists.

"It howled half a dozen times," he says. "It was a big, moaning animal with huge lungs. It wasn't a wolf, and it wasn't a bear. I just assumed it was somebody, Indians maybe, playing a trick on us. But when we went to look, there was nobody there."

When I ask Leonard if he thinks Sasquatches exist, he says he is unsure but that he's open to it.

The conversation tapers off. I can tell he's more interested in talking about hunting. He redirects my attention to yet another DVD he has pulled from the pile.

"This is my second appearance on *The Best and Worst of Tred Barta.*"

I nod.

"You know who Tred Barta is, right?" he asks.

"To be honest, I've never heard of any of these people, Leonard."

Barta, he tells me, is a famous Colorado hunter and the host of a reality-TV series on hunting. In each episode, Barta and a local guide go in search of big game: bear, elk, moose, boar, caribou— anything. His weapon of choice is a longbow that shoots homemade wooden arrows.

"This episode's special," Leonard says, as he slides the disc into the player. "Right after my first show, where I helped Tred hunt a grizzly, he got cancer in the spine and was paralyzed from the waist down. Tred later did this special episode where I guided him in his wheelchair to hunt a black bear."

"Hunting in a *wheelchair*?"

"Yeah," he says, fiddling with the controls. "And I almost broke my back doing it."

The episode, entitled "Bella Coola Black Bear," shows a verbose, chair-bound Barta (think Gilbert Gottfried), being driven around in a pickup truck through the bush and attended to by a retinue of woodsmen and their dogs. Leading the crew is Leonard, who appears as he does in all the shows: quiet, strong, with that same cherubic grin. He is gentlemanly, a Canadian Crocodile Dundee, with a fat Ottoman-style ginger mustache, a cowboy hat, a red-and-black-checkered bomber jacket, waders over jeans, and an assortment of weaponry. A long stem of grass hangs casually from his mouth.

"The terrain here was too rough for that wheelchair, so we took him to the Chilcotin. Up to the plateau."

The show is both captivating and bizarre. It's a window onto a culture that is completely alien to me. What fascinates me more is seeing Leonard watch himself in what must have been his golden age as a guide.

In 1992, Leonard moved from Ocean Falls to Bella Coola to set up a guide outfitting business. His lifelong dream was to become a big-name bear-hunting guide, catering to the growing stream of Americans and Europeans willing to pay top dollar to come to Canada to shoot a bear. Hunters in British Columbia are categorized by residency. Resident hunters (British Columbians) may be awarded a license by lottery to hunt on their own, unguided, in the province. Nonresident hunters (outsiders) have to pay to accompany a guide outfitter, who has his own territory, a kind of hunting juris-diction. Each territory has an exclusive license, which the outfitter has bought, allowing him to lead nonresident hunters in that area.

When Leonard began, he acquired the license for one guide area in what would later be part of the Great Bear Rainforest. Over the years he started buying the licenses for the adjacent territories from their aging guides for around $150,000, in Canadian dollars, apiece. The nearly guaranteed business meant that he easily got the bank loans he needed to make those added purchases. Leonard also doled out big money to buy and refurbish a number of boats for his hunting navy. Among them was a seventy-five-foot World War II patrol boat turned highliner fishing seine that Leonard named *Pacific Grizzly*. It would become the flagship of his flotilla—a live-aboard base camp with room to accommodate six hunters at a time.

Soon Leonard was in possession of five hunting territories with adjoining borders—an enormous region. Although many guides competed with him for business across British Columbia, Leonard's area was special, offering hunters a scenic coast, fjords, freshly caught seafood for dinner, and some of the largest bears found anywhere on the planet.

"We had about ten thousand square miles on the central and north coast—from Cape Caution up past Klemtu," Leonard recalled nostalgically. "We were allowed to harvest forty-two bears in five years and were getting $15,000 for the hunt and $10,000 for the kill. It was probably the highest-priced hunt in all of North America."

For much of the 1990s, Leonard lived his dream. He found himself running a full-blown bear- and mountain-goat-hunting business, with several employees, in a northern rain forest paradise through which as many as fifty hunters passed each year. In that time he acquired a reputation as a rugged storybook character. His many exploits and brushes with death fueled the folklore surrounding his person. In one well-known yarn, Leonard was running full tilt through the rain-soaked forest in pursuit of a black bear. When he reached a bend in the game trail, he came across one of the largest boar (male) grizzlies he'd ever seen. Leonard hit the brakes to turn tail, but he slipped, sliding feet first right beneath the grizzly—between its front paws. At that moment, Leonard and the grizzly were face-to-face, just inches apart. For a second, the bear just stared at him, perplexed. And then, according to Leonard, "the bear let out the loudest, most horrible growl straight into my face. It was like a hurricane blast of the rankest fish smell you could imagine. I thought I was a goner for sure. But I guess I got the old man on one of his better days."

After roaring point-blank at Leonard, the grizzly uninterestedly walked over him and ambled away, out of sight.

Leonard somehow managed to survive the worst that nature, the land, and the elements threw his way. But ultimately the challenge posed by that other force to reckon with on the planet—humans—brought about his downfall as a bear-hunting guide.

Though Leonard sat on a hunting mother lode, his business and livelihood also straddled environmental, cultural, and political fault lines that were on the cusp of shifting irrevocably. Although he couldn't see it, his timing and location couldn't have been worse.

"So Leonard's got the greatest deal going for years," Ian McAllister said, describing the situation to me earlier. "It's like the Wild West. Nobody's up there monitoring. He can do what he wants. It's a pretty sweet deal. And then we come along."

By the turn of the millennium, conservationists like McAllister and Captain Brian Falconer, who were fighting to create the Great Bear, opened up another front in their environmental crusade: the grizzly trophy hunt. Their crosshairs came to rest first on Leonard and his business. They brought heavy domestic and international pressure to bear on the hunt. When the lobbying campaign coincided with a sharp decline in the salmon runs on which the bears depended—including the salmon collapse and bear starvation episode at Owikeno Lake—the government stepped in to drastically reduce the bear-hunting quotas in Leonard's territory.* By 2002, Leonard was able to hunt only a meager two bears per year. The quota, a pittance, was too low for him to pay off his debt, let alone make a living.

"It was just a kick in the teeth to be knocked down to two bears a year," Leonard bitterly recalled, "They may as well have just signed my papers to go bankrupt."

Ellis and McAllister each claim it was the other who suggested the sale of Leonard's guide territory. In either case, the outcome was the same: Leonard decided to give up his operation. Raincoast managed to raise the $1.3 million sale price agreed to by the parties after two years of negotiations. The money allowed Leonard to pay off his remaining debt and keep a small portion, which he used to start his bear-viewing business.

Since then, life has been a struggle for Leonard. He complains that tourism work provides little more than a hand-to-mouth existence. And as the battle now rages to stop all trophy hunting of grizzlies in the Great Bear, Leonard remains a potent symbol of the hunt. Some people on the coast dislike him and believe that he continues to hunt grizzlies in the shadows, something Leonard vehemently denies.

I turn my attention back to the Tred Barta video. The hunting posse close in on their black bear, which the barking dogs indicate is up in a tree. I glance back at Leonard, who's sitting on the edge

---

* In 2001, the provincial New Democratic Party government imposed a moratorium on bear trophy hunting across all of British Columbia until better scientific data about its impact on populations could be collected. Several months later the party was defeated in a snap election. The first act of parliament of the victorious Liberal Party was to rescind the moratorium.

of his chair and watching with a grin as he and the other guides carry Barta's wheelchair to the base of the tree. Barta draws in his bow and fires several arrows in succession at the black bear, felling it. Cheers and hugs erupt as music for the closing credits comes up. Barta turns to the camera and declares this experience to be the greatest in his hunting career. He profusely thanks Leonard, who is smiling beside him.

After a few more words about the valor of hunting and spending time outdoors, the camera zooms in on Barta. The show host locks his gaze to the lens, assumes a celebrity pose, and delivers the signature mantra that closes every episode of his series:

"If *I* can do it—*you* can do it."

The next day, I leave my cheap riverside motel in Bella Coola proper and ride up the empty highway on a rented bicycle to the Four Mile reserve—a Nuxalk residential community located that distance up the valley from the main town site. It's an idyllic day, one of those perfect, temperate end-of-summer afternoons, with swirling horsetail clouds and a cool breeze blowing in from the ocean and filtered through evergreens.

I turn onto a side road and enter the reserve, riding leisurely past homes situated on spacious, unfenced lots separated by swaths of bushy overgrowth. The placid neighborhood is alive with groups of romping children. From Four Mile, the view looking up the Bella Coola valley is crystal clear. An adjacent side valley, the Thorsen, beckons with the mist-obscured, sugar-icing-coated glacier at its head.

I've reached the supposed ground zero of Bigfoot—the waking version of the lofty wilderness of my daydreams as a kid. It's hard to downplay the links and associations with Sasquatch here.

Because of that, the idea of looking for the physical animal is tough to resist. For, in a real sense, Bella Coola is Bigfoot.* For Sasquatch enthusiasts, the town's very name, its contours of sound, evokes the creature's spirit. Whereas Bigfoots are said to appear occasionally in neighboring communities, they are omnipresent here, constantly flitting between hidden recesses and blind spots. Residents allege the animals are bolder here than anywhere else on the coast—so much so that they'll walk through your front yard if need be.

Reports span the length of the Bella Coola valley and all adjoining creek and river systems. Ask around and you'll hear incidents of every variety, involving howls, whoops, screams, loud crashing in the bush, and road crossings; figures standing or crouching in the open at night, peeping into windows, banging on houses, throwing rocks, throwing sticks, and knocking on wood; and putrid lingering odors and tracks in the mud or snow. Some reports are just weeks old. Others have been circulating for more than half a century.

The majority of encounter sites cluster in and around the town of Bella Coola and Four Mile reserve, as well as on the highway and adjacent river running between the two communities. Drivers, cyclists, and pedestrians on the two-lane road have reported seeing Sasquatches crossing it in both directions. Fishermen on the river have seen the animals on its shores.

Nothing strikes me as particularly significant about this—at first. The area around and between the two communities is the busy, more populated stretch of the valley. Residents here are mostly

---

* Bella Coola earned its wider reputation as a Sasquatch hub when journalist John Green and field investigator Bob Titmus, both pioneering Bigfoot researchers, started documenting the numerous reports here in the 1960s. The town's Bigfoot profile was further raised when the memoirs of a colorful twentieth-century Nuxalk bear-hunting guide named Clayton Mack were published in the 1990s. Mack's two books, *Grizzlies and White Guys* and *Bella Coola Man*, contain the transcribed oral accounts of his own early adventures. Mack, a respected wilderness hand who spent most of his life in the bush guiding hunters (including Norwegian explorer Thor Heyerdahl), claimed to have seen and heard the creatures on a number of occasions.

Nuxalk, and Sasquatch awareness runs high (whereas up the road in the non-native community of Hagensborg, as in Ocean Falls and Denny Island, there is far less belief in the creatures—and there are significantly fewer reports). Whether or not Sasquatches exist, it makes sense that there would be more reports in this thorough-fare zone than in the rest of the valley. But when I look at Google Earth to get a better handle on the terrain, I notice something interesting: the entrances to four side valleys are located in the hot zone of reports. Three of those valleys are on the south side of the Bella Coola River, between Four Mile and the ocean. The fourth, the Necleetsconnay valley, faces them all on the north side. Each of these valleys is home to glacier-fed, salmon-bearing creeks and is a world unto itself. Their confluence at the lower reaches of the Bella Coola River is a nutrient-rich crossroads.

Could the cluster of alleged Sasquatch activity in this area be indicative not just of human demographics—a cluster of belief—but also of the proximity of those valleys to one another? In other words, could the higher number of reports be the result of real Bigfoots constantly moving among the valleys, crisscrossing back and forth between habitats and food sources? The Necleetsconnay, a narrow valley hemmed in by steep mountainsides and canyons running ten miles north from Bella Coola, strikes me as the most promising of the bunch. I bushwhacked its lower reaches on my previous visit alongside Clark Hans, who, decades earlier, had seen a Sasquatch on a ridge while duck hunting with his cousins. The Necleetsconnay merges with the Bella Coola River delta about a mile northwest of town, where the remains of old Nuxalk village sites are found. It is an area of numerous reports.

I share my ideas later that day in Four Mile with Nuxalk Sasquatch investigator Loren Mack. He concurs with my observations, adding that there are "known routes between the valleys" on which the creatures travel. He shares with me his own treasure trove of plaster casts and stories outside his trailer.

"Keep in mind," he says afterward, "that we have at least two *different* creatures here according to our traditions. You have the *Sninik*. It's tall and pale-looking, with clammy skin and thin patches of fur. It crouches in the bush with its knees coming up as high as its head. It makes whooping noises. Then you have the *Boqs*, which are darker and much smaller. Child-size. They're more tricky and dangerous. They're the screamers."

It's another reference to the Little People of the Wuikinuxv and the *Bukwus*, the little woodsman, of the Heiltsuk tradition.

"But neither of those," I say, "accurately describes the classic Sasquatch: the big, tall, often dark, hairy animal most often described."

"Those Sasquatches are the hybrids," he says. "There are other beings in our traditions, too."

As I get to know the locals discussions of this sort continue, culminating in a growing feeling, again, that the creatures, whatever their size, color, or shape—whatever their nomenclature—likely exist.

Tempering those stories is my discussion with Peter Mattson, known affectionately to his friends and acquaintances as "the Swede." Mattson is an eccentric émigré, a ski bum from Europe, who runs the Tweedsmuir Park Lodge and its heli-skiing operation at the head of the valley.

"In all the years I've been here, we've never seen a trace of them," he says in his cut-and-dried Scandinavian accent. "And with all the flying that we do, especially taking our backcountry skiers and snowboarders over the mountains in the winter, you'd think we'd have seen tracks in the snow by now. But we haven't."

"Ever?"

"*Never.*"

"Not *one* track?"

He shakes his head. "Not a track, not a toe-print, not even a hair."

I've slipped back into the dualistic mind-set involving Sasquatch —"exists" versus "doesn't exist"—out of both habit and desperate hope. At the same time, the metaphorical image of the Sasquatch in the outline of the mountains near Ocean Falls remains alive in me. In quieter moments I allow myself to think about Bigfoots in a more symbolic and philosophical way. And though I've considered psychology, in the hope that it would help illuminate either proof or disproof of the creature, I still feel there's an aspect of our behavior that's unexamined, having to do with our need to plumb the depths of the unknown.

What is the deepest intent of Bigfoot hunters and investigators? What is my own?

Life is full of unknowns that preoccupy us. We constantly grapple with things we don't know or can't see—the blank spots on our conceptual and literal maps: *What, if anything, lies around the next corner? Past the edge of the visible universe? Beyond tomorrow? After death?*

For the literal questions, we often do our best to actually, directly or indirectly, see for ourselves. Explorers fling themselves into little-known regions. Scientists conduct experiments. Companies and governments employ analysts, consultants, spies. Individually, we might take our question to a private investigator—or a psychic. When an answer is particularly elusive, we make do with guesses: we use our imagination, we concoct hypotheses and stories that jibe with our worldview. We create placeholders until we know for sure. In answering more existential questions, philosophical systems, including religious and cultural cosmologies, fulfill a similar function. They're connectors, bridges to little-understood or unknowable aspects of life.

In answer to certain mysteries, various cultures have employed pantheons of deities, demigods, and preternatural beings. Christian lore has angels—celestial beings that act as intermediaries between heaven and earth. In Islamic and pre-Islamic Middle Eastern lore, the *djinn* are intelligent, shape-shifting, and meddlesome essences that harbor a capacity for either good or evil. Elfin- and fairy-type beings (which, like the *Thla'thla* or *Dzonoqua,* are given to kidnapping children) are still revered in Celtic cultures. In the countries of Scandinavia, races of little people called *Tomte* and *Nisse* are said to roam the countryside. One Norse being, the *Hulder* or *Skogsrå,* is a female forest spirit that can lure a man into her subterranean cave, from which he will never emerge. Move in any direction on the world map, and the beliefs, the stories, the lore accrue. At one level these beings represent a direct link—and a kind of proof within the circular logic of belief—that there is a deeper, unexplained mystery in the origins of life and the universe. And that as humans we aren't alone in this painfully empty cosmos.

Within these precincts of cultural expression, the Sasquatch may find its deepest function and appeal. In First Nations cultures, the creatures associated with Bigfoot, even if they are also flesh-and-blood animals, are imbued with religious and supernatural significance. Like prophets, holy people, or saints, these creatures, auspicious in the extreme, appear to deliver messages, herald events, impart lessons, or dole out justice—in the cause of cosmic equilibrium. They are the subtle, secretive and cunning emissaries from some other reality, which all humans, not just people in traditional cultures, seem to yearn for.

Though Sasquatches on one level embody a kind of primitivism —the "backward" and "uncivilized" qualities that make them characters in bad horror films and goofy commercials—the creatures are gifted with a slate of talents that place them on a level *above* humans:

Profound physical strength and endurance
Unfathomable stealth and speed
Ability to appear and disappear at will
Hypnotic and fear-inducing projections of gaze and voice
A hyper-symbiotic relationship with nature

Their highly evolved and even magical sleight of hand gives them the appearance of superheroes or demigods. In a manner consistent with higher beings, Sasquatches set themselves apart from humankind. They dwell in out-of-the-way places which are difficult for us to get to and where we don't belong. Like Greek gods huddling on Olympus, they remain aloof and want little to do with our lot. Like our very own shadows, they move away from us when we pursue them. But they can also appear randomly in our midst. And when they do, as with any deity, the appearance is auspicious in a life-changing way. Ask any eyewitness.

"The basic urge toward mysticism," the late Anglo-Afghan storyteller and experiential philosopher Idries Shah once wrote, "is never, in the unaltered man, clear enough to be recognized for what it is."[21] The Sasquatch enthusiast, hunter, or scientist will give any number of logical motives as his or her excuse for pursuing the animal. And those may be true. But anyone hooked on Bigfoot is almost surely drawn as well to the phenomenology and magical mystery surrounding the alleged creatures. We could even call this impulse religious—not in the conventional meaning of the word, but more in the pure sense of having a reverential relationship with and attitude toward something sacred, set apart, forbidden.

When I honestly plumb my own motivations, I can see that my fascination stems from the seemingly superhuman implications of the Sasquatch. And because the part of me that likes to believe—and wants to believe—still clings to the idea, I feel driven to physically go out and look.

"Let's go on an expedition," I blurt out to Leonard Ellis, who is showing me around the valley for the day.

The cacophony at the crowded Bella Coola farmers market recedes ever so slightly. Leonard stops dead in his tracks and turns to look at me as if I'd just uttered a magical phrase. He breaks into a smile that is almost mischievous.

"What are you thinkin'?" he asks.

"Hike up the Necleetsconnay."

Leonard becomes pensive. He looks disappointed. "Necleetsconnay will be a heavy bushwhack. Also, lots of bears in there this time of year because of the salmon."

"But there are bears everywhere right now."

"Bigger risk in there," he says. "It's a narrow valley, so we'll be squeezed in pretty tight with them. More chances of a run-in."

I nod, not knowing how to counter that.

"I'd have my gun but . . . yeah . . . it's not the best scenario."

The conversation ends there. But I can see the gears turning inside Leonard's head.

"You know, instead of Necleetsconnay we can hike up to my cabin for a few days," he says, weighing my reaction. "It's pretty remote. About as remote as you'll get anywhere around here. It's a difficult hike even for me, and not something I do with tourists—anything can happen. So you'd have to really be up for it."

"Where is it?"

"Stillwater Lake. The cabin used to belong to Stanley Edwards—the son of Ralph Edwards. You've heard of the Edwards family, right?"

I had.

Ralph Edwards was a famous homesteader from North Carolina who in 1913 settled on the shores of Lonesome Lake, deep in the valley of the Atnarko River—a tributary of the Bella Coola. Battling seemingly insurmountable odds, the self-taught woodsman, fisherman, and farmer hacked down a tract of old-growth forest, built a complex of cabins and a farm with electricity, and raised a family there, living in seclusion for decades. Pioneering and self-sufficient, the family survived on knowledge culled from a vast library of how-to books lugged, with everything else, into the wilderness. Ralph is best known for building an airplane and for saving the last population of trumpeter swans, a critically endangered bird species living at the lake, from extinction—for which he was awarded the Order of Canada.*

His exploits were made famous in a 1957 biography, entitled *Crusoe of Lonesome Lake*, by American Pulitzer Prize–winning writer Leland Stowe. The cabin and property Leonard owns had belonged to Stanley Edwards, Ralph's son, an eccentric offshoot who had settled and lived a hermit's life at neighboring Stillwater Lake.

"I bought the property after Stanley was found dead in an outhouse several years ago," Leonard says. "One of the bridges on the trail to the cabin got washed out in a big flood a few summers back, and I haven't been down there since. The bridge was just rebuilt. I need to go check on the place."

---

* Edwards taught himself advanced mathematics and aeronautical engineering, getting his pilot's license after only twenty-eight hours of instruction at age sixty-two—the oldest person in Canada ever to qualify at the time. But he never got his homemade plane to fly.

My enthusiasm for Leonard's idea, an otherwise hugely tempting offer, is somehow dampened by my desire to go up the Necleetsconnay.

"Well?" Leonard says, sensing my hesitation. "Are you up for a few days in the bush with the old man?

I smile and reluctantly put aside my other plans. "Let's do it."

Plans begin to take shape. But before anything happens, tourists stampede into town and sign up for Leonard's bear tours. He tells me his remaining free time is being snapped up—and that he's not sure if, or when, we'll make it to his cabin.

Frustrated and still wanting to explore the rain forest, I decide to look for a replacement guide. I seek out Clark Hans, the Nuxalk artist who, on my previous visit, had showed me around the confluence of the Necleetsconnay and Bella Coola Rivers. But Clark is away, working on Vancouver Island, and no one knows when he'll be back.

Unsure of what to do next, I head to the banks of the river on the edge of town. I sit at a picnic table and watch the silt-heavy river coursing like a runaway lava flow. The sky, earlier blue, is covered with dark roiling clouds riding a blustery wind. Dozens of agitated gulls are aloft, circling high over the town.

"Looks like a storm blowing in," a voice says behind me.

I turn around and see a short, middle-aged man wearing a blue bandanna on his head, beige overalls, and kneehigh brown rubber boots. The muzzle of a rifle sticks out of a canvas bag thrown over his shoulder. He looks like a cross between an early twentieth-century hunter and a beatnik hobo.

"You can tell it's a storm," he says, pointing up, "when the birds fly like that."

We introduce ourselves. The man tells me his name is James Hans.

"*Hans*? You must be related to Clark," I say.

"Clark's my cousin."

As I tell James more about myself, I remember that Clark had been duck hunting with cousins the day he had his Bigfoot encounter and fled across the river.

"Were you with Clark when he saw a Sasquatch, years ago? He told me the story."

"Yeah," he confirms, pulling his bag off his shoulder and placing it on the ground. "We got separated that day, so I didn't see the Sasquatch. But we all got smoked when we got back to town. Our people think that if you see or come near a Sasquatch, something bad will happen to you. That you'll get out of your right mind. Our family didn't want any of us to lose our spirit."

"Have you ever seen one?" I ask.

"Seen *and* heard them. Once down the inlet at Taleomy. Another time over here in Piisla. I also seen one on the river near Four Mile, at night, up close, with a flashlight. We came back, and my grandmother smoked us that night too."

"You must spend a lot of time in the bush," I say.

"I grew up around Nickle-Sqwanny," he says, pointing toward the Necleetsconnay valley. "My parents used to carry me around there in a packsack when I was a kid. Now I go there all the time by myself to hunt deer and ducks and go exploring around."

A rumble of thunder echoes up from the inlet, rising above the sound of the river.

"I'm gonna go before it rains," James says, reaching for his bag.

"Hold on," I say. "When are you going out next? Into the bush, I mean?"

"Not sure. I just go when I go. I decide the same day."

"Could I come along next time? I'm staying at the motel here," I say, pointing down the road.

James hesitates. He's on the cusp of saying yes, but then something holds him back. I realize, as I'm sure he does, that he knows absolutely nothing about me.

"Let me think about it," he says, uncertain, taking a step back.

"I spent time with Clark. He'll vouch for me if you contact him," I say, grasping at the opportunity. James deliberates to the first drops of rain.

"Can you swim?

"Swim?"

"Yeah, I'm thinking of drifting the river in my rowboat sometime this week. The water's pretty rough and cold. In case anything happens, you'll need to make it quickly to shore."

"I'm a good enough swimmer."

"All right," James says. "I'll drop by the motel and let you know."

At the moment it starts to pour, a wooden skiff floats into view on the river. It's carrying two men untangling nets, likely fishermen, who suddenly freeze and stare at me, as the unceasing torrent carries them downriver into tree cover and out of my field of view.

When I turn to look at James again, he's gone.

Days later, James and I are driven by his wife fifteen miles up the valley to a gravel side road running to a small tributary of the main river. A billowing drizzle bordering on rain hangs over the length of the valley. James takes the wheel from his wife when we arrive and backs the truck, and the trailer carrying his rowboat, down a steep incline to the creek. I walk down the knoll ahead of the trailer and am instantly throttled by the smell of rotting fish. It is rancid, like the humpback whale breath I inhaled while traveling on *Achiever.* I see then that the shoreline is littered with the pale, bloated carcasses of spawned-out chum salmon. It looks like the aftermath of a biblical plague.

James and I have become better acquainted since meeting days before. A forty-nine-year-old Nuxalk man, he is married to an archaeologist, is the father of seven kids, and once worked, like Leonard, as a bear-hunting guide. James is gentle and kind, but there's also an underlying intensity to him. He seems to move back and forth between the present moment and some other place in his awareness—as if he inhabits two worlds simultaneously. His long experience on the land is manifested as fluid ease and confident mastery.

"My family and I sometimes go into the bush to have supper at night," he told me earlier. "We've even walked home in the dark without a flashlight. Some people think I'm pretty nuts doing that. But I was raised not to be afraid of the dark. My dad used to say, 'If an animal is going to get you, it's not going to wait until it's dark out.'"

The drizzle graduates to rain. We push the rowboat into the water and climb in after donning our rain gear. James takes the oars and rows us, through the flotsam of dead salmon, toward the river. We exit the tributary and collide head-on with the rushing Bella Coola River, which sweeps us into its unstoppable trajectory.

"What can I do to help?" I ask, seeing James suddenly strain to control the rowboat.

"Look for logjams and snags," he says, pulling at the wooden oars. "Especially when we get nearer to town in a few hours."

I feel a tinge of anxiety upon realizing how vulnerable we are. In spite of the oars, we're almost totally at the mercy of this powerful river. But my fear is mitigated by the sight of James's reflexes, deftness, and navigational savvy—and the realization that bucking the flow, through fear or hesitation, can be just as dangerous as the hazards that lie in our path.

Once I relax, a new perspective opens up. The valley and mountains transform. The space becomes vast, virtually a cosmos. I realize I'm experiencing the Bella Coola valley from a wholly new vantage point: its central axis and beating heart—the river itself. Not only am I seeing the valley from within, but by riding the current I'm actually taking part in its fundamental life force: the perpetual movement of water.

That edginess I'd sensed earlier in James now possesses him. He appears lost in a hybrid universe of his trancelike imaginings and the physical world. I too slip into my own hypnotic rhythm, coaxed by the now deceptively disarming flow of the river and the thickly forested slopes that seem to respire magic. Gusts of cold air blowing down from the alpine zone, sudden downpours, and collisions with frenzied salmon are the only interruptions to this dreamlike drifting. And then something really strange happens: I start to lose all sense of bearings, boundaries, markers, direction. I can neither see the town nor imagine it. The road, totally obscured from view, ceases to exist in my mind even as a notion. In fact, all intimations of human presence have vanished, as if they were never there to begin with. The separation between past, present, and future also melts away. I realize that I'm floating down the river in its timeless, eternal form. Seen from its own vantage point, the valley has assumed its true character and scope.

People talk about seeing with "new eyes." Prior to this river journey, I saw the valley strictly from the perspective of the town and the road—with the rain forest extending away from it as something peripheral. All of this illuminates a heinous flaw in our thinking, the mental parceling and the fragmentation we impose on things; what we know are the nodes, waypoints, and details of the grid—but there's so much more. And it's not just the literal, geographical grids but also the figurative ones: the ruts in our minds—the grid of fixed ideas and mental trajectories running from A to B to C. We don't realize that all the other territory is there—until we stumble upon it, a kind of Noble Beyond.

As we near town, the river accelerates. Rapids, logjams, and eddies appear. Darkness rapidly falls, and the detailed, nuanced world of the rain forest, with its thousand gradations of life and tonality, falls into a shadowy, silhouetted caricature that becomes hard to decipher.

James is alert, rowing furiously to avoid things I can barely see coming. The river meanders. Our boat begins to spin in circles. At a big bend in the river the boat catches the edge of a logjam in the shadows. James hollers and over a course of milliseconds I see my life flash before me as the back of the boat gets thrust upward by the beastly, runaway currents.

"Come to my side!" James shouts, as he grapples with the log. I shift toward him, but the boat continues to tilt up and sideways. But before we are upended, the vessel somehow breaks free, and we are drawn again into the dashing flow.

James rows desperately toward the south bank of the river. Around another bend we see the lights of homes on the street where James and I met a few days earlier. He rows us in that direction, to a section of shore sheltered from the current by an outer sandbank.

Without saying a word, we climb out of the boat, sodden and jacked up on adrenaline. Together we drag the skiff out of the water and hide it in the trees, before stumbling, almost punch-drunk, onto the road. The long chasm of the Necleetsconnay valley, now to our backs, looks on indifferently, cloaked in an ever-deepening darkness.

Leonard phones the next day to say he's had some tour cancellations and wants to make another go at getting to his cabin at Stillwater Lake.

Later that week we're rolling up the highway in an early 1980s pickup truck resurrected from Leonard's fleet of weed-besieged, decommissioned vehicles hidden behind his cabins. It's an immaculately clear late-summer morning, the cool air redolent of pine and mountain herbs.

"This is the real thing," Leonard exclaims, as the wind, blowing through the window, rustles his curls. "Grizzly bears and heavy bushwhacking. You can't get anywhere more remote."

In the back seat are Leonard's teenage son, Daniel, and their black Labrador retriever, Josie. Leaning on the seat between Leonard and me is a sleek 12-gauge shotgun.

When I arrived at Leonard's place earlier, I found Daniel stuffing a backpack with food. With his heavyset build, curly blond hair, and slightly defiant gait, he is a youthful clone of Leonard.

"I decided to bring the boy," Leonard said matter-of-factly, pulling me aside. "It's good to have an extra hand to help carry the grub. And in case we need to get a few things done."

"Like what?" I asked, sensing he had something specific in mind.

"One of Daniel's friends happened to hike by the cabin a few weeks ago and told him that someone, or some*thing*, had broken into it. Made a big mess apparently."

As we push up the valley, the mountains become bolder and more imposing. Forested behemoths with trisyllabic names like Nusatsum, Defiance, and Stupendous, topped with crowns of bare rock, stand sentry at the entrances to enigmatic side valleys that flank them. We cross into Tweedsmuir Provincial Park and continue to follow the winding road. Just before the highway ascends to the Chilcotin Plateau, Leonard pulls onto an unimaginably rough dirt road that is pockmarked and littered with rocks. We're thrown around like an airplane in a patch of bad turbulence. For hours, enduring whiplash, we follow this rocky wagon trail along narrow ledges overlooking the sparkling Atnarko River, alive with spawning salmon. The road drops again to a spot where a few cabins sit by the shore.

Leonard slows down. "That's Bill Robson's cabin over there," he says, indicating the property of a man he had introduced me to a week earlier, who had said he had heard heavy bipedal footsteps and panting there at three o'clock one morning.

A little farther down the road, Leonard stops the truck and points out of the passenger window. "And that there is the old outhouse where they found Stanley Edwards dead."

We all stare silently at the wooden structure, as if paying our respects. I'm overcome with the image of the white-bearded hermit, the former owner of Leonard's cabin, dressed in his trademark yellow construction vest and helmet, sitting slumped over in the outhouse—the culmination of a lopsided, maladapted life of solitude. An attempt to become a kind of Sasquatch.

We leave the vehicle at the end of the dirt road and navigate a dry, rugged path through a forest that bears little resemblance to the perspiring coastal jungles that I've traveled through up until now. The wilderness here, marked by thick-barked, fire-resistant Douglas fir, is rain-deprived, with far less undergrowth. Beneath our feet is a powdery concoction of sand and conifer needles. Leonard says we are walking through the old riverbed of the Atnarko—before its course was diverted by a cataclysmic flood in 2010.

The mood is unexpectedly tense. Leonard, who is shouldering an uncomfortable-looking external frame backpack from the seventies and carrying his shotgun, has been going on about his plight as a persecuted hunter.

"People are spreading all kinds of rumors about me, including saying I'm still guiding for bears. They can't get their minds around the fact that I've stopped. I feel I'm being bullied and picked on."

The degree of waffling Leonard does in his attempt to come to terms with what happened to him is striking. In one breath he tells me he's happy that he no longer has to shoulder the stress of his old hunting business and that "bear viewing and ecotourism are the way to go." But in the next breath he lashes out at the anti-trophy-hunting forces he blames for his downfall. Leonard adds bitterly that another environmental campaign protecting wolves has caused them to explode in number, with the result that they've killed off all the deer and mountain goats in the region. "These environmentalists are swinging things all to one side," he grumbles. "Just eat tofu and don't do nothin'. That's all they're good for."

Daniel too is not in the best of moods. He doesn't speak much to me, and speaks even less to Leonard, with whom he seems almost angry. I get the sense he doesn't want to be here. He glares at Leonard every time his father stops for a rest break.

As the trail ascends the mountainside we come across a group of four hikers—two women and two men—the first and only people we see on our trip. Leonard knows them and is drawn into small talk. Their eyes shift surreptitiously between Leonard, his shotgun, and then me. Leonard mentions he is taking me—"a writer from Ontario"—to his cabin. But the comment seems to only deepen their curiosity, shown on their faces.

"They were behaving strangely," I say, after they walk off.

"Probably spooked by the gun," Leonard grumbles. "They're the sort of people who only carry bear spray."

"Is that a bad thing?" I ask.

"It's a bad idea. Bear spray only works at fifteen feet at most. If a pissed-off bear is that close to you, you're in real trouble."

"I can see that carrying a gun is a good idea. But doesn't that also come at the risk of dropping your guard?"

"Whaddaya mean?"

"I imagine with a gun there's less need to pay attention and be careful. And so you're more likely to have to use it in the end. And vice versa with bear spray."

Daniel is standing with his back to us, looking into the woods, pretending not to listen.

I go on: "The bear-viewing operations I know of here seem to do fine without firearms."

"How any bear operator, or tourist provider, can take guests into bear territory with just spray is beyond me. Anything can happen out here. If I don't have a gun, I won't go into the bush."

"Maybe those people have learned how to behave around bears without provoking them."

Though my comment wasn't intended as a slight, I can see that Leonard has taken it as one. His tone turns didactic.

"What you need to know, John, is that those coastal bears are well fed and habituated to people. The guides and the bears know one another personally. The tours even give 'em names, like Tom, Frank, and Susan—like they're old chums. But if you run into an Atnarko grizzly, you'll see how mean and grumpy they can be. I brought a group near here, and an old boar got too close. It was running near a cedar stump. To protect my guests I shot the stump and it exploded. You know what the bear did?"

"I can guess."

"That's right. The bear decided it had better walk away—and he did."

I can see the episode running through Leonard's mind, and a cool look comes over his face. "Lucky for him."

Our hike to the cabin begins smoothly. But after a few hours, a set of worrying omens descends in sequence. The first comes when Leonard takes his fourth rest break in under an hour. He sits on a log by the trail, and lets out a long moan ringing with pain and relief. Daniel looks daggers at his father.

"What's the matter?" I say to Leonard. "You're always stopping."

"I'm just outta shape," he says, staring at his boots. "It's nothin'."

Daniel holds his own stare. "Ask him about his knee," he says to me coldly.

Leonard looks up at his son with exhausted annoyance, and turns to me. "I had a little surgery in this knee here back in the spring. It's just buggin' me a little."

"You should have mentioned that before we left," I say, feeling a tinge of fear.

"I didn't think it'd be an issue."

Daniel cracks a patronizing grin. "Who'd have imagined the great Leonard Ellis getting his ass kicked on a hike. Let's go, Dad."

The second omen comes when we arrive at the mouth of Stillwater Lake, a long, narrow body of water hemmed in by steep, forested mountainsides draped with rockslides. Our plan is to borrow canoes at another cabin here and cross to Leonard's property at the head of the lake. But when we find the boats, we discover they're cracked and banged up.

"They're no good," Leonard says, with a tired sigh, before standing and looking out toward the lake.

"Can we get there on foot?" I ask.

Leonard ruminates. "The west shore of the lake, on the right, is the slightly shorter route, but it's got too many rockslides. I've done it once before. We wouldn't make it to the cabin before dark."

"And the east side?"

"There's bits of old trail there. Never hiked it all the way." Leonard thinks some more before shrugging off a concern he is weighing. "It should be fine. Let's take it."

"This ought to be interesting," Daniel says, drawing each word out, with a nervous grin.

The moment we set foot on the lake's eastern bank, our hike enters the domain of punishment. It takes on shades of Percy Fawcett's doomed expedition in the Amazon. We're forced to navigate waves of successive rockslides teeming with sharp-edged, slippery boulders resting precariously one on top of another. Alerted to our presence, every known biting insect—wasps, hornets, black flies, horse flies, deer flies, mosquitos—swarms us. Josie, Leonard's dog, whimpers and cries, as she too barely manages to avoid falling between the jagged boulders. Small sections of what look like trail appear, mercifully, through the thick brush, only to vanish, Houdini-like, without a trace, into the next clearing teeming with black boulders.

I'm trailing behind the others when I hear Daniel's voice up ahead, childlike, imploring, and stripped of cynicism.

"Holy fucking shit, Dad! Look!"

I catch up to find the two crouched beside the largest bear track I—and apparently they—have ever seen. It's in dirt and is bigger than the head of an oversize tennis racket. It could be the footprint of an elephant. And there are more in the distance, heading in the direction where we're going.

"Giant old boar," Leonard says, gravely, stroking his chin. "Ever see anything like that before, Daniel?"

Daniel shakes his head slowly, fixed on the print. "Uh-uh."

Leonard stands and looks around in a pose of alert vigilance. "We need to move. It'll be dark soon and that cabin's still a ways away."

We push on, constantly looking over our shoulders. Contrary to Leonard's expectation, the shoreline we're navigating rises, turning into a steep, rocky cliffside. We're forced to turn inland, uphill, where Leonard says he's certain there is a way back down to the lake.

Hours later, after hiking through heavy, face-scratching brush, we reach the top and are rewarded with a stunning view over the densely forested head of the lake, blooming in several shades of green, in which Leonard's cabin is concealed. But that moment of sweetness is spoiled by the gut-wrenching realization that there's no apparent way down. Upon reconnoitering, Leonard says there is only a three-hundred-foot cliff over the water to our side and a steep avalanche chute of dirt and rock up ahead whose bottom he can't see. We could keep climbing and follow the mountain ridges around the lake, he adds, but we could hike forever and not find a safe way down.

I'm feeling frustrated, worn out, and exhausted. Daniel is on the cusp of blowing a fuse. Leonard, who is now limping from the raw pain in his knee, is beside himself with confusion, busy doing mental calculations. He tells us he's going off to investigate on his own and for us to stay put. When Leonard doesn't return after forty minutes or so—and doesn't respond to our calls—Daniel and I go looking for him on the bluff above us. We find him there, sitting morosely on a huge rock overlooking the lake, in a pose like Rodin's *Thinker*.

It's now early evening. Seeing Leonard, my guide, at a complete loss sends a shudder running through me. I realize we likely won't make it to the cabin before dark.

"We need to decide whether to find a place to camp for the night—or whether we should head back," I say, feeling something approaching panic well up in my chest.

"There's no going back," Leonard snaps. "We won't make it in time. And there's no way I'm camping out here for the night with that big boar wandering around—and while my cabin is just down *there*."

"So what do you propose?"

"We go down that avalanche chute," he says, pointing to a precipice just ahead of us.

A look of wild disbelief comes over Daniel's face. "Dad, you're crazy! There's no way we'll be able to get down there! It's way too steep!"

"Going down's not the problem," Leonard says, more calmly now, trying to downplay things. "The issue is coming back up. We just gotta make sure we can climb the chute again when it's time to leave."

"How? How do we make sure?" Daniel says, with desperate, mocking sarcasm.

"The first rule I learned while goat huntin' is that if you can climb down without killing yourself, you should be OK to get back up. So, there's only one way to find out."

I concur with Daniel that it's a bad idea and decide to challenge Leonard. "What if we make it down without killing ourselves, but we still can't climb back up?" I ask. "What happens then?"

Leonard shrugs. "Maybe there's a boat at the cabin? That's the only other way out of here. That west shore is even nastier than this. And the way things are going with my knee . . ."

Daniel fumes and shakes his head again, glaring down at his father as Leonard strains to get up from the rock he's sitting on. Leonard grabs his pack and shotgun and starts hobbling toward the chute.

Josie follows him, but when they reach the top of the grade, she stops in her tracks and turns around feebly.

"I'll check it out and let you know," Leonard hollers. Using his shotgun like a cane, he disappears down the slope, past a few small trees.

Daniel and I sit silently, staring at the ground, for what feels like ages.

"What's with your dad?" I say, finally giving in to the temptation to ask.

The teenager makes a slightly dour face before glancing at me embarrassingly. "He likes to push himself sometimes."

I'm stranded atop a rocky bluff in a remote and rugged wilderness. My frazzled and injured guide wants to fling us down a steep mountainside in a desperate bid to reach shelter. Our sense of vulnerability has long ago turned into fear. But running parallel with it, like an undercurrent, is a sort of excitement.

I've given little serious thought to Sasquatches in the last few days. But in this moment, perched atop an avalanche chute, with the weight of adversity bearing down, I get a flash of insight, however irrelevant and unhelpful: this visceral fear I'm experiencing, the thrilling kind, which bursts our reservoirs of adrenaline, is what Bigfoot enthusiasts seek. It is an excitement born of adventure, glory, and self-sacrifice.

Somewhere in that mist-laden landscape between Koeye and the Hoodoo Valley, when the surrealism became almost intolerable, I was struck by a notion that has remained with me ever since: there is a process of personal mythmaking in play here. What began as a research trip, albeit an adventuresome one, to solve a puzzle, has morphed into an all-consuming journey, an epic, whose hero is none other than me. And whether I admit it or not, that was probably the intention all along.

All of us yearn to be heroes in narratives of our own making, if only to live lives brimming with purpose. Most of us take up that call, at one time or another, to a greater or lesser extent. Others make it a recurring part of life. It's the underlying motive, almost a default setting, that pushes rational people to sometimes do seemingly irrational things. Anywhere there is an opponent, or obstacle, standing between the hero and his or her goal—where difficulty and adversity lie—there is a mythical quest with its attendant moments of high drama.

Journalist Will Storr says that a "compulsion for emotional narrative" underlies this deep desire to fling ourselves into the push and pull of human circumstance. He describes the mind as a kind of "Hero-Maker," seeing the world in terms of stories in which we are cast into the virtuous leading role. Our minds, Storr says, are addicted to story templates because that is how we experience life. "The mind reorders the world," he writes, "turning the events of our days into a narrative of crisis, struggle, resolution, and casts us in the leading role. In this way our lives gain motivation. . . . We are coaxed into hope, into heroic acts, into braving impossible odds."[22]

The Sasqualogist, whether lay investigator or scientist, is no different from the other self-styled heroes. His or her particular brand of journey rests heavily on literal adventuring—questing—through a physically wild landscape, with all of its exciting fears and challenges to test one's mettle. But this quest, it seems to me, is also metaphorical. He or she is in pursuit of what may be the most elusive prize that ever existed—a modern-day holy grail. And the obstacles are duly massive. The Sasqualogist wrangles against snickering hordes of skeptics and debunkers (who are themselves heroes of their own mythical journeys). He or she struggles to awaken an indifferent public and a contemptuous scientific establishment. The literal monster the Sasqualogist must slay, apprehend, or capture on camera is a much greater Goliath, in physical and mental acuity, than the biblical giant of that name.

Bearing this in mind, I wonder: Can there ever be victory for this sort of heroism—a seemingly futile kind propped up by hope? One in which all previous heroes on the same path have fallen by the wayside—self-sacrificed, beaten by the beast, like warriors at some indefensible Thermopylae. Beyond the nobility in superhuman effort against insurmountable odds, what could possibly goad a would-be hero into that sort of quest (especially when there are so many others to choose from)?

It may be that its prize is like no other: the capture of a supernatural being.

And so here I am now, among them—yet have always been among them—lost in the mythical landscape of imagination from which I derive my personal significance: another kind of Noble Beyond. But now that I'm awakened to it, I'm less than sure that this is the kind of hero I want to be—or that Sasquatch is the prize I want to spend my precious days failing to attain.

Our journey down the avalanche chute begins as a sluglike procession, as I, Daniel, and a whimpering Josie inch down what feels like a 70 percent incline on our backsides, while straining with Herculean effort to keep from gaining velocity and becoming flying objects. For a while it seems to work—until the ground gives way.

In that moment, the entire hillside comes alive in an animated rippling of dirt and rock that gathers momentum, moving faster and faster. I look behind me to see Daniel and Josie, wide-eyed with horror, being pulled down the mountain in a rip-roaring cloud of dust. I slide faster and faster until my desperate efforts to stop cause me to lose my balance and tumble over and over.

Time slows and all becomes gray, as I endure what feels like head-to-toe rug burn—and the terrestrial equivalent of being dragged under a huge wave of cresting seawater.

After who knows how long, and how far a fall, I awaken to the sound of rushing pebbles and dirt coming to a standstill beside me. I'm lying on my side facing downhill. Standing maybe twenty feet in front of me, with the lake behind him, covered in the fine dust that bathes people pulled from collapsed buildings, is Leonard. He's holding his shotgun and pack and has a satisfied grin on his face. I hear Daniel cursing bitterly just above me, as Josie, now a gray Lab, steps on my head to get to Leonard's side.

"Told ya we'd make it down," he says. "Leonard Ellis doesn't give up."

The final push to the cabin, through a spacious grove of Douglas fir, is desperate and incoherent, a race against darkness in free fall.

Because of his knee, Leonard can no longer shoulder his heavy pack, which Daniel now carries in addition to his own. Even though we wear head lamps, visibility in the woods is frighteningly low. It is a shadowy, monochrome world of forms—one of those malign forests from fairy tales. To make matters worse, Daniel and Leonard are sparring about which of the many crisscrossing trails that have suddenly appeared leads to the cabin. But just as hope begins to fade, perhaps for good, we start to see evidence of human activity: piles of wooden planks, fences, hand tools, pieces of machinery.

"Stanley's unfinished projects!" Leonard says, trying to hide his relief. "We're almost there."

Ordinarily, after an ordeal of this sort, the homecoming, the arrival at relative comfort and shelter, is sweet enough to negate what has been endured. But when we finally get to the old enclosure, my heart sinks to depths I had no idea existed. Our head lamps and the last light of dusk reveal a thin shell of a cabin totally at odds with the rustic comforts I'd held out for: it is a patchwork log-and-plywood shack, with open windows covered in tarps, surrounded by homemade wooden scaffolding and ladders. A renovation work in progress! As Leonard and Daniel drop their packs and dust themselves off, I peer around back, hoping to find the "real" cabin. Instead, I discover three partially completed shelters interspersed in a large clearing.

"Jumpin' Jeezus!" Leonard yells.

I return to the cabin and step inside to find Leonard and Daniel, with their head lamps on, standing between some bunk beds and what appears to be the kitchen area. The place looks as if it has been ransacked. Cans of food, empty jars, pots and pans, rice, coffee, pasta, and mouse shit litter the floor. A large wooden chest is on its side, its lid nearly torn off.

"Bears?" I ask.

"Probably," Leonard grumbles. "Though how a bear can nearly rip the lid off a locked grub box I have no idea."

I pick up an empty dill-pickle jar at my feet. "Are bears able to open screw-top jars?" We exchange uncomfortable glances.

"Something—or someone—came through here," Leonard says. "Right now it doesn't matter who. Let's clean this place up before it gets dark. I'll light some lanterns and start a fire outside. You two get some water from the creek for washing."

I have no idea how we muster the energy and enthusiasm, but for the better part of an hour, in the last trickles of daylight, we tackle the mess. By the time total darkness falls, the inside of the cabin is in surprisingly good order, swept almost clean, and we are on our bunks spinning with exhaustion.

At first I'm kept awake by Leonard's thunderous snoring, the sound of Josie licking her shredded paws, and the audible fluttering of bats flying in and out through the cabin windows and doing hard turns over my head. As I begin to drift off, I hear a heavy movement around the cabin. It is the sound of lumbering and rustling of foliage. The presence, I'm certain, is no small animal. But I'm far too spent to care. I keep my eyes closed and will the sound to go away as I fade into my own version of well-deserved oblivion.

I stumble groggily out of the cabin the next day, my body stiff, every muscle aching. Leonard and Daniel are nowhere to be seen. Everywhere around me is a spacious and airy wood, filled with Douglas fir, pine, and birch running deep in all directions. Daylight unveils and defangs what felt like a diabolical forest the night before.

It is eerily calm.

I walk around the cabin to the partial clearing behind it. There I find the structures I could barely make out the night before. One is a very large, open two-story shed for firewood containing what must be a five-year supply of logs. Two more partially constructed buildings, whose final intended form I can't divine, sit nearby. The rest of the property, littered with hardware-store esoterica, looks like a hurricane disaster site. Wooden planks of every variety, size, and type cover the ground, as do tools, equipment, metals, plastics, machine parts, books, and bobbles. The only thing more astonishing than the sight itself is the implication that Stanley Edwards had carried it all here.

"What a mess," I say, as Leonard appears. I find and pick up an old hardcover book lying beneath one of the sheds. It's a German-language translation of Leland Stowe's *Crusoe of Lonesome Lake*.

"You shoulda seen the place when I bought it," Leonard says. "Stanley was a hoarder, a real hermit."

Daniel climbs down from the loft in the shed containing the fire-wood. He's holding a gray 1970s bomber jacket, which he displays to us, glowing with pride.

"Look, Dad. Stanley's old coat. Looks like I'll be wearing a bit of history."

Leonard smiles. "Well, boys, the good news is, we've got a boat. We don't have to hike back up that mountain. I can't find any paddles, so I'm gonna see if I can rustle up some good two-by-fours. Why don't you guys gimme a hand."

During the whole trip I've been ambivalent about Leonard's past. It has been hard not to be. I'm not a proponent of the grizzly trophy hunt. But I also don't see in Leonard the nefariousness that some others do. Some will say it's because I'm naive. Perhaps it's because as an outsider I don't have a stake in these issues and am not driven by the emotions that sometimes surround them. But high emotion, especially in service of—or in opposition to—a cause, paradoxically narrows our vision into a two-tone outlook on life: "right versus wrong," "with us or against us," or "us versus them." We stop dis-cerning the many subtleties and shades that also exist within the spectra of life. The "other" can become a dehumanized enemy. It's easy for Leonard's opponents to see him only in terms of his differ-ences and his ideas surrounding aspects of hunting—and vice versa. But if one can manage to look at him more dispassionately, one might find someone who also has much in common with his foes.

This complexity was apparent when I spoke separately with both Leonard and Ian McAllister at Pacific Wild. While the two men complained, sometimes bitterly, about each other, I was able to see similarities between them and could also discern a strange but powerful linkage, and sensed that, although they were opposed, each was somehow key to the other's fate—and the fate of the region they struggled over. It was as if a strange cosmic collusion were in play that required both their positions, at odds, to create something new.

Leonard's purchasing and cobbling together of the adjoining bear-guiding territories made it possible for the environmentalists to eventually buy him out and help bring some protection for the bears within a large area in one swoop. In doing so, and encouraging bear-viewing ecotourism in those places, the conservationists and First Nations have fostered an economy Leonard both contributes to and derives his newer work and sustenance from. And so there is a much larger dynamic in play than what heated, irreconcilable enemies can see.

As the three of us dig through piles of wood looking for makeshift oars, Josie trots off into the trees, virtually unnoticed. Moments later we hear her barking. It doesn't seem important until Leonard yells in a growling voice more alarming than any I've heard from him to date: "Joseeee! Come'ere! Come'eeeeeere!"

The dog scurries into view from behind a Douglas fir.

And then everything comes undone. Suddenly, and without any sense of transition, there is a large grizzly sow with a cub forty feet ahead of us at the edge of the clearing. The sow is flailing, roaring, and gnashing her teeth. She is a blur of rippling brown fur and beady eyes set in a wide head. The cub is dancing skittishly around her. I stand there looking at everything blankly, not understanding, trying to process what is going on—and how it came to pass. The moment of surprise is drawn out and stupefying.

Following an invisible cue, as if some order of battle were under way, the bear cub shinnies up the trunk of a tree with the nimbleness of a squirrel. All of us fan out in the slow, cautious, semi-crouched motion of wrestlers about to grapple. Part of me wants to run and keep running. But I remain calm enough to remember that this would be the wrong thing to do. I take small steps back in the direction of the buildings, urging the others to do the same. But no one is listening. Daniel is the first to flip into panic mode.

"She's gonna charge us, Dad! Shoot 'er! *Shoot 'er!*"

I have no recollection of Leonard's shotgun anywhere that morning. But now he has it raised—as if he has just pulled the weapon out of his back pocket. The man has menacingly come to life. He is roused and bristling with aggression—a mirror of the snapping beast in front of us.

"Go on! Get outa here! Go on! *Geeeeeeeeeeeeeeet!*" His growls, decibel for decibel, are just as frightening as the bear's.

Panic infects me in turn. "Let's go!" I yell, stepping backward, feeling the last of my composure fall apart. "Let's walk out of here! Now!"

"This is *my* property!" Leonard barks over his shoulder. "There's no going anywhere!" He returns to his aim, grappling tensely with the weapon.

Meanwhile, the grizzly's movements are erratic, chaotic. She lunges several feet before hitting an invisible wall, howling and roaring as if she's struggling to break free from a net that ensnares her.

"Dad! *What are you doing?*" Daniel yells, holding back tears, as the bear takes a few steps toward us. "She's not stopping!"

Leonard curses to himself, keeping his shotgun raised and moving it around, jerkily. Something is wrong.

"Quick, Dad! Shoot 'er! *Shoot 'er!*"

The bear takes half a step back and prepares to charge.

"*Daaaaaaaaaaaaaaaaaaaaaaaaaaaad!*"

Hair bristling, the bear bolts, like an unstoppable missile. The world slows as I give myself over to my reflexes, trusting them to sidestep a thunderbolt.

The gun goes off. There is a deafening clap of thunder. An open-palmed thrust of pressure to my chest. An explosion of earth.

A thick spray of dirt flies into the bear's face as if a miniature meteorite has crashed to earth. The animal slams on the brakes and recoils with a roar.

Leonard lets out his own nasty, vituperative roar, the mother of all impervious rages, hurled in the dialect of some dark underworld that I hope never to hear again.

"GEEEEEET OUTTTAAA HEEEEEEEEEEEEEEEEEERR-RRRRRRRRREE!"

When the forest is done quaking, and some semblance of nature's indifference returns, all of us, including the bear, find ourselves just standing there, emotions largely discharged, wondering what to do next.

The sow is uncertain. She wears a look of shy embarrassment and lowers her head to the ground, pivoting it from side to side, fluttering her lips. After a few pendular swings she resignedly lumbers into the trees.

My heart is galloping uncontrollably. I try to speak but can't.

"Jeezus," Leonard says.

We stand there watching her, a shadow drifting between trees, as she is joined by her offspring. The pair vanish deeper into the woods before reappearing again, farther off, in the adjacent creek, crossing to the other bank. The three of us huddle, dazed and fired up on adrenaline. Josie picks up a rusty old food can, brings it to Leonard's feet, and starts to play with it as if nothing has happened.

"Boy, that was close," Leonard mumbles, looking both agitated and euphoric and trying to regain his composure.

"What took you so long to shoot?" Daniel asks, his relief tinged with annoyance.

"The gun jammed. We'd have been dead meat if I hadn't let off that warning shot," Leonard says, before turning to me with a look as admonishing as it is sarcastic.

"So, Sasquatch Man. Seen enough yet? Ready to go back?"

9

The Reckoning

*The search is not for a wild man but for how wildness has left men,
then to bring that wildness back.*

—Daniel C. Taylor, *Yeti: The Ecology of a Mystery*

We're crammed into an old wooden rowboat, with Leonard in the back, paddling against the wind with two-by-fours cut by Stanley Edwards himself. Only Leonard speaks, periodically directing our strokes through the thick blooms of aquatic weeds. He's irked about the way the trip has gone and returns to his laments about his plight and life. My mind is overloaded, and I block out most of what he's saying. But one sentence penetrates:

"Without meaning, a man's life falls apart," he says.

Our run-in with the sow and cub the previous day marked the end of our expedition—and my trip. It was as if some denouement, or climax, had been reached. It felt like a powerful, unspoken truth: that there was nothing more to do. My travel companions, I think, sensed that too.

At first I can't help feeling that I'm returning empty-handed—that the Sasquatch has run circles around me.

But it really hit home more than once during this side trip with Leonard that it doesn't matter much in the grand scheme of things whether the Sasquatch actually exists or not. The possibility of a physical Bigfoot may be important for people like John Bindernagel and other scientists, who are working within a certain materialist worldview involving mammals, natural histories, and primate lineages. But to me the implications of the Sasquatch have amounted to a different significance: what it tells us about ourselves.

When I think of everything I've considered related to the Sasquatch —belief and skepticism, scientific pursuits, traditional tales, personal mythmaking, pseudo-religious awe, pattern-matching, and the attempt to explain the unexplained—I realize these are all expressions of meaning. And that our pursuit of the Sasquatch, our various interpretations of it, are a reflection of this deepest of human motivations.

Without meaning, a man's life falls apart.

I've seen during this trip that we have an innate, fundamental need for meaning—for our lives to be meaningful. Everything—our beliefs, our disbeliefs, our worldview, our perception, our actions, what we do and why we do it—is driven by this default search.

This applies to John Bindernagel and his quixotic quest to convince his skeptical colleagues of the existence of the Sasquatch. You can see it in the coastal First Nations communities reviving and preserving their culture, and resisting the systemic interests that sometimes seek to exploit them. It is evident in the work of conservationists like Ian McAllister and Captain Brian Falconer, as they struggle to maintain the integrity of the world's most intact ecosystem. It also applies to Leonard Ellis, in his connection to a hunting tradition, a life in the outdoors, and the struggle against the challenges inherent in that environment. By finding meaning we build connections between seemingly disparate things, creating a greater whole. Out of life's chaos we form a bigger and more coherent picture, one that feels more unified and connected. Meaning is a compass and rudder for our lives. It helps to make our suffering more tolerable.

Whatever its reality, the Sasquatch is a compelling symbol replete with potential meanings. Wild-man myths abound the world over. They do so largely because many of us seek a connection to the way we once were—to the more primal stages of our development, which, though partly superseded, still remain in us. To others, Sasquatches are anything but obtuse throwbacks to our lower selves; instead, they embody a supernatural cunning and higher capacity. They exist on a higher plane, personifying the unknown—or yet to be discovered—aspects of the universe. For some indigenous people, the creatures are preternatural custodians of nature, who, as characters in traditional stories, have something to teach. By deifying Sasquatches, some of us look to comfort ourselves with the idea that we share the universe with a comparable higher intelligence, that there's an order to things that we can sense but not properly articulate, and that we're being watched and perhaps taken care of.

The scientists, amateur sleuths, and explorers looking for the creatures are driven by the thrill of discovering something great. They find meaning in these investigations into new and unknown realms on the fringes of knowledge itself and in manning the outposts on the dangerous and exotic frontier dividing what we know from what we don't know. These are modern-day mythical journeys.

My own quest in search of an explanation for the Sasquatch phenomenon overlaps with this mythical quest. The fruits of these travels—the characters, the stories, the unlikely coincidences and strange connections—have created a deluge of meaning for me. I've developed a deeper understanding and appreciation of the environment and the need for humans to maintain its integrity in the face of the growing forces of consumption that imperil it. I've also walked away with a heightened admiration of and a closer connection to the First Nations communities I've visited, about which I knew little prior to the trip.

Though no incontrovertible proof has emerged for Bigfoot's physical existence, I find myself awakened to a new significance of the creature. I've learned to see the Sasquatch as a powerful symbol of the natural world—a diminishing realm from which most of us are becoming increasingly estranged. On one level, Sasquatches personify the more refined spectra of nature that we cannot, or often do not, see. They remind us that there is much more to the natural world, writ large, than meets the eye. They also show us, almost by holding up a mirror to ourselves, that the eye with which we see is limited. The artificial lines we humans have created, the fragmentation we have wrought upon the whole, separate us from the wilds to which we are inextricably linked.

The more we humans denude our environment, the more elusive the Sasquatch becomes and thus the more we grasp for it—not quite realizing that we are chasing after an aspect of our own nature that is vanishing with the disappearance of our earth's nature. It is no wonder that the indigenous residents of the Great Bear generally don't pursue Sasquatches or make too big a fuss about the creatures, beyond paying them the normal respect. The compulsion doesn't exist because, in a way, the essence of the creatures already lives within them. It exists in their surroundings, and in their intent—and actions—as responsible stewards of their lands and waters.

So, do Sasquatches *physically* exist?

At a certain point in my journey, I had come to understand that binary thinking on the matter—"exists" versus "doesn't exist"—was a quagmire. In the spirit of avoiding that mental posture and in the name of real open-mindedness, perhaps, I've come to see that we need to consider one more possibility in this conundrum of conundrums: human logic, suitable for explaining a certain level of physical existence, simply doesn't apply here. In other words, maybe the Sasquatch, whatever it is, exists in a reality lying beyond our ordinary perceptual capacities. Naturally, we try to explain phenomena in terms we understand. In certain cases, however, our accepted and understood definition of cause and effect may be limiting or downright wrong. The greatest experiential scientists in human history—mystics from various philosophical traditions—and our own quantum physicists of the modern era concur that the universe is not only other than what we perceive it to be, but also so convoluted and paradoxical in its behavior as to contradict our own systems of reasoning. Reality extends far beyond our familiar conceptions of space, time, and causality into a wholly different field.

Given all the different interpretations and perspectives, perhaps the best, most reliable description of a Sasquatch that we can muster in words—right now—is one that borders on the philosophical, or even metaphysical: it is a meeting place, a point of distillation, or a moment, in which the spirit of nature, including some long-lost part of ourselves, and an observer come together in an experience that is far greater than the sum of its parts.

Contrary to what we like to believe, some questions have no answers. And in the case of the Sasquatch we may simply never know. To be married to one idea, one meaning, and remain locked into it without direct knowledge, just to create certainty and mental stability, is much closer to delusion than most of us realize. It's also as far away as we'll drift from the noblest of Noble Beyonds: the fundamental reality veiled from us by our subjective senses.

Epilogue
The Noise

I have suffered from some acute bouts of reverse culture shock over the years following trips to meccas of cacophony—places in India, Egypt, and parts of Latin America. In those cases I returned to Toronto tuned to the manic frequencies of my host country, which rendered me completely out of phase with my quieter home environment. My first days back were often buffeted by a silence so pronounced it would throb in my ears. People on the street wandered around in slow motion, like objects drifting weightlessly through interstellar space.

By contrast, my reentry into big-city life following my trip to the Great Bear Rainforest—a torturous ordeal of reacclimatization surpassing any before it—is the complete reverse experience. I've taken a swan dive from a moss-covered, crystalline pinnacle of stillness and clarity into a roiling, incongruous uproar.

The Noise.

That was the name Alex Chartrand Jr., in Wuikinuxv, had given to the irreverential hullabaloo, the godless clamor, the grinding machine gears of the city—the hallmark of a place where no Sasquatch would possibly reside. For people like Alex, accustomed to the subtler, gentler setting of the natural world, which is conducive to a more humane pace—the Noise of the outside world was a grating fact of life. I took his mention of it as a light rebuke, a poking of fun—not unlike the scores of other jokes about Toronto I'd endured from British Columbians during my journey. But in some way, it was also a warning about my impending return. Traveling to a different reality, and then returning to one's own, highlights the things we were numb to before.

The day I leave the Great Bear, I realize something is seriously amiss when, arriving at the connecting airport at Port Hardy, I see women's high-heeled shoes and for a few seconds have no idea what they are. In the landscapes through which I had trod, high heels were necessarily absent. As a result, they'd disappeared from my mind as a notion—and temporarily as a memory.

When I arrive for the night in Vancouver, an ordinarily subdued city, devoid of the edginess and chutzpah common to other large urban centers, I'm met with a circus of stimuli on the order of places like Tokyo or Bombay. When I left the plane my first impression, apart from the jolting sight of concrete and an indescribable smell of impurity, was of a faint background buzz, a constant humming.

The Noise ramps up when I catch a cab with a loud, opinionated driver who has lived in Vancouver for twenty years but has never heard of Bella Bella or any other coastal community north of Campbell River. It continues as his car radio babbles maniacally, entreating me to hire a lawsuit attorney and to eat at KFC. It intrudes in the forms of cranium-shattering roars of motorcycles and wailing sirens. One of the stranger experiences is walking along Georgia Street, a wide downtown thoroughfare, and seeing vehicles barreling past me, just feet away (the cement trucks are particularly bad). Up the coast, the slightest rustling in the bushes had been enough to startle me. My sensitization to the Great Bear's delicate frequencies amplifies the sounds of distant road construction and the garbled, angry hollering of drunkards in the alleyways beneath my hotel at night. The Noise slips through every crack, like granules in a sandstorm.

My assumption that Vancouver has prepared me for Toronto is proved wrong at the airport when I arrive to collect my luggage at the baggage carousel. Above it, a large flat-screen TV broadcasts a barely coherent jumble of sensationalized news and stock-market tickers, as travelers gaze hypnotically between it and their smartphone screens. If anything, the Noise is at a more jarring pitch here, the collective neurosis more pronounced.

What equilibrium I gained during my travels is shattered, gradually, by the city's *dis*equilibrium. It's underscored by the unenviable state of its people—the often rushed, routine-bludgeoned masses avoiding eye contact and wearing frowns of dissatisfaction. Weeks in, sadly, I feel the coastal magic begin to evaporate. It's hard not to be affected by the collective. I am reminded of an old Middle Eastern proverb: *All that enters a salt mine becomes salt.*

It is then that I truly come to appreciate the Sasquatch's reflexive desire to give the train wreck we call civilization a wide berth. I find myself wanting to return to the forest, to burrow ever deeper in search of places unaffected by this chorus of human short-circuiting: the Noise. Certain conversations with people, I find, especially trigger that feeling.

"I heard you were in BC over the summer," a friend of a friend says, yelling in my ear over the music blaring in a packed bar on Ossington Street one night, weeks into my re-assimilation. I am out with friends. The sea of coked-up and marijuana-anesthetized humanity laps at our edges. "What were you doing there?" he asks.

"I was traveling the coast collecting stories of Sasquatch encounters."

"*What* encounters?" he asks, half-hearing and turning his ear to me again.

"*Sas-quatch!*" I say.

He looks at me, and I am met with a blank stare that melts into a smile and then laughter. "*Sasquatch?* I bet everyone who lives out there is kind of a Sasquatch, eh? *Hahahahaha!*"

I continue to look him in the eye, straight-faced, with an unshakable seriousness. His laughter tapers into a chuckle, which then slowly morphs into a shocked and sobering look of incredulity. He sees that I'm not joking and composes himself.

"No, really," he stammers. "What were you doing there?"

POSTSCRIPT

Early in the morning on October 13, 2016, the US-based tugboat *Nathan E. Stewart*, heading south from Alaska through Heiltsuk territorial waters, missed its turn into Seaforth Channel and drove straight into the rocks off Athlone Island. The three-hundred-foot fuel barge it pushed was empty, but the tug carried more than two hundred thousand liters (fifty-three thousand gallons) of diesel and other industrial oils, which started to leak into the Pacific. Within hours, the tug was below water with an ever-growing fuel slick surrounding it.

The wreck sat beside one of the most ecologically abundant areas in the territory, Gale Passage, a place known to the Heiltsuk as Q'vúqvai. It is a narrow waterway between islands containing ancient village sites where, for millennia, people harvested seafood such as clams, crabs, and seaweed for the traditional herring–egg harvest. Though the size and scope of the leak were only a small fraction of what was envisaged for a supertanker accident, with all its attendant coastal devastation, the imperiling of Q'vúqvai was by all accounts a nightmare come true.

With barely any training, funds, or equipment—and without warning—residents of Bella Bella and Denny Island became the first responders, doing anything and everything in their power to contain the spill. It was a heroic, round-the-clock operation that lasted many weeks—one made more difficult by the delayed and largely confused response of the government and other outside agencies.

The Heiltsuk weren't able to stop the diesel leak and its spread. Containment and absorbent booms proved ineffective, often breaking in rough weather and storms. A cluster of islands on the outer coast has been contaminated for an unknown period of time—a heavy blow to the community's food sources, culture, and economy.

In spite of this tragedy—and perhaps in a small way because of it—the pendulum is swinging again toward more responsible decision-making for the coast. Successive governments at both the federal and the provincial levels have charted a slightly different course from their neoconservative predecessors. Between my travels and the time this book went to print, the Great Bear Rainforest agreement was ratified, in 2016, bringing additional protection to the region. Two of the more controversial pipeline-tanker initiatives slated for the coast—including Enbridge's Northern Gateway project—have been canceled. In May 2018, a federal law known as the Oil Tanker Moratorium Act, designed to restrict the largest ships carrying crude and other oils from plying the north coast of British Columbia, was passed in Canada's House of Commons.

And in a dramatic turn of events, in December 2017, the provincial government aligned with many indigenous communities on the coast, and much of the general public, to ban the trophy hunting of grizzly bears across all of British Columbia. The lion's share of responsibility for this shift in policy rests in the work of a core group of people, some of whom appear within these pages.

Not all individuals and communities on the coast, or across the province, support these changes. The cyclical nature of governments combined with deeply polarized politics nowadays means there are no firm guarantees that some of these decisions won't be overturned. But optimism remains high among those who seek to maintain these changes.

Meanwhile, the world of Sasquatch research lost one of its pillars.

On January 18, 2018, wildlife biologist and Bigfoot-studies doyen John Bindernagel died after a two-and-a-half-year battle with cancer.

In the years between his diagnosis and his death, Bindernagel tripled his efforts to get his research into the public domain, posting his video lectures on YouTube and appearing as a guest on TV and in podcasts. Up until his final days, he was meticulously filing and documenting eyewitness reports. In the end, he never realized his dream of encountering a Sasquatch at close range or seeing his theories vindicated by mainstream science.

Addenda

Addendum 1

Incident at the Deer Pass Cabin, as Related by Mary Brown

There was another situation about three years ago at the Deer Pass cabin in Troup Passage. I run the Restorative Justice Program, and one of the programs that we have is isolation for people who are in trouble with the law, or who are going down the wrong path. Their families come together and say, "We need to help this person get back on track."

This case involved a young man. He was nineteen years old. He was put into isolation at the Deer Pass cabin in August.

We occasionally go to check on people put in isolation. On the first visit, I brought one of the councillors with me. When we saw him, he seemed fine. He said, "You know, I'm a little scared, but I'm managing. I hear things at night, but I think it's just wolves in the bush."

The second week we went up there to check on him again. We could tell that this time the young man was spooked. He told us, "I can hear things. I'm starting to smell things. It's really stink. I think there's something out there. I don't know if it's a bear—or what it is."

We returned again during the third week. As soon as I walked up the trail to the cabin, I saw that there was a huge bonfire burning outside it. It scared me because we only do small campfires there because there's a lot of trees around.

I ran up and said, "Hey, what's going on?" When I got there I found the young man just sitting by the fire. As soon as he saw me, he literally fell to his knees and embraced my legs and screamed, "You gotta take me in! You gotta take me in! There's something out here!" He was crying and was absolutely terrified.

I said, "Get ahold of yourself. Try to calm down and we'll talk about this."

So we spent a little while talking and he was kind of jumping all over the place from story to story about what he heard, what he smelled, and what was there. He was scared stiff and insisted that he'd learned his lesson.

Then, in the middle of his rant, as though he'd just remembered, he screamed, "Look!" and pointed to the top of the cabin. I looked up and thought, "What the heck is that?" There's two windows at the Deer Pass cabin and it was right above one of the windows: an enormous handprint! It looked like whatever had made it rubbed its hand in the soot of an earlier fire.

He said that something had come during the night and was banging on the side of the cabin. The attack, he said, started early in the night, while he was inside. It began with rocks and branches being thrown at the walls. He said he was absolutely terrified and as the night progressed, more things started happening. Banging. Shaking.

He said, "I swear it was a *Thla'thla*! I swear it was because what could put a handprint up there?"

I looked at it again. It was huge, and you could still see it because the dirt or soot was still on the walls. It wasn't a perfect handprint by any means, but you could see it was a handprint and there was more than one along the walls of the building. And there was no way that this young man could have gotten up there. The Deer Pass cabin is high. It sits on stilts. The space beneath the cabin is used for wood storage. There's no ladder at the cabin and it was just too high. The print was just too big.

He then went on to say that the creature was mocking him. It was terrorizing or scaring him. It could have gotten into the cabin at any time if it wanted to through the windows and door.

He said the creature finally went away after he screamed at the top of his lungs: "Leave me alone! Please just leave me alone! I'm not going to hurt you! Just leave me alone!" And I guess when it heard the fear in his voice, it disappeared.

Addendum 2

Hoodoo Valley Postscript

A year after my trip, I visited the Great Bear Lodge, a remote bear-viewing camp at the southern edge of the Great Bear Rainforest. I traveled on the invitation of one of the owners, Marg Lehane, an Australian I'd met in Winnipeg a few months before.

One evening, after an unforgettable but completely drenching day viewing grizzlies in the field, Marg and I found ourselves chatting over a glass of wine beside a huge wall map of the region. As we compared notes about the beautiful places we had both visited in the Great Bear, I related the stories I'd heard in Wuikinuxv about the Hoodoo Valley—which I pointed to on the map. When I told her that logging companies had reported strange incidents there over half a century ago, I could see the gears turning in her head. She admitted to knowing nothing about the place, but said that a colleague of hers might have been in the area at the time. She

promised to ask him whether he knew anything, and she would
put us in touch if he did.

Weeks passed and our conversation slipped my mind. But then
one day I received an email from her:

> *When you were at the lodge, we talked about a valley in the Rivers Inlet*
> *area with some unusual happenings. My business partner knows the exact*
> *valley you were referring to. He went into the valley after the two logging*
> *operations there went broke to retrieve some of the machinery, and said that*
> *it was a creepy experience. He would be more than happy to chat with you*
> *about what he knows.*

Later that day I began a correspondence with seventy-two-year-
old Lance McGill, who lives on Vancouver Island. This is his state-
ment concerning his knowledge of the Hoodoo Valley:

> That valley, the Sowick valley on Owikeno Lake, is a really beautiful
> place. It's chock-full of fir, cedar, and hemlock. My family was in
> the construction business. And I'd first heard about it when my dad
> bought a Caterpillar D7 off the first logging company to go broke
> in there in the late 1950s. I can't recall the company's name, but
> they apparently had a hell of a time in there. All sorts of mishaps.
> Nothing went right.
>
> Between 1965 and 1967 I was working for a logging company
> called Kerr and Dumaresque, which was pulling timber in various
> parts of Owikeno Lake. While it was there, another logging show,
> run by Carlson Logging out of Port Alice, got the rights to go
> into Sowick—that problem valley. I actually knew Carl Carlson,
> the owner. We'd sometimes come across him and his crew on the
> lake or in the village. So we knew directly from them what was
> happening there.

As with the previous logging company that had gone into that same valley, nothing—and I mean nothing—went right for Carl and his boys. Their trucks and machinery constantly broke down. They malfunctioned or crashed for no apparent reason. There was an uncanny number of accidents. Many people got hurt, some really badly. They couldn't get their camp set up properly. The natives wouldn't work for them. The few that did got freaked out and never came back. It's normal for things to be a bit rough and difficult on a logging show. But this was way beyond normal. No matter what those guys tried to do in that valley, everything went wrong.

When Carl's yarder donkey exploded and caught fire—the engine was turned off and it was raining cats and dogs at the time—he decided to pull the plug on the operation. "That was the last straw," he told me later. "I'm never going back in there for any kind of money," he said. He thought the place was haunted or cursed. The incident with the yarder happened on the same day that all those guys got out of there in a panic. It was as if they were fleeing from Godzilla or something. They ran for their lives, leaving everything behind.

It was shortly after that when I was approached by Carl to go in there and recover some of the equipment he'd left behind. No one else would do it—no one from his old crew. Neither would the natives living in Rivers Inlet. I wasn't superstitious in any way. Nor did I believe in the supernatural—or things being haunted. So when he desperately asked me to help him it was easy to say yes. I asked my friend Bill Trailing to come with me.

When people in Rivers Inlet heard I was going in there, every single one of them told me I was nuts. "Birds don't sing in that valley," one of them told me. Another guy from the Johnson family told me a story about three native hunters who went missing in there years before. The village later sent a search party for them and found their bodies with their heads missing. I dismissed all of it as colorful stories, superstitions. To me, everything that had happened in there was just a bunch of old-fashioned bad luck—pure and simple.

As I just mentioned, I'm not a religious or superstitious person. But when Bill and I got into that valley, we both felt something horrible. It was a creepy feeling, like something cold blowing on the back of your neck. The forest was dead silent. No breeze. Nothing moved. Even though we were outside, it felt as though we were sitting indoors in a silent room. To this day I can't explain it. It was a strange feeling that everything was wrong. That we weren't welcome there. Even weirder was this sort of presence. I felt that we had company with us, that someone or something was always watching.

I thought maybe I was imagining things, or had been influenced by all the people I had spoken to. But when I talked about it with Bill, he said he felt the exact same thing. In fact, neither of us had felt anything like it before—or after. It was so negative that we decided to cut the job short and just leave the valley that same day, with what few small things we managed to gather.

From what I understand, all the big machinery is still in there. No one's been back to retrieve it. To this day, no one from the village will go in there. I don't blame them. After experiencing what we did, neither would I.

Acknowledgments

In the years devoted to creating this book, I have incurred an enormous debt of gratitude to the many people who helped make it possible. I wish to thank everyone in the communities I visited who appears in this story and the many others whom I met, traveled with, and/or spoke to behind the scenes. Their combined input helped me to develop a modicum of understanding of the rich and complex region I knew so little about before. I'm especially grateful to those who spared their time and energy to share their very personal Sasquatch-related experiences, and with a stranger at that. In the end, I was able to mention only a small fraction of those anecdotes. Nonetheless, each was part of the larger patchwork of stories that influenced my understanding of this phenomenon.

I owe huge thanks to the Heiltsuk, Wuikinuxv, Kitasoo/Xai'xais, and Nuxalk First Nations and their members, who embraced me with an openness and hospitality that paved the way for many a new friendship.

Very special thanks go to those in the region who hosted me and/or facilitated aspects of the journey recounted herein. In Bella Bella and Koeye: Jess Housty, Alvina Duncan, William Housty, Marge Housty, Larry Jorgensen, Qqs Projects Society, Chief Harvey Humchitt and his family, Ian McAllister and Pacific Wild, Captain Brian

Falconer, Raincoast Conservation Foundation and the crew of *Achiever*, Shearwater Fishing Lodge, Shawn Nagurny, and Chris the sea bus pilot. In Wuikinuxv: Lena Collins, Alex Chartrand Jr., and Chris Corbet. In Klemtu: Tim McGrady, Spirit Bear Lodge, and Clark Robinson Sr. In Ocean Falls: Rob and Corrina Darke. In Bella Coola: Leonard Ellis, Daniel Ellis, Michel Bazille, Bella Coola Grizzly Tours, Clark Hans, and James Hans and his family. In Courtenay: the late John Bindernagel and his wife, Joan.

Producing a travelogue is not a simple linear progression of research, travel, writing, and editing in that exact order. In my case, those streams ran in parallel until the very end. I made additional visits to the Great Bear, sometimes for freelance assignments, at other times to work on the manuscript, but always with the intention to deepen my knowledge about the region. I'd like to thank: Geoff Moore, the Cariboo Chilcotin Coast Tourism Association, and Destination British Columbia for assisting with my first trip to the area. Ingmar Lee and Krista Roessingh on Denny Island for putting up with the itinerant wannabe west coaster from Ontario who occupied their guest cabin on more than one occasion. Maple Leaf Adventures; Tom Rivest and Marg Lehane at the Great Bear Lodge; Desiree Lawson and Aaron Ditchfield; Howard Humchitt; and the Simon Fraser University bird crew, all for various micro-adventures, voyages, creek walks, and jaunts along the coast.

For suggestions on some of the psychology literature I have journalist, editor, and author Denise Winn to thank. A few friends came to my aid, lending their editorial insights while pushing me across the finish line. I especially want to thank: Andrew Boden, Ivan Tyrrell, and John Bell, who made useful comments and recommendations in the final draft stages.

My agent Carolyn Forde—by coincidence an erstwhile fan of Art Bell's radio programs on the unexplained—was fortunately drawn to this story. I am very grateful for her faith in the project and for her tenacity in finding a home for it.

I offer thanks to the team at Grove Atlantic in New York for believing in this book and for doing what we comfortable, risk-averse Canadians are not well known for—taking the leap. It was an enormous pleasure collaborating with everyone there—especially with editors George Gibson, Corinna Barsan, and Emily Burns, whose revision alchemy transformed the work for the better. Their infectious and imperishable enthusiasm for the project helped keep the work enjoyable at every stage. I'd also like to thank Julia Berner-Tobin, Deb Seager, and Kait Astrella, also at Grove Atlantic, for their help.

I also offer my heartfelt appreciation to B.C. author, naturalist, and artist Briony Penn, who provided the wonderful maps found at the front of the book, and the devil's club illustration that divides sections of the work.

I finally extend my gratitude to friends and family for their support over the years. And to LH for the many rambles she accompanied me on in the backcountry around Squamish, Chilliwack, and Harrison Lake, where Sasquatches, as it turned out, were never too distant.

References

Alley, Robert J. *Raincoast Sasquatch*. Surrey, BC: Hancock House, 2003.

Arberry, A. J., ed. *Mystical Poems of Rumi 1*. Chicago: University of Chicago Press, 1974.

Barker, John, and Douglas Cole. *At Home with the Bella Coola Indians: T. F. McIlwraith's Field Letters, 1922–24*. Vancouver: UBC Press, 2003.

Beck, Fred, and R. A. Beck. *I Fought the Apeman of Mt. St. Helens*. Privately printed, 1967. Also online at http://www.bigfootencounters.com/classics/beck.htm.

Berger, Knute. "It's Too Soon to Close the Door on Bigfoot's Existence (Hear Us Out)." *Seattle Magazine* (online), October 2017. http://www.seattlemag.com/news-and-features/its-too-soon-close-door-bigfoots-existence-hear-us-out.

"The Bigfoot Classics: Albert Ostman's Story." *Bigfoot Encounters* (website). http://www.bigfootencounters.com/classics/ostman.htm.

Bindernagel, John. *The Discovery of the Sasquatch: Reconciling Culture, History, and Science in the Discovery Process*. Courtenay, BC: Beachcomber Books, 2010.

———. *North America's Great Ape: The Sasquatch*. Courtenay, BC: Beachcomber Books, 1998.

Blu Buhs, Joshua. *Bigfoot: The Life and Times of a Legend*. Chicago: University of Chicago Press, 2010.

Boas, Franz. *Bella Bella Tales*. Boston: American Folklore Society, vol. 25, 1932.

Bortoft, Henri. *Taking Appearance Seriously: The Dynamic Way of Seeing in Goethe and European Thought*. Cornwall, UK: Floris Books, 2012.

————. *The Wholeness of Nature: Goethe's Way Toward a Science of Conscious Participation in Nature.* Herndon, VA: Lindisfarne Books, 1996.

Burton, Sir Richard Francis, *The Kasidah of Haji Abdu El-Yezdi.* London: Bernard Quaritch, 1880.

Byrne, Peter. *The Search for Bigfoot: Monster, Myth or Man?* New York: Pocket Books, 1976.

Campbell, Joseph. *The Hero with a Thousand Faces.* Novato, CA: New World Library, 2008.

Capra, Fritjof. *The Tao of Physics: An Exploration of the Parallels Between Modern Physics and Eastern Mysticism.* Boston: Shambhala Publications, 1975.

Chamberlain, Ted. "Reinhold Messner: Climbing Legend, Yeti Hunter." Interview. *National Geographic Adventure,* May–June 2000.

Clancy, Susan. *Abducted: How People Come to Believe They Were Kidnapped by Aliens.* Boston: Harvard University Press, 2007.

Clarke, David. *How UFOs Conquered the World: The History of a Modern Myth.* London: Aurum Press, 2015.

Coleman, Loren. *Bigfoot! The True Story of Apes in America.* New York: Paraview Pocket Books, 2003.

Davis, Wade. *The Clouded Leopard: Travels to Landscapes of Spirit and Desire.* Vancouver: Douglas and McIntrye, 1999.

Deikman, Arthur J. *Meditations on a Blue Vase.* Napa, CA: Fearless Books, 2014.

————. *The Observing Self: Mysticism and Psychotherapy.* Boston: Beacon Press, 1982.

Denholm, Derrick Stacey. *Ground Truthing: Re-Imagining the Indigenous Rainforests of BC's North Coast.* Half Moon Bay, BC: Caitlin Press, 2015.

Dickie, Gloria. "The Value of a Bear: Why Some Indigenous Communities in BC Won't Rejoice over the NDP's Decision to Ban the Grizzly Hunt." *The Walrus* (online), April 18, 2018. https://thewalrus.ca/the-value-of-a-bear/.

Drury, Clifford M. *Nine Years with the Spokane Indians: The Diary of Elkanah Walker 1838–1848.* Norman, OK: Arthur H. Clark Company, 1976.

Dubos, René. *So Human an Animal: How We Are Shaped by Surroundings and Events.* New York: Scribner's, 1968.

"Encountering Another Being II." Video excerpt from *The Seed Beneath the Snow*, a documentary film about economist and ecologist David Fleming, posted by Empathy Media, n.d. https://vimeo.com/236955585.

"Fight with Big Apes Reported by Miners." *The Oregonian* (Portland, Oregon), July 13, 1924.

Frankl, Victor E. *Man's Search for Meaning*. Boston: Beacon Press, 2006.

Gill, Charlotte. *Eating Dirt: Deep Forests, Big Timber, and Life with the Tree, Planting Tribe*. Vancouver: Greystone Books, 2011.

Gill, Ian. "Koeye Reclaimed, a Century Later." *The Tyee*, September 19, 2014. https://thetyee.ca/Opinion/2014/09/19/Koeye-Reclaimed/.

Glavin, Terry. *The Last Great Sea: A Voyage Through the Human and Natural History of the North*. Vancouver: Greystone Books, 2003.

Gleick, James. *Genius: The Life and Science of Richard Feynman*. New York: Vintage, 1993.

"The Great Pismo." YouTube video, posted by Tom Corcoran, November 18, 2012. https://www.youtube.com/watch?v=eYshI7RohLk.

Green, John. *On the Track of the Sasquatch*. Agassiz, BC: Cheam Publishing, 1971

———. *Sasquatch: The Apes Among Us*. Surrey, BC: Hancock House, 1978.

———. *The Sasquatch File*. Agassiz, BC: Cheam Publishing, 1973.

———. *Year of the Sasquatch*. Agassiz, BC: Cheam Publishing, 1970.

Griffin, Joe, and Ivan Tyrrell. *Human Givens: The New Approach to Emotional Health and Clear Thinking*. Chalvington, UK: HG Publishing, 2003.

Haidt, Jonathan. *The Righteous Mind: Why Good People Are Divided by Politics and Religion*. New York: Vintage, 2012.

Halpin, Marjorie, ed. *Manlike Monsters on Trial: Early Records and Modern Evidence*. Vancouver: UBC Press, 1980.

Heffernan, Margaret. *Willful Blindness: Why We Ignore the Obvious at Our Peril*. London: Bloomsbury, 2012.

Hunter, Don, and René Dahinden. *Sasquatch and Bigfoot: The Search for North America's Incredible Creature*. Toronto: Firefly Books, 1993.

King, Thomas. *The Inconvenient Indian: A Curious Account of Native People in North America*. Toronto: Anchor Canada, 2012.

Kopas, Cliff. *Bella Coola: A Story of Effort and Achievement*. Vancouver: Mitchell Press, 1970.

Kopecky, Arno. *The Oil Man and the Sea: Navigating the Northern Gateway.* Vancouver: Douglas and McIntyre, 2013.

Krantz, Grover S. *Bigfoot Sasquatch: Evidence.* Surrey, BC: Hancock House, 1999.

Macfarlane, Robert. *The Wild Places.* London: Granta Books, 2009.

Mack, Clayton. *Bella Coola Man: The Life of a First Nations Elder.* Pender Harbour, BC: Harbour Publishing, 2002.

———. *Grizzlies and White Guys: The Stories of Clayton Mack.* Pender Harbour, BC: Harbour Publishing, 1996.

Mackinnon, J. B., *The Once and Future World: Nature as It Was, as It Is, as It Could Be,* New York: Random House, 2013.

Matthiessen, Peter. *The Snow Leopard.* New York: Penguin Books, 1978.

McAllister, Ian. *Great Bear Wild: Dispatches from a Northern Rainforest.* Vancouver: Greystone Books, 2014.

———. *The Last Wild Wolves: Ghosts of the Great Bear Rainforest.* Vancouver: Greystone Books, 2007.

McAllister, Ian, Karen McAllister, and Cameron Young. *The Great Bear Rainforest: Canada's Forgotten Coast.* Pender Harbour, BC: Harbour Publishing, 1998.

McAllister, Ian, and Nicholas Read. *The Great Bear Sea: Exploring the Marine Life of a Pacific Paradise.* Victoria: Orca Books, 2013.

McCarthy, Shawn. *CSIS, RCMP Monitored Activist Groups Before Northern Gateway Hearings.* Globe & Mail online, November 21, 2013. https://www.theglobe andmail.com/report-on-business/industry-news/energy-and-resources/csis-rcmp-monitored-activists-for-risk-before-enbridge-hearings/article15555935/.

McIlwraith, T. F. *The Bella Coola Indians.* Toronto: University of Toronto Press, 1948.

McLeod, Michael. *Anatomy of a Beast: Obsession and Myth on the Trail of Bigfoot.* Berkeley: University of California Press, 2009.

Meldrum, Jeff. "On the Plausibility of Another Bipedal Primate Species Existing in North America." *Capeia,* October 20, 2017. https://beta.capeia.com/zoology/2017/10/20/on-the-plausibility-of-another-bipedal-primate-species-existing-in-north-america.

———. *Sasquatch: Legend Meets Science.* New York: Forge Books, 2007.

Messner, Reinhold. *My Quest for the Yeti.* New York: St. Martin's Press, 2000.

Murphy, Christopher. *Sasquatch in British Columbia: A Chronology of Incidents and Important Events.* Surrey, BC: Hancock House, 2012.

Napier, John. *Bigfoot: The Yeti and Sasquatch in Myth and Reality.* Boston: E. P. Dutton, 1973.

Nickell, Joe. "Bigfoot Lookalikes: Tracking Hairy Man-Beasts." *Skeptical Inquirer* (online), September–October 2013. https://www.csicop.org/si/show/bigfoot_lookalikes_ tracking_hairy_man-beasts.

Ornstein, Robert. *The Evolution of Consciousness: The Origins of the Way We Think.* New York: Simon and Schuster, 1991.

———. *Multimind: A New Way of Looking at Human Behavior.* Los Altos: Malor Books, 2003.

———. *The Psychology of Consciousness.* New York: Viking, 1972.

Ornstein, Robert, and Ted Dewan. *Mindreal: How the Mind Creates Its Own Virtual Reality.* Los Altos, CA: Malor Books, 2010.

Powell, Thom. *The Locals: A Contemporary Investigation of the Bigfoot/Sasquatch Phenomenon.* Surrey, BC: Hancock House, 2011.

Pyle, Robert Michael. *Where Bigfoot Walks: Crossing the Dark Divide.* Berkeley, CA: Counterpoint Press, 2017.

Raban, Jonathan. *Passage to Juneau: A Sea and Its Meanings.* New York: Vintage, 2000.

Ramachandran, V. S., and Sandra Blakeslee. *Phantoms in the Brain: Probing the Mysteries of the Human Mind.* New York: Harper Perennial, 1998.

Ramsey, Bruce. *Rain People: The Story of Ocean Falls.* Kamloops, BC: Wells Gray Tours, 1971.

Regal, Brian. *Searching for Sasquatch: Crackpots, Eggheads, and Cryptozoology.* New York: Palgrave Macmillan, 2011.

Rivers Inlet Ecosystem Study (website). http://riversinlet.eos.ubc.ca.

Sargant, William. *Battle for the Mind: A Physiology of Conversion and Brain-Washing.* Los Altos, CA: Malor Books, 2015.

Schulz, Kathryn. "Fantastic Beasts and How to Rank Them." *New Yorker* (online), November 6, 2017. https://www.newyorker.com/magazine/2017/11/06/is-bigfoot-likelier-than-the-loch-ness-monster.

Shackley, Myra. *Wildmen: Yeti, Sasquatch and the Neanderthal Enigma.* London: Thames and Hudson, 1983.

Shah, Idries. *Caravan of Dreams.* London: Octagon Press, 1988.

————. *Learning How to Learn*. London: Penguin Arkana, 1983

————. *Seeker After Truth*. London: Octagon Press, 1982.

————. *The Sufis*. New York: Doubleday, 1964.

Showler, Suzanna. "On the Trail of Ignored Beasts." *Maisonneuve* (online), February 20, 2014. https://maisonneuve.org/article/2014/02/20/trail-ignored-beasts/.

Sleigh, Daphne. *The People of the Harrison*. Abbotsford, BC: Abbotsford Printing, 1990.

Storr, Will. *The Heretics: Adventures with the Enemies of Science*. London: Picador, 2014.

Stowe, Leland. *Crusoe of Lonesome Lake*. New York: Random House, 1957.

Taylor, Daniel C. *Yeti: The Ecology of a Mystery*. Oxford: Oxford University Press, 2017.

Tizon, Alex. "The Killing of the Bears." *Seattle Times*, January 30, 2000.

Twigger, Robert. *White Mountain: Real and Imagined Journeys in the Himalayas*. London: Weidenfeld and Nicholson, 2016.

Vaillant, John. *The Golden Spruce: A True Story of Myth, Madness, and Greed*. New York: Vintage, 2006.

Wallace, David Rains. *The Klamath Knot: Explorations of Myth and Evolution*. Berkeley: University of California Press, 2003.

Wexler, Bruce. *Brain and Culture: Neurobiology, Ideology, and Social Change*. Cambridge, MA: MIT Press, 2006.

Winn, Denise. *The Manipulated Mind: Brainwashing, Conditioning and Indoctrination*. Los Altos, CA: Malor Books, 2000.

Wohlleben, Peter. *The Hidden Life of Trees*. Vancouver: Greystone Books, 2016.

Wolf, Edward, and Seth Zuckerman. *Salmon Nation: People, Fish, and Our Common Home*. Vancouver: Ecotrust, 1999.

Endnotes

1. Regal, Brian. *Searching for Sasquatch: Crackpots, Eggheads, and Cryptozoology.* New York: Palgrave Macmillan, 2011, p. 59.

2. Bindernagel, John. *North America's Great Ape: The Sasquatch.* Courtenay, BC: Beachcomber Books, 1998, p. 4.

3. Bindernagel, John. *The Discovery of the Sasquatch: Reconciling Culture, History, and Science in the Discovery Process.* Courtenay, BC: Beachcomber Books, 2010, p. 129.

4. Davis, Wade. *The Clouded Leopard: Travels to Landscapes of Spirit and Desire.* Vancouver: Douglas and McIntyre, 1999, p. 209.

5. Ostman's full-length, verbatim account of his kidnapping can be found online at *Bigfoot Encounters* (website). http://www.bigfootencounters.com/classics/ostman.htm.

6. Marc Myrsell, Sasquatch Chronicles Podcast, Episode 357: 1924 Ape Canyon, September 3, 2017.

7. Nickell, Joe. "Bigfoot Lookalikes: Tracking Hairy Man-Beasts." *Skeptical Inquirer* 37.5, September–October 2013.

8. Messner, Reinhold. *My Quest for the Yeti.* New York: St. Martin's Press, 2000, p 5.

9. Ibid. pp. 7–8.

10. Ibid, p. 156.

11. See Daniel C. Taylor's excellent book, *Yeti: The Ecology of a Mystery.* Oxford: Oxford University Press, 2017.

12. Chamberlain, Ted. "Reinhold Messner: Climbing Legend, Yeti Hunter." *National Geographic Adventure*, May–June 2000.

13. Ornstein, Robert. *The Evolution of Consciousness: The Origins of the Way We Think*. New York: Simon and Schuster, 1991, p. 150.

14. Shah, Idries. *Seeker After Truth*, London: Octagon Press, 1991, p. 116.

15. Wexler, Bruce. *Brain and Culture: Neurobiology, Ideology, and Social Change*. Cambridge, MA: MIT Press, 2006, p. 5.

16. Ramachandran, V. S., and Sandra Blakeslee. *Phantoms in the Brain: Probing the Mysteries of the Human Mind*. New York: Harper Perennial, 1998, p. 134.

17. Storr, Will. *The Heretics: Adventures with the Enemies of Science*. London: Picador, 2014, pp. 94–95.

18. Haidt, Jonathan. *The Righteous Mind: Why Good People Are Divided by Politics and Religion*. New York: Vintage, 2012, p. 104.

19. Deikman, Arthur. *Meditations on a Blue Vase*. CA: Fearless Books, 2014, p. 246.

20. Dubos, René. *So Human an Animal: How We Are Shaped by Surroundings and Events*. New York: Scribner's, 1968, p. 158.

21. Shah, Idries. *The Sufis*, New York: Doubleday, 1964, p. 23.

22. Storr, *The Heretics: Adventures with the Enemies of Science*, pp. 369, 375.

Index

INDEX